REAL WORLD APPLE GUIDE

BY JESSE FEILER

M&T BOOKS

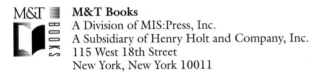

M&T Books
A Division of MIS:Press, Inc.
A Subsidiary of Henry Holt and Company, Inc.
115 West 18th Street
New York, New York 10011

Apple Guide requires System 7.5 or later.

Printed in the United States of America

Limits of Liability and Disclaimer of Warranty

Some of the figures in Chapter 25 are from: Josef Albers's *Interaction of Color*, Interactive CD-ROM edition. Copyright © 1994 by Yale University Press and its licensors. All rights reserved.

Library of Congress Cataloging-in-Publication Data

```
Feiler, Jesse.
   Real World Apple Guide / Jesse Feiler.
      p,   cm.
   Includes index.
   ISBN 1-55851-429-5
   1. Macintosh (Computer)--Programming. 2. Apple Guide. I. Title.
QA76.8.M3F45  1995
005.265--dc20                                          95-1878
                                                          CIP
```

Editor-in-Chief: Paul Farrell   **Managing Editor:** Cary Sullivan
Development Editor: Laura Lewin   **Copy Editor:** Joanna Arnott
Production Editor: Anthony Washington

TRADEMARKS

About the author

Jesse Feiler is Software Director of Philmont Software Mill. With Joseph Roberts, Art Director, he designed and developed Philmont Symposium System-affordable, interactive, multimedia presentation software, consisting of Symposium Creator and Symposium Explorer. Together, they were responsible for Josef Albers's *Interaction of Color interactive* CD-ROM *edition*, published by Yale University Press.

Before founding Philmont Software Mill, Mr. Feiler served in a number of technical and managerial roles at the Federal Reserve Bank of New York, with responsibilities ranging from personal computers to mainframes, and from in-house information services to monetary policy operations and bank supervision support. He has also served as a consultant, author, and/or speaker for (among others) the American Booksellers Association, Campbell-Ewald, the Bruce Goff Estate, MADA/Software Frameworks Association, Young & Rubicam, the Association of American Publishers, MacTech Magazine and Apple Computer, Inc.

He is active in the community, serving on the boards of the Philmont Public Library, the HB Playwrights Foundation, and the Mid-Hudson Library System. He is a member of DQ.

Philmont Software Mill maintains an area on eWorld accessible with the following path: Computer Center : Straight to the Source : Philmont Software Mill (shortcut "Philmont"); or from other networks at ePhilmont@eWorld.com. Files related to Philmont Symposium System and Apple Guide in general are located there; a continually updated copy of the References & Resources stack included on the CD-ROM in this book is provided there as well.

Foreword

Apple Guide isn't really about computers: it's about people. How people do things, how they learn, and how computers can assist them in the tasks that they do. The developer of Apple Guide assistance—programmer, instructional designer, consultant, or solution provider—focuses on the user and the tasks that need to be done. Although a great deal of computer syntax is provided in this book, a significant amount of attention is paid to people and the ways in which they use computers. Some of the things that we take for granted in computer interfaces change with Apple Guide; many of the things that users put up with grudgingly can disappear with Apple Guide. It's about time that we turned from teaching people how to use our hardware and software (in other words, how to do things *our* way) to teaching ourselves to understand people and the way in which they use our products.

The examples in this book are drawn from a number of sources, including the Macintosh Guide assistance that shipped with the first release of System 7.5. Philmont Symposium System (Symposium Creator and Symposium Explorer), which Joe Roberts and I developed, incorporated Apple Guide from a very early point, providing a great deal of experience with Apple Guide as it evolved. A number of examples (and a lot of adventures) can be found in this book. Josef Albers's *Interaction of Color interactive CD-ROM edition*, published by Yale University Press, was one of the first multimedia publishing projects to incorporate Apple Guide for both the application program and its content. Joe and I were fortunate enough to work on that project, and Yale University Press has been kind enough to allow us to reproduce a number of screen shots here.

Since Apple Guide is so involved with people and their actions, the successful Apple Guide designer must study people—always a delicious undertaking. We are a fascinating species, and we revel in examining ourselves and our behavior—whether in scholarly tomes, supermarket tabloids, or outside the post office on a Saturday morning. In the References & Resources stack found on the CD-ROM included with this book, a number of references are given to books in various areas that have been particularly useful. Fortunately, there is reference material aplenty for every taste: Donald A. Norman writes entertainingly about cognitive psychology in his many books, while Jane Austen and Tolstoy are available to those who take a different approach to understanding the things that people do and how they go about planning them. In my case, I have been very fortunate to have learned a great deal about human behavior from Uta Hagen and the late Herbert Berghof—brilliant actors, teachers, and friends.

Others who have been of tremendous assistance include:

Tony Meadow, of Bear River Associates, who asked me to write a book a number of years ago. (Of course, the book he asked me to write was about databases, but…)

John Powers and Glenn Katz, from the initial Apple Guide development team and now of guideWorks, provided a great deal of information—and an interesting demonstration of Apple Guide that is found on the CD-ROM that comes with this book.

Alan Bloom, Barbara Butler, and Christopher Kell provided valuable insights into the manuscript from their unique perspectives.

At M&T Books, Laura Lewin, Jono Hardjo, and Andy Neusner were enormously helpful.

Joanna Arnott, Copy Editor, and Anthony Washington, Production Editor, braved the wilds of <Gestalt> commands vs. Gestalt functions vs. Gestalt selectors and emerged (I hope) mentally and emotionally unscathed. Their contribution to the book is substantial, and greatly appreciated.

Bob Hagenau, of Apple, was of enormous help to this project, particularly in helping to make the CD-ROM that comes with this book a reality.

Joe Roberts, distinguished communications designer, gifted teacher, colleague, and good friend must receive enormous thanks.

Finally, although it pains me to say it, the cats Blanche and Ernest were of no help whatsoever.

Preface

For more than a decade, Apple has been the leading innovator in personal computer technology. More than any other vendor, Apple has been concerned with the "user experience," with what a nontechnical person has to go through to set up a computer and to learn how to use the hardware and software. Apple has also considered the needs of more experienced users.

Apple has long been concerned with the many difficulties in using computers— even the Macintosh, which some studies indicate is still the easiest computer to learn. After spending a lot of time studying how people use computers and what can go wrong when they do, Apple has come up with a strategic direction for its user interface: to move away from passive interfaces toward active ones.

A passive interface requires that the user know a lot about the hardware, system software, and application software in order to do anything. On the other hand, an active interface requires that the computer (the hardware, system software, and application software together) try to figure out what tasks the user is trying to accomplish and assist her or him in making it happen.

Apple Guide is one of the latest innovative technologies to appear from Apple Computer's labs; it is a first step on the road to active interfaces. It is not a help facility, like Balloon Help, a help system that helps users to quickly understand what user interface elements and their functions are. Apple Guide is not like the numerous help systems available on Macintosh, Windows, and other platforms that provide either a book metaphor or hypertext capabilities. These systems can be helpful to some people in some situations, but they are basically electronic versions of the paper documentation.

Using a traditional help system is like reading the paper documentation, or in some cases, a bit easier than that since you can move around within the help file using hypertext-like links. But you still have to know what you're looking for and you have to know the vocabulary used by the application developers.

Using Apple Guide is like having an expert looking over your shoulder (but when you want it) walking you through the steps. It can show you which menu to select by circling it. It can highlight buttons, and so on. You learn how to do something by actually doing it, not just reading about it. This is cool stuff.

And you don't have to write code, or even change your code, to be able to provide Apple Guide assistance for others to use. In fact, anyone can write Apple Guide files for any program. If you're a writer, you now have a new market—you can write and sell your Apple Guide files for anyone's software. If you work for a software publisher, you can provide higher-quality help and reduce the number of tech support calls that you receive. If you work in an organization, you can create Apple Guide files to walk people through your work processes even if they involve more than one application.

I met Jesse Feiler, a long-time Macintosh developer, about six years ago. He was giving some tutorials on supporting relational databases from an object-oriented application framework, a rather painful thing to do back then. He did a marvelous job of explaining how these two worlds could be combined with clarity and humor. I've always hoped that he would write so that he could reach a larger audience. I am very pleased to present this book, which explains—with clarity and humor—a significant new technology from Apple.

Tony Meadow
Bear River Associates, Inc.

Table of Contents

PART 1: WHAT IS APPLE GUIDE?

PART 2: CREATING GUIDE FILES
WITH GUIDE MAKER

PART 3: CREATING AND MODIFYING APPLICATIONS TO USE APPLE GUIDE

PART 4: ADDING APPLE GUIDE TO CUSTOM SOLUTIONS AND CONTENT

Introduction

The most important thing to remember is:

IT'S NOT HELP

At one time what is now called Apple Guide was called Apple Help.

Sometimes, Apple Guide has been called a context-sensitive help system.

People have been known to refer to Apple Guide as a replacement for Balloon Help. It's not a replacement for Balloon Help, and—as was said before—it is not help.

Apple Guide is active assistance, a new interface layer interposed between application and user, which not only is able to provide information but actually performs tasks as necessary. It is not help.

WHAT'S WRONG WITH HELP?

Help seems such a positive term. You think of Clara Barton and Florence Nightingale and of Boy Scouts helping old people across the street or collecting food for hurricane victims. Help seems so good.

Help has two negative connotations, however. First, some people don't like to be helped. Whether it's the senior citizen who's perfectly happy to stand on the bus, the driver who doesn't need help with directions from a spouse, or the woman in the famous commercial who said, "Mother, please! I'd rather do it myself," we have all seen (and been) people who don't need or want, and even sometimes resent, help.

In the world of computer software, there's another negative aspect to "help." Developers pride themselves on creating application programs that are powerful, yet easy to use. To provide extensive help somehow implies that these applications aren't quite so easy to use.

Of course, needing help to do something doesn't imply that you're stupid or incompetent, nor that the task you're trying to do is complex or difficult. When you tie up a package with string, there's that one critical moment where a third hand to press a finger on the knot is a godsend. When you take clean sheets out of the dryer, folding them is immensely easier if there's someone who can take the opposite corners and walk them toward you.

For all its positive aspects, the word "help" is a mixed blessing, and the people at Apple decided to avoid it wherever possible in talking about Apple Guide.

APPLE GUIDE AND ASSISTANCE

Apple Guide provides quick answers to questions with shortcuts, "what is...," and so forth, and longer answers in the form of tutorials and step-by-step walk-throughs of procedures. Apple Guide can even bypass the commands that you do: many Apple Guide screens have a "Do It for Me" button on them. This is much more than help; it is the first step toward the next generation of computer interfaces: active assistance.

The Macintosh graphical user interface was a great innovation: its possibilities are laid out in front of you in the form of icons, buttons, and menu commands. You just point and click (with the occasional drag thrown in). It makes the Macintosh very easy to use. And it's rather attractive: your computer starts up and smiles at you. When the desktop appears, the icons of your documents, folders, and applications are clearly labeled and placed just where you put them the last time you used your computer.

In 1984, this was a revolutionary breakthrough. To some people it made the use of a computer possible for the first time. To some hardened users of computers it looked like a silly game. ("I know how to use a computer; I don't need little pictures.") As the years have passed and more and more operating system vendors have incorporated major aspects of the Macintosh operating system interface into their products, the value and popularity of the interface have become indisputable.

Advances in computer interface design are driven by three things: improvements in computer processing power (which make the advances possible), competitive needs (which make the advances necessary), and the imagination of software engineers (which makes us happy). It is not a coincidence that Apple Guide made its first appearance in System 7.5, which was the first major revision of the operating system to be released after the advent of the Power Macintosh line, powered by the RISC-based PowerPC chip. Likewise, the competitive environment for operating systems heated up as a new version of Windows incorporated many features of the sort that had previously been seen only in the Macintosh operating system. Meanwhile, software engineers looked at an environment in which color, on-screen video, and stereo sound were taken for granted; and at a public who had assimilated the basic elements of the graphical user interface (buttons, mouse, menus, and so on) and were ready for new adventures.

Focusing on You and Your Work

Two major points characterize the new user interface that makes its debut with System 7.5. Whereas the original Macintosh interface focused on making the computer and its software very easy to use, the new approach is focused on making it very easy for you to do what you want to do. Note the difference: in the second formulation, the focus is on you and the work that you want to do. In the first, the focus was on the computer and its software, and making them easy to use. Apple likes to talk about "moving from ease of use to ease of doing."

Active Assistance

The second point characterizing the new user interface is that it is active. This doesn't mean that your Macintosh is suddenly going to get up and tap dance around your desk. It means that the computer can do more than merely respond to each command that you give. This activity may take the form of performing automated tasks so that one command launches a long and complex series of operations, or it may take the form of watching and recording your actions so that they can be repeated with a single mouse-click at a future time.

This complex and active interface can also provide a level of assistance that was previously unavailable. No longer do you have a passive help screen that says, "Choose **Open** from the File menu." With Apple Guide you have a screen that says, "Choose **Open** from the File menu" while a red circle (a *coach mark*) is drawn around the File menu. As if that weren't enough, when you pull down the File menu, the item **Open** is shown in red. As if that weren't enough, if you don't choose **Open**, Apple Guide says, "Oops! You must choose **Open** from the File menu." And to top the whole thing off, if you still don't choose **Open**, Apple Guide says, "Please wait a moment; Apple Guide is choosing **Open** from the File menu," and it's done for you.

Apple Guide is much more than help, and it is a critical, intrinsic part of a new approach to the user interface.

APPLE GUIDE SERVICE

Apple Guide is a form of active assistance, but what, exactly, does it provide? What does it do? These aren't idle questions: the expectations of users and developers are critical as they use and develop software. Just as "help" has negative connotations and denotes only a subset of what Apple Guide can provide, it is important to define what Apple Guide does provide in a way that makes clear to all what to expect.

The word is *service*. "Service, the ultimate luxury." "Service with a smile." (The nearly universal reaction of people when they first see a coach mark drawn is a smile.)

Service is not a mass-market mechanism: it is provided to individuals or small groups. It is a personal transaction. Providing good service requires an understanding of what a person is attempting to do and what he or she is likely to do next. By its nature, Apple Guide assistance provides different assistance to different people at different times.

Service at its best is unobtrusive but always available. Perhaps the classic example is the oft-repeated tale of Queen Victoria. Supposedly she never looked behind her when she sat down. Whenever she sat down, a chair was immediately slid under the Royal Rump.

Finally, service makes us feel good. It makes our lives easier, and it brings us back to the people and places that have provided good service. "Service" reminds us that it is the computer that serves us, that the machine should adapt to the needs of the user. In contrast to "help," which may connote difficulty, incompetence, or lack of skills, "service" is always a positive experience.

Types of Service

Following are some examples of service, all of which are analogous to the kinds of service Apple Guide can provide:

- Service can consist of help: "Is it spelled 'wierd' or 'weird'?"

- Service can consist of expert coaching: "Cut the branch off just above that little bud. OK, next time you can cut even closer to the bud. That's good. If you hold the pruner at more of an angle, it'll be easier to make the cut."

- Service can consist of doing things for you: "Beulah, peel me a grape."

- Service can consist of preparing or suggesting things: each night at the Ritz-Carlton in Boston, the *TV Guide* magazine in your room is placed on the night table with a book mark at that night's schedule.

- Service can consist of watching to make sure that you don't make mistakes: "No, the Men's Room is the second door on the left. That's the Ladies' Room."

Tasks Versus Tools

Just as the Macintosh user interface is advancing from ease of use to ease of doing—from a focus on the tool to a focus on the task—application developers and solution providers must make a similar transition. One of the consequences of dealing with tasks as opposed to tools is that tasks are more complex. If you compare word processor A with word processor B, you can make a chart (using spreadsheet C) that easily compares them feature by feature, tool by tool. The computer magazines do this month in and month out.

In your daily life, however, you are likely to give greater weight to the comment of a colleague who says that for doing the kind of work you both do, word processor B seems to work better. For example, the pagination and hyphenation routines are less important than the fact that word processor B can easily produce auto repair shop bills that are acceptable to insurance adjusters' claim form needs. The task supersedes the tool.

In this task-based environment, service to the user is as important as it is in any business. And service, such as Apple Guide can provide, is what brings customers back and makes them happy. Service doesn't imply weakness or incapacity on the part of the person being served, although that may be the case. It doesn't imply tasks that are complicated or difficult, although that may also be true. The three attributes of service—that it is personal, unobtrusive yet readily available, and makes you feel good—are not attributes that have historically been associated with computers and their interfaces. Interestingly, these attributes were attributed to computers in the popular press in the early 1950s as "electronic brains" were starting to capture the public's imagination. Forty years later, we are starting to fulfill the expectations that people had of computers from the beginning.

OPPORTUNITIES WITH APPLE GUIDE

Apple Guide can enhance tremendously the user's experience with an application or solution.

Apple Guide for Applications

From the beginning, Apple Guide was designed to be tightly incorporated into an application as easily as it can be added to an application after the fact. Apple Guide can be used to augment—or in some cases replace—paper documentation.

Apple Guide for Custom Solutions

Because Apple Guide assistance can be developed not only by application developers but also by third parties, the opportunity exists for third parties to provide custom solutions for vertical markets and individual corporations, as well as to provide custom Apple Guide assistance for these markets and corporations. In this way, the broad functionalities of mass-market products can be customized and fine-tuned for specific uses.

Apple Guide for Content

It is worth noting that there is a special opportunity to develop Apple Guide for content. This is similar to the opportunities for Apple Guide assistance provided for custom solutions. In the case of Apple Guide for content, however, the assistance is provided for a database or for the content of interactive multimedia on CD-ROM or other media.

Examples of Apple Guide Assistance

To put things in perspective, following is a possible scenario showing how Apple Guide can be used with applications, custom solutions, and content.

- The developer of a database application program provides Apple Guide assistance to help users use the program. This assistance provides definitions of basic database terms (records, fields, keys of retrieval, and so on) and tutorials that guide the user through creating, retrieving, sorting, and printing database records.

- A solution provider creates a database for libraries using the database application program. Apple Guide assistance is added to define data elements used in this customized database (Library of Congress number, MARC record, author, title, publisher, shelf location, and so on). A tutorial is created that guides the user through the process of cataloging a book. The tutorial assumes that the user has used the application's tutorial to learn the concepts of creating and storing a generic record.

- An end user adds further assistance for the library that uses this database. A tutorial here might guide staff members through the processing of accessioning a book. That tutorial would build on the concepts in the previous two tutorials (general data entry and book cataloging) but would add specific points that matter to the library: are mysteries shelved with fiction or separately?, are all new acquisitions shelved on the "New Books" shelf or only newly published books?, and so on.

Opportunities for Apple Guide Authors and Designers

Companies are springing up that specialize in providing Apple Guide assistance to vertical markets and individual corporations as well as to in-house developers. The skills that are needed to create Apple Guide assistance include not only a knowledge of the software for which the guide files are being created but also a knowledge of technical writing and—most important of all—an understanding of the people who will use the guide files and the tasks that they will perform.

The Difference between Developing Apple Guide and Other Assistance

Developing successful guide files requires an understanding not only of Apple Guide's syntax and standards, but also of the principles that underlie people's expectations of service from their computer and applications.

Developing help using traditional tools, such as manuals and on-line help, often is a thankless task. As anyone who has fielded technical support calls knows, people don't read the manuals. As anyone who has tried to look up something in a manual knows, the manual is never organized properly to answer your immediate question. (Fate takes care of this.) With Apple Guide, you have a vehicle that helps you provide service that is personal, unobtrusive, and readily available—characteristics not shared by manuals, on-line help, or even Balloon Help.

As designed by Apple and implemented by successful guide file authors, Apple Guide provides this service, and also makes people feel good. This is not an idle comment: when people first see coach marks drawn on their computer screen, they invariably smile. There is a positive gut-level response to this technology. Some guide files never advance beyond this basic level, providing help that is merely a rehash of printed documentation, or worse, help that consists only of references to pages in a manual. But with a full understanding and appreciation of Apple Guide's possibilities and users' expectations, you can build on the positive feeling that accompanies the first coach mark. It's a feeling that derives from the clear and unambiguous information that the coach mark conveys ("Click here") as well as from the equally obvious recognition that with something so simple and explicit, users can relax, knowing that they are in safe hands.

Not only can Apple Guide satisfy the user, it can make the Apple Guide developer feel good, too. Working with a technology that starts with a user who is smiling and comfortable is a welcome change for many developers and help authors!

HOW THIS BOOK IS ORGANIZED

There are five parts to this book. Each provides information about a different aspect of Apple Guide and includes short examples and code excerpts. The CD-ROM accompanying this book provides a Cookbook with tips, recipes, shell files for Guide Maker, and a number of examples. Much of the code that is excerpted in the book is presented in whole on the CD-ROM; additional e xamples are provided beyond those given in the book. Also on the CD-ROM is a folder containing Apple Guide resources (Apple Guide itself, Guide Maker, fonts, interfaces, etc.) as well as a folder containing demonstrations of Apple Guide.

Part 1: What is Apple Guide?

The first part of this book discusses Apple Guide from the points of view of the user and the designer of Apple Guide files. You learn about the aspects of Apple Guide the user sees and uses as well as the behavioral principles that underlie its use. Precisely because Apple Guide is not help, it is important to understand how people use this technology. It is strongly recommended that everyone read this part of the book!

Part 2: Creating Guide Files with Guide Maker

In the second part, you will learn how to create Apple Guide files using Guide Maker, Apple's Apple Guide authoring tool which is provided on the CD-ROM, complete syntax for Guide Scripts is provided here. This chapter is designed for the author of Apple Guide files (as opposed to the user or designer). If you are not going to write Apple Guide files yourself, you can skim this section.

Part 3: Creating and Modifying Applications to Use Apple Guide

In the third part, you will see how applications can be modified to interact with Apple Guide. It is not necessary to modify an application for Apple Guide, but doing so provides added value to users and third-party developers. Specific techniques for using Apple Guide with MacApp and OpenDoc are presented. This section is addressed to programmers and system engineers.

Part 4: Adding Apple Guide to Custom Solutions and Content

The fourth part of the book deals with adding Apple Guide to custom solutions: 4th Dimension, HyperCard, WordPerfect, Microsoft Word and other products. The challenge of adding Apple Guide to a solution that involves the use of several different applications is also presented here. This section is best understood by people with an understanding of one (not all) of the products discussed. A knowledge of programming isn't necessary. This section is addressed to value-added resellers, consultants, and solution providers.

Part 5: Reaching Out to the world: Localization and Windows Help

Because we live in a world of connections and communications, the fifth section of this book deals with the issues of localizing Apple Guide for different countries, cultures, and languages as well as with the issue of converting Windows Help files. This section is addressed to Apple Guide authors who are localizing assistance or converting Windows Help.

N O T E   All the example code is provided on the CD-ROM that comes with this book. Some of the examples are Apple Guide files, which are designed to run with specific third-party applications, such as 4th Dimension, HyperCard, Microsoft Word, FileMaker Pro, or WordPerfect. The source code for all guide files is available, but you will be able to use the Apple Guide files only with those applications that you already have. Examples for a fairly wide range of applications have been provided so that you should be able to experiment with at least some of them.

TERMINOLOGY—APPLICATIONS, DEVELOPERS, AND AUTHORS

Apple Guide can be provided for an individual application. It can also be provided for what are called "custom solutions," which are a combination of commercial application(s), custom application(s), and fourth-generation languages (such as 4th Dimension or HyperCard) designed to fill a specific individual's or company's needs. Except for sections of the book that deal specifically with applications or custom solutions (Parts 3 and 4), *application* is used to refer to commercial applications, custom applications, and custom solutions.

Similarly, although applications are normally developed by developers and custom solutions are normally developed by consultants or solution providers (not to mention value-added retailers), all of these people are referred to as *developers*.

Apple Guide files can be developed by developers (in the broad sense used above), by technical writers, by end users, or by teachers. These people are referred to as *Apple Guide authors*.

SUMMARY

Apple Guide is not just another help system and not another bell or whistle added as an after-thought to differentiate one program from another or to keep up with the Joneses of competitive developers. When properly designed with an understanding of the range of its capabilities and the possibilities of its use, Apple Guide provides an enhancement to the traditional user experience of the graphical user interface, which is so great that it is able to transcend most of what we take for granted about how people use computers.

CHAPTER 1

What Is Apple Guide?

Apple Guide provides assistance in the form of help, coaching, doing things for you, preparing or suggesting steps to take, and watching to make sure that you succeed at what you're trying to do.

APPLE GUIDE BASICS

The principal delivery vehicle for this assistance is an Apple Guide window, shown in Figure 1.1.

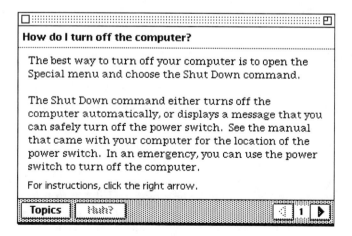

Figure 1.1 An Apple Guide window.

Apple Guide windows float in front of all other windows on the computer's monitor. They have a consistent appearance, with a small drag bar at the top, a title in a shaded area at the top of the window, a navigation bar at the bottom, and the contents (called a panel) in the center.

Panels can contain text; they also can contain PICT graphics (see Figure 1.2) or QuickTime movies.

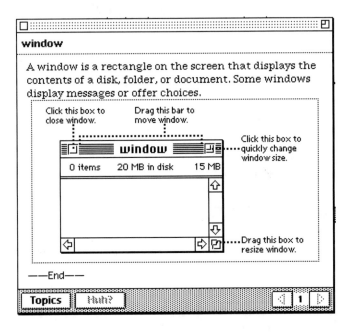

Figure 1.2 An Apple Guide window containing text and a PICT graphic.

Apple Guide is provided for itself; in Figure 1.3 an Apple Guide panel shows the parts of an Apple Guide window. (**Macintosh Guide** is the command that appears in the Guide menu for the Finder. It is an Apple Guide file, not a synonym for Apple Guide itself.)

Figure 1.4 demonstrates how the navigation bar at the bottom of the Apple Guide window can vary. There are often four buttons in the bar: a **Topics** button to return you to the list of Apple Guide topics, a **Huh?** button to provide additional information about the panel's contents, and left- and right-pointing arrows to advance or step back in the sequence of panels. Between the two arrows is the panel's sequence number.

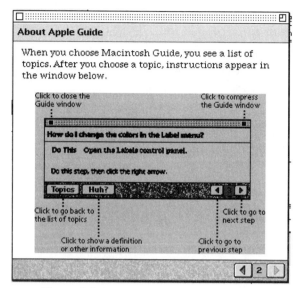

Figure 1.3 A panel from Macintosh Guide.

In Figure 1.3 the Apple Guide window shows only the two arrows; further, the right arrow is grayed out. This is the last panel in a sequence and the user cannot advance.

In this particular case, the user does not have the option of returning to the topics list with a **Topics** button. There also is no **Huh?** button on this panel.

Often a prompt is displayed at the bottom of the panel telling the user what can be done next (see Figure 1.4).

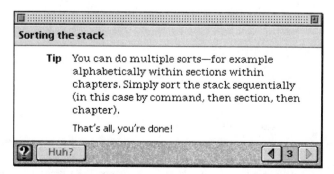

Figure 1.4 An Apple Guide window with a prompt.

The prompt can tell the user when the end of a sequence has been reached—as was shown in Figure 1.2.

Text in panels is usually shown in a special font (Espy) designed for Apple Guide, but the Apple Guide author can vary the font, size, color, and style, as shown in Figure 1.5.

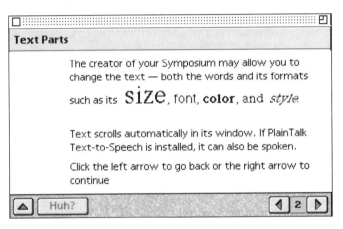

Figure 1.5 An Apple Guide window with styled text.

Some formatting conventions are suggested for Apple Guide panels. The standard **Tag** format is applied to the word "Hours" in Figure 1.6, and the standard **Body** format is applied to the rest of the text.

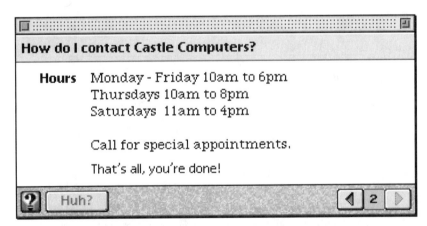

Figure 1.6 An Apple Guide window formatted with the **Tag** and **Body** formats.

In addition to text, PICT graphics, and QuickTime movies, panels can contain buttons, such as the radio buttons shown in Figure 1.7. In this case, the next panel shown (when the user clicks the right arrow) varies, depending on which radio button was selected.

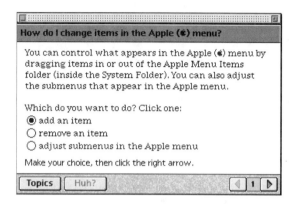

Figure 1.7 An Apple Guide window with radio buttons.

Regular buttons and check boxes can also be used in panels.

Text (as well as specified areas of graphics) can be *hot*, which means that clicking on it takes the user to another panel. Hot text is often shown in bold type (see Figure 1.8).

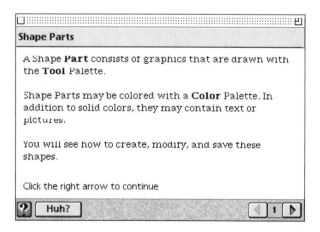

Figure 1.8 An Apple Guide window with hot text in bold type.

The **Huh?** button is often used to provide additional information or a definition. In Figure 1.8, the designer of the Apple Guide assistance has chosen to use hot text to give users additional information. The **Huh?** button is used to describe this, as shown in Figure 1.9.

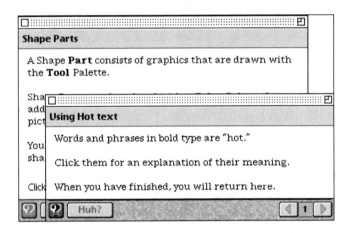

Figure 1.9 A Huh? window in front of the Apple Guide window from which it was opened.

Huh? panels are shown on top of the basic panel; their navigational arrows are grayed out. They are closed with the close box, but they can be kept open for reference by the user as he or she continues with the basic sequence of panels.

In addition to the information in the Apple Guide window, Apple Guide can draw coach marks on the screen (see Figure 1.10). In addition to circles, arrow, underline, and x-mark coaches can be used. When a coach mark is used on a menu, the menu is circled on the menu bar.

When the menu is pulled down, the command in question is often underlined and shown in a different color (see Figure 1.11).

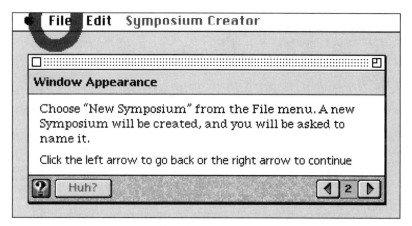

Figure 1.10 A coach mark on a menu.

Figure 1.11 A menu item coached with an underline.

When Apple Guide coaches a user to perform an action, it can check whether that action has been carried out by using a context check. If the action has not been carried out, an Oops panel can be displayed. Figure 1.12 shows an Oops panel and demonstrates the use of a regular button in a panel.

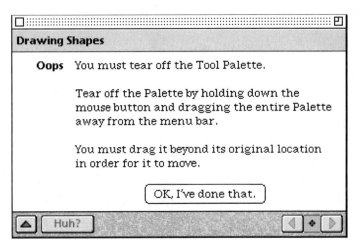

Figure 1.12 An Oops panel with a standard button.

Using AppleScript or the Apple Guide API, Apple Guide can send commands to the application. This enables the Apple Guide author to perform a task for a user. Sometimes the task is performed automatically, but other times it is performed only after the user has failed to do it. Figure 1.13 shows a panel that appears when Apple Guide is performing such a task. The user is asked to click the button when the task is completed. (The button in Figure 1.13 is a 3D button; compare it to the standard button in Figure 1.12.)

Coach marks can be used to highlight items in windows or on the desktop as well as for menu commands. Figure 1.14 shows a coach mark drawn on an application's window.

On gray-scale and color monitors, the underlying image can still be seen through the colored coach mark; on black-and-white monitors, the underlying image is obscured. For this reason, coach marks are automatically drawn differently on black-and-white monitors, as shown in Figure 1.15.

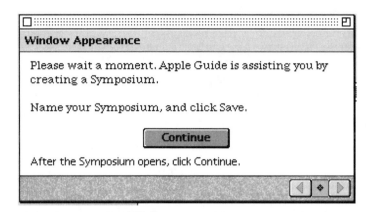

Figure 1.13 An Apple Guide panel with a 3D button.

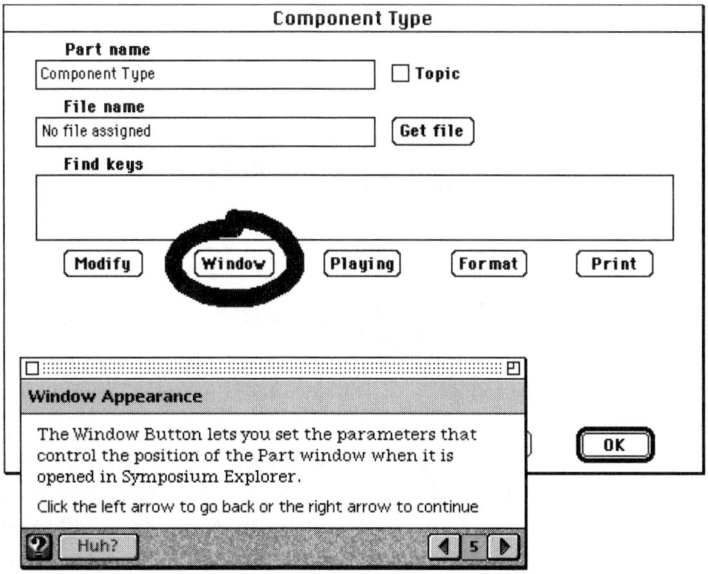

Figure 1.14 An application window with a coach mark drawn on it.

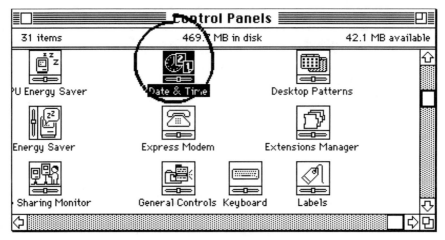

Figure 1.15 A coach mark drawn on a window in the Finder, displayed on a black-and-white monitor.

Apple Guide is usually invoked from the Guide menu. In Figure 1.16 the Finder's Guide menu is shown.

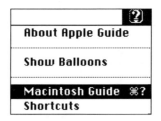

Figure 1.16 The Guide menu.

After an Apple Guide command is chosen from the Guide menu, an Access window is opened. (Several styles of Access windows are available; the Full Access window shown here is the most powerful.) The first time an application's Access window is displayed, an introductory message is shown in the Access window (see Figure 1.17).

The Full Access window allows users to find assistance by choosing topics, as shown in Figure 1.18.

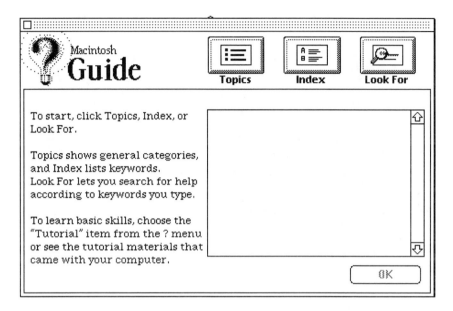

Figure 1.17 A Full Access window with howdy text shown.

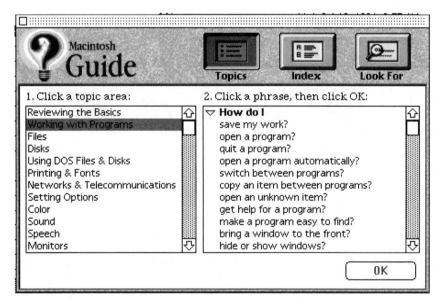

Figure 1.18 A Full Access window showing topic areas and topics.

An index provides an additional method of finding assistance (see Figure 1.19).

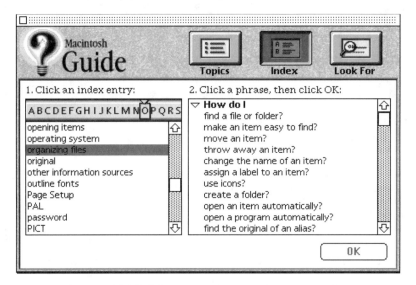

Figure 1.19 A Full Access window showing index entries.

Finally, the user can type in a word or phrase to search for specific assistance (see Figure 1.20).

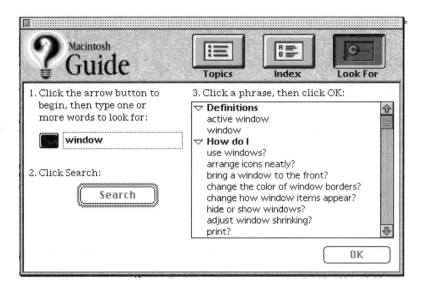

Figure 1.20 A Full Access window with the **Look For** button clicked.

The Simple Access window shown in Figure 1.21 provides a more direct means of getting to assistance and is appropriate for smaller or less complex guide files. (The window shown here is the Finder Shortcuts Apple Guide window.)

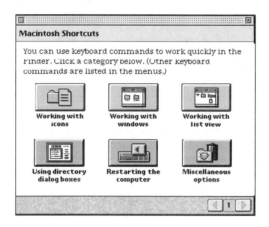

Figure 1.21 A Simple Access window.

The Single List Access window shown in Figure 1.22 provides an intermediate degree of complexity between the Full Access and Simple Access windows.

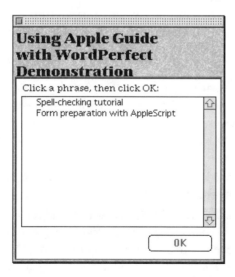

Figure 1.22 A Single List Access window.

CUSTOMIZING APPLE GUIDE

The basic Apple Guide elements have been shown in the previous pages. The words "often," "frequently," and "usually" are liberally sprinkled through this discussion. Almost every aspect of Apple Guide is modifiable and customizable.

For example, in the Full Access window shown in Figure 1.18, the phrase "1. Click a topic area:" is the default for the Topic Areas Instruction command. You can specify another phrase for your assistance. The phrase, "2. Click a phrase, then click OK:" is the default for the Topics Instruction command. You can also change this phrase. In the upper-left part of the window, Apple Guide provides a default graphic and the name of your assistance. You can provide your own graphic or specify a different name for the assistance.

By using all of the options that Apple Guide provides, you can create an assistance system that is more complex and confusing than the application you are trying to support! The standards and suggestions for design (both behavioral and graphical) presented here can help you avoid this. Many of the standards are Apple's own. Some of the suggestions have arisen from changes in Apple Guide during its development; alternative ways of doing things have been tried in Apple Guide's evolution, and it would be foolish not to learn from them.

Most important of all, however, is that you as a designer of Apple Guide use it yourself and learn to critique the guide files that you create and use. Is something annoying? Can you never remember where a certain tip is located? By watching yourself as you use Apple Guide you will learn a great deal about how to design—and how not to design—Apple Guide assistance.

NOTE

A good example of the evolution of the design of interface elements is shown in the Topics button at the left of the navigation bar at the bottom of the panels shown in this chapter. The behavior of this button (returning you to the access window) is unchanged, but the visual representation has evolved.

The standard now is to use the Apple Guide lightbulb icon for the Topics button, as shown in Figure 1.14.

In an early version of Apple Guide, the Topics button was a stylized up arrow, as shown in Figure 1.12. User testing revealed that people familiar with HyperCard treated this as a return arrow in HyperCard—returning you to the main sequence from a Huh? Panel, rather than an arrow to return to the access window.

Accordingly, the arrow was revised to the much clearer button shown in Figure 1.1, with the word "Topics" on it. This solved the problem, but was not strictly speaking correct when the user had selected another button in the access window: clicking on it returns you to whichever access window display you have chosen—either Topics, Index, or Look For.

At this point, the Apple Guide lightbulb icon came on the scene. It neither conveys a misleading message (as the arrow button did) nor a possibly inaccurate one (as the Topics button did).

The point of this little history is encourage you to watch, listen, and learn from your users. No design is perfect the first time, and it is the quality of the designer's observation and the imagination and responsiveness of the revisions that make for the best possible guide file.

SUMMARY

Apple Guide's basic features provide a full interface that can deliver active assistance to users. Based on the most basic elements of the Macintosh interface (windows and buttons), Apple Guide requires no new knowledge from the user or Apple Guide developer as far as the mechanics of Apple Guide assistance are concerned.

The basic elements of Apple Guide can be deployed in a variety of different ways, all geared towards the common goal of providing users with the assistance that they need, when they need it, and in a way that satisfies their needs—both for immediate assistance as well as for the skills to learn how to accomplish their tasks in the future.

CHAPTER 2

Apple Guide Concepts and Definitions

Apple Guide can be thought of as a new interface layer interposed between the user on the one side and the computer and its applications on the other. Just as an application's interface elements (menus, dialog boxes, buttons, and so forth) help the user access the program's underlying functionality, the Apple Guide interface helps the user access the application interface itself. (Using AppleScript and the Apple Guide API, Apple Guide also can access the program's functionality directly.)

Functionally and physically, Apple Guide appears closer to the user than the application's interface itself. The coach marks appear on top of windows and menus; Apple Guide presentation panels float above all application windows. From a behavioral point of view, Apple Guide also is closer to the user than the application itself. Particularly in the case of mass-market productivity tools (spreadsheets, word processors, desktop publishing, communications, and so forth), the application's interface must be designed to be as easy to use as possible for the broadest array of people.

Custom Apple Guide solutions and add-ons can provide assistance couched in the language of the user. Think for a moment of a secretary in a lawyer's office using Microsoft Word to type a contract; now think of a minister typing a sermon using the same software. Once again, think of a librarian typing a list of patrons with overdue books. Each person is using the same software—same menus, same dialog boxes—for a very different purpose. Most likely, each person will even use a different word to describe what they're creating. (Only computer types will say they're creating documents; from the example users' points of view, they're creating a contract, a sermon, and a list.) It is this assistance, sensitive to the contexts of the users, that Apple Guide excels at providing.

In this section, the Apple Guide terms and concepts are defined. Some of these have been mentioned before, but they are all included in this section to provide a central point of reference. The terms and concepts are grouped into five functional areas:

- Access windows
- Presentation panels (this area includes coach marks)
- Sequences and their controls (this area includes context checks)
- Setup (this area covers items that are relevant to an entire guide file—its application and name, for example—as well as default settings)
- Mixins (this area discusses the ability to add and delete elements of Apple Guide assistance to and from different files at run-time

The description of Guide Script syntax in Part 2 groups Apple Guide commands into the same areas.

N O T E   Most guide files are created using Guide Maker, which is on the *Real World Apple Guide* CD-ROM. The concepts and definitions in this chapter are those of Apple Guide; concepts and definitions specific to Guide Maker are discussed in Chapter 15, "Using Guide Maker and Organizing Source Files."

ACCESS WINDOWS

When a user opens a guide file, the Access window is the first window shown. On its first presentation, this window usually contains special text with instructions on its use. Figure 1.18 shows one type of Access window, the Full Access window. The other types of Access windows are the Single List Access window and the Simple Access window.

When a user selects a topic from an Access window, Apple Guide closes the Access window and opens a presentation window for the appropriate topic.

Howdy Text

Howdy text is the text shown when an Access window is first presented. Figure 1.17 shows the howdy text for Macintosh Guide. When an Access window is reopened, the howdy text is not displayed. The howdy text is seen again only when the computer is restarted. Figure 1.18 shows the same Macintosh Guide Access window as in Figure 1.17 with its normal contents.

Full Access Window

The Full Access window is the most powerful entry to Apple Guide and is the most frequently used. The buttons in the upper right—**Topics**, **Index**, and **Look For**—control the contents of the central panes. Figure 1.18 shows a Full Access window with the **Topics** button selected; Figure 1.19 shows the same window with the **Index** button selected; and Figure 1.20 shows how the window looks when the **Look For** button is clicked.

Guide files with more than 20 topics should use a Full Access window.

Topic

An Apple Guide topic is a single section of assistance. When a user chooses a topic (by either double-clicking it or selecting it and clicking **OK** on the Access window), Apple Guide closes the access window and opens a presentation window. In Figure 1.18, "save my work?" in the right pane is a topic. Topics appear in both Full and Simple Access windows; in Full Access windows, they appear in the right pane when any of the **Topics**, **Index**, or **Look For** buttons are clicked.

Header

Topics can be grouped under a header in a Full Access window. In Figure 1.19, the phrase "How do I" is a header. Headers are presented in bold type and have a triangle next to them. By clicking on the triangle, the user can show or hide the topics in the header. Headers must have at least one topic in them. It is not necessary to have headers for topics.

Topic Area

When the **Topics** button is clicked, the left pane of a Full Access window displays a list of topic areas. Topic areas are the highest level of organization for assistance in a Full Access window. Topic areas are comparable to the chapters in a book. By clicking on a topic area in the left pane, the appropriate topics (and headers, if provided) are shown in the right pane. The user can expand or collapse headers using the triangles. When a specific topic is double-clicked (or when the topic is selected and the **OK** button is clicked), the topic is opened in its own presentation window.

Topic Areas Instruction

The line of text that appears above the list of topics in a Full Access window when the **Topics** button is clicked can be customized. This line is called the topic areas instruction. Figure 1.18 shows the default, "1. Click a topic area:".

Topics Instruction

The line of text that appears above the right pane of the Full Access window, regardless of which button is clicked, is called the topics instruction. (Figures 1.18, 1.19, and 1.20 show the default, "2. Click a phrase, then click **OK**:".)

Index Instruction

The line of text that appears above the list of topics in a Full Access window when the **Index** button is clicked is called the index instruction. (Figure 1.19 shows the default, "1. Click an index entry:".)

Look For Instruction

The line of text displayed at the top of the left side of the Full Access window when the **Look For** button is clicked is the look for instruction. (Figure 1.20 shows the default, "1. Click the arrow button to begin, then type one or more words to look for:".)

Single List Access Window

The Single List Access window is basically the same as the right panel of the Full Access window when the Topics button is clicked. The Single List Access window contains a list of topics (and optionally headers). The third hierarchy of organization that is available in the Full Access window (topic areas in the left panel) is not used in the Single List Access window.

Single List Access windows are appropriate for guide files that are not very large or complex. Apple recommends that guide files with between 7 and 20 topics use Single List Access windows.

NOTE

When designing Apple Guide assistance, remember that during the course of development, it is common to add topics to guide files. Even if you don't add topics yourself, upgrades to the application software may add new features that require new topics. If you are unsure whether to use one type of access window or another, it is a good idea to use the larger one. For example, you should consider using Full Access rather than Single List Access, and Single List Access rather than Simple Access.

Simple Access Window

The Simple Access window contains no list of topics, headers, or topic areas. It can contain buttons (like in the Finder Shortcuts Simple Access window shown in Figure 1.21), or it can contain text, QuickTime movies, or PICT graphics. In fact, there is no such thing as a Simple Access window; a Simple Access window is any Apple Guide presentation panel. It can contain any of the navigational tools (buttons, arrows, and so forth) to guide the user to further information, or, it may contain the information itself.

PRESENTATION PANELS

Apple Guide assistance is shown in panels. The panel (sometimes called a presentation panel) is a special type of window. Each panel should contain one thought: an action for the user to take (Figure 1.6 shows a Do It panel), a tip (see Figure 1.4), one item of information, or an error message (Figure 1.12 shows an Oops panel).

In System 7, panels are a constant width of 341 pixels (the total window width is 344 pixels). Apple Guide automatically expands the panels vertically if needed to accommodate the contents. (Commands are available to the Apple Guide author to set maximum and minimum panel heights.)

Panels have three areas: the title area (at the top, below the drag bar), the navigation bar (at the bottom), and the content area (in the middle). Like most windows, they can be dragged, closed with a standard close box, and zoomed. (Clicking the zoom box compresses the window: only the title area and navigation bar are visible; the content area is removed.)

Title Area

The title area contains a title for the topic or sequence that is being presented, not a title for each panel. The topic shown in an Access window may be a brief phrase, such as "move a window?" that completes a sentence started by the header, such as "How do I." The appropriate title for the sequence of panels shown in this topic would be "Moving Windows" or "How do I move a window?" A title that is too wide for the title area of a panel is wrapped to a second line, and the title area is expanded appropriately.

Navigation Bar

The navigation bar at the bottom of the window always contains left and right arrows, which are used to go to the next or previous panel in a sequence. Either (or sometimes both) of these arrows may be automatically dimmed by Apple Guide for the beginning (no previous) or end (no next) of a sequence. The sequence number of the current panel is shown between the two arrows.

Up to three navigation buttons also can be placed in the navigation bar.

Navigation Buttons

The navigation bar can contain up to three special navigation buttons designed by the Apple Guide author. The **Huh?** and **Topics** (the Apple Guide light bulb icon) buttons are common examples of navigation buttons. Navigation buttons are specified for a given sequence, not for individual panels in that sequence. However, just as the left or right arrow may be dimmed on a given panel, one of the navigation buttons may be dimmed for a specific panel. (The fact that only one navigation button—other than the arrows—can be dimmed on a specific panel has design implications. When you plan for navigation buttons in a sequence, remember that their normal state is active and that the exception is to dim one of them on a given panel.)

Navigation buttons either launch a specific action (like returning to the Access window) or start a sequence that is appropriate for a given panel (such as a Huh? sequence).

Because the navigation bar is always a fixed width and height, navigation buttons must always be 18 pixels high.

Content Area

In the center of the presentation panel is the content area. This area can contain text, PICT graphics, QuickTime movies, or buttons.

N O T E

These things are all objects in the very specific sense used in object-oriented programming. Because objects can be overridden to create new objects that share some of the first object's attributes and behavior, it is possible to see how Apple Guide panels could incorporate new functionality.

Each panel should present one point: a point of information, an error message, or an instruction to the user. Limiting panels to one point makes it easier for the user to navigate through Apple Guide and makes the reuse of panels more probable. When you plan your first guide file, you may not consider reusing the individual panels. As your Apple Guide assistance grows, you will find that some panels—particularly those that define or identify parts of the interface—can be used in several places. Bear in mind that reusing panels does not mean showing them to the user repeatedly. The same panel may quite properly reside in several places in a guide file: as a Huh? panel to explain something in response to a user's request, in an Oops sequence to explain something—this time in response to a user's error, or in a basic sequence to present the information directly. The panel's reappearance to the user is based on logical and understandable user actions (even if they are errors). If you find that certain basic information is needed in a variety of sequences, consider a slight restructuring of your guide file so that the basic information is placed in its own sequence, accessible either from an access window or via a Huh? Button. The alternative is to force the user who may be looking at a variety of sequences to skip through the same basic information in each sequence. In most cases, the subtle nuances of difference that may occur will be lost as the user quickly glances at the panel saying, "Oh, I've seen that before."

At the bottom of the content area is a prompt, which is an instruction to the user of what to do next.

Prompt

Apple Guide's assistance to the user is unobtrusive yet always available, in the best tradition of good service. The navigation bar with its arrows (and optional navigation buttons) provides all the controls many users need. In addition, a section at the bottom of each panel's content area is provided for a prompt—an instruction to the user of what to do next or what options are available.

The prompt area can be eliminated from an individual panel if necessary. If a large graphic is included, or if a QuickTime movie is placed on a panel (particularly if it contains its own instructions to the user), eliminating this prompt area may be appropriate. Removing the prompt should be done only after careful consideration. It is usually redundant because the navigation bar is always visible, but it is important. Some people are comfortable following only written instructions; others ignore most of the words and click on buttons or arrows as if there were no tomorrow. Fortunately, most people fall between these extremes.

Prompt Set

Apple Guide enables you to create a set of prompts that you can associate with a given sequence (or by default, with all sequences). A prompt set consists of four prompts:

- a prompt for the first panel in a sequence, such as "Click the right arrow to begin"
- a prompt for the intermediate panels, such as "Click the right arrow to continue, or the left arrow to back up"
- a prompt for the last panel in the sequence, such as"-End-"
- a prompt for panels with controls (like check boxes or radio buttons) in them, such as "Make your choice, then click the right arrow to continue"

Control

A panel can contain controls that the user clicks on: check boxes, radio buttons, and two kinds of buttons. ("Control" is used here in the same sense in which it is used in the Macintosh interface. As defined in the Macintosh Human Interface Guidelines, "Controls are graphic objects that cause instant actions or audible results when the user manipulates them with the mouse. Users set controls that change settings to modify future actions. Controls also enable users to make choices or assign parameters in a range. Controls display existing choices so that they are visible to users.")

Controls can be placed in specific locations on panels and can cause immediate actions, such as showing another panel (buttons). Or they can be used by Apple Guide in determining what panel or sequence of panels to be shown next (radio buttons and check boxes).

Standard Button

A standard button is shown in Figure 1.12. Its title and location are specified by the Apple Guide author, but its design is the standard button shape used throughout the Mac OS interface. It is 20 pixels high and at least 59 pixels wide; it can be wider if the button's title requires. When clicked, the button is highlighted and an action takes place, often opening another panel, but sometimes sending an Apple Event to an application. A "Do It for Me" button often is used on a panel to allow the user to have Apple Guide perform the task.

3D Button

For a 3D button, the Apple Guide author provides a graphic to be used in drawing the button. (3D buttons are shown in Figures 1.13 and 1.21.) Graphics must be provided for the button for when it is in the up position and for when it is clicked, both for color and black-and-white versions. Like standard buttons, 3D buttons cause immediate actions.

Radio Button

Radio buttons never occur singly: they are used when one of several options must be selected. They have no immediate effect: when the user clicks the right arrow, Apple Guide takes one action or another depending on which radio button is checked.

Check Box

Like radio buttons, check boxes provide several options; however, check boxes allow multiple choices to be made. Check boxes also can occur singly. The boxes are evaluated when the user clicks the right arrow.

Text Block

A text block is a body of text that can be referenced by name. To set the howdy text that is shown in an Access window the first time it is opened, you need to create a text block.

Format

You can define a format, which is a combination of font, size, style, and color, and give it a name. These formats can be reused throughout a guide file, providing a consistent look. Multiple formats can be used within a panel. Figure 1.6 demonstrates the use of the default **Tag** format (used for "Do This") and the default **Body** format (used for the rest of the text).

If a format does not specify a value for a specific attribute, the attributes of the text as entered into Guide Maker are used. Thus, for example, the format used in Figure 1.8 does not specify a style; the text as entered is either plain or bold (for the hot text words). The format specifies the font, size, and color.

Hot Items

Clicking a button in a panel causes an immediate action to occur, usually either an Apple Event sent to the application or the opening of a new sequence. Any object in a panel can be "hot" in this sense. The Apple Guide author can specify a given rectangle that will be hot, a word that will be hot (on its first, last, or all occurrences), or a specific object (PICT graphic, text block, and so forth) that is hot.

N O T E

The designer of assistance who uses hot items must confront several issues. The first and most important is designing an interface that makes the items clearly hot but does not otherwise distract from the content. The bold words in Figure 1.8 stand out; some people would say that they stand out to the extent that they make the text harder to read. Italicized words stand out less, but since italic often is used for emphasis in normal text, the user may not realize that the text is hot. Often, a button in either the panel or the navigation bar (such as a **Huh?** button) provides a more appropriate interface element.

Coach Marks

Coach marks are the most visible manifestation of Apple Guide. They can be used to highlight menu items (see Figures 1.10 and 1.11), to highlight objects in windows (see Figure 1.15), or to draw attention to specific areas in windows.

Coach marks come in four styles:

- red circles, which should be used to show the user where to click
- an underline, which should be used to show the user where to type text
- an arrow, which is most appropriate for pointing to an area that is otherwise defined by a graphic on the screen (such as a window) and that needs to be pointed out to the user either for clarification or for the user to do something other than click or type (drag, for example)
- a green x, which can be used to indicate where typing should begin or to indicate the first line of a multiline data entry field

Before providing the user with a Technicolor assortment of coach marks, the Apple Guide designer should consider these standards, adding additional standards where appropriate. As always with the interface, the color of a coach mark should not be used solely to distinguish its meaning from another coach mark. On a gray-scale monitor, all coach marks are the same color.

Coach marks are removed from the screen as soon as the user does anything—such as click, move the mouse, or type—that generates an event. Each panel should contain only one coach mark, because a panel should address only one issue.

In addition to menus, windows, and items in windows, coach marks can be drawn for areas that are specified in two other ways. An AppleScript sctipt can be written and included in the guide file that returns a rectangle for the coach mark. In the following AppleScript script, the location of a field called "name" in a stack called "Invoice Stack" is returned:

```
tell application "HyperCard"
copy (bounds of background field "name") to x
copy (loc of window "Invoice Stack") to y
set item 1 of x to (item 1 of x) + (item 1 of y)
set item 2 of x to (item 2 of x) + (item 2 of y)
set item 3 of x to (item 3 of x) + (item 1 of y)
set item 4 of x to (item 4 of x) + (item 2 of y)
return x
end tell
```

NOTE   This script is discussed in detail later. Apple Guide expects coach mark locations to be provided in global coordinates relative to the upper-left corner of the screen. Because HyperCard returns coordinates relative to the window containing the object, this script adjusts them to global values.

It is always preferable to find a coach mark location by associating it with an object rather than specifying pixel coordinates. That way, if the object moves as a result of a modification by the user or developer, the coach mark's integrity is preserved.

Finally, using the Apple Guide API, a developer can modify an application to return a coach mark location. This can provide a high level of customization, as, for example, when a misspelled word in a document is identified with a coach mark. In some cases, the application's response to a request for a coach mark location will cause it to take some additional action. If there is a misspelled word in a document, for example, the response to a request for a coach mark might scroll the word into view and provide the coach mark location.

SEQUENCES

Panels are arranged in sequences by the Apple Guide author. A simple sequence often corresponds to a topic in a Full Access or Single List Access window. Sequences can contain other sequences. The order of panels in a sequence is specified by the Apple Guide author but can be modified as the user goes through the sequence. These modifications can occur when the user chooses one option or another (see Figure 1.7), or when Apple Guide evaluates a context check and chooses one branch of an IF statement or another.

Conditions

Apple Guide can evaluate logical conditions and use the results to control the panels shown in a sequence. When check boxes or radio buttons are used in a panel, Guide Maker allows the author to check to see which controls are on and to use these results to determine the next panel.

In addition to providing the standard IF-THEN-ELSE type of branching common to programming languages, Apple Guide allows for the persistent evaluation of conditions. This is roughly comparable to the use of WHILE statements in programming languages, but it differs in that when the condition becomes false, a special sequence—an Oops sequence—is activated.

An example of the use of a persistent evaluation of conditions would be a sequence requiring that a certain window be open and remain open while the user is guided through its contents.

There are three conditions that Apple Guide recognizes: <Show If>, <Skip If>, and <Make Sure>.

<Show If>

The <Show If> condition shows a panel in a sequence if the context checks in the condition evaluate to TRUE. It is evaluated only when the forward arrow in the navigation bar is clicked. Because the <Show If> condition is not evaluated when the backward arrow is clicked, the panel in question might be displayed at times that the Apple Guide author thinks it would not be displayed (or vice versa).

NOTE   This is one of the many reasons why testing Apple Guide sequences is so important and tricky. When testing guide files, make certain that you see what happens when you don't follow directions: when you make the wrong choice, back up with the backward arrow, don't click any of the check boxes on a panel, and so forth.

<Skip If>

The <Skip If> condition is evaluated under the same circumstances as the <Show If> condition; its result is the opposite.

<Make Sure>

<Make Sure> conditions are persistent conditions that function like WHILE statements in programming languages. They are evaluated when either the forward or backward arrow is clicked. As a result, they can guarantee that a panel is not inadvertently shown when the backward arrow is clicked. <Make Sure> conditions are evaluated after <Show If> or <Skip If> conditions are evaluated for a given panel.

<Show If> and <Skip If> conditions simply determine whether a given panel (or group of panels) is shown. When the condition evaluates to TRUE or FALSE, Apple Guide has the panels at hand to display (or not display). With the <Make Sure> condition, Apple Guide needs to alert the user when the <Make Sure> condition is not true. A special sequence—often consisting of only one panel—is associated with each <Make Sure> condition. This sequence, called an *Oops sequence*, is displayed when the <Make Sure> condition is false. After the problem is corrected (either by the user or automatically by Apple Guide), the user clicks a button that invokes the standard *goback* event to return to the original sequence.

The user may not necessarily return to the panel that failed the <Make Sure> condition. The <Make Sure> condition is evaluated (and reevaluated) with every click of the forward and backward arrows in normal sequence, as well as when the standard goback event is processed (as when the user clicks an **OK** button in an Oops sequence). During this time, conditions on the computer may have changed: the user may have done what was requested but also switched to another application and written a document, a fax modem may have sent or received a fax, and so forth.

To determine which panel in a sequence should be returned to from an Oops sequence, Apple Guide starts with the panel that failed the <Make Sure> condition and searches it and the preceding panels to find the first panel (counting backward) that:

- has no <Make Sure> condition attached to it, or
- has a <Make Sure> condition that evaluates to TRUE attached to it, or
- is the first panel of the sequence.

The <Make Sure> and <Skip If> conditions often are combined to guarantee the integrity of a multistep process. This is one of the most powerful aspects of Apple Guide. You do not know what the user has been up to when he or she starts to use an Apple Guide topic. If the user has started to do something and then gotten stuck, the appropriate application may be launched, the specific window may be open, and half the information that needs to be entered may have been entered. By combining <Skip If> and <Make Sure> commands, you can jump over panels that coach the launch of the application, the window opening, and so forth. The first panel that the user sees will (if all goes well) contain the instructions for the precise next step that needs to be performed. The same sequence, however, will coach the user step by step through each of the initial panels if the <Skip If> and <Make Sure> commands detect that the application has not been launched, the window is not opened, and so forth.

Context Check

The elements of conditions are context checks. Context checks ultimately can be evaluated to a TRUE or FALSE value.

Guide Maker contains two standard context checks: checkBoxState and radioButtonState. These are used to check the values of radio buttons and check boxes on the current panel.

Context checks can be evaluated in two other ways. In the first, an external code module can be written and included as a resource in the guide file. Context checks may be comparable to simple questions (Is file sharing turned on?) or they may be complex questions that require Apple Guide to include information in the question (Is the window named "Preferences" open?). In the second case, one or more parameters must be passed to the external code module. When the context check is evaluated, the external code module is executed.

External code modules usually are not written by an Apple Guide author. They must be written and compiled into code modules by a programmer. External code modules often are available to provide answers to general context check questions: is file sharing turned on, is a window with a specific title opened, and so forth. External code modules of this sort are used extensively in the standard Apple Guide for the Macintosh set of files. Context checks that use external code modules have the advantage of being able to be implemented without modifying the application for which assistance is being provided.

NOTE The file Standard Resources on the *Real World Apple Guide* CD-ROM (located in the Cookbook folder) contains the external code modules used in Macintosh Guide. For a list of these external code modules, their purposes, and their parameters, refer either to Chapter 12, "Sequences II—Conditions and Context Checks" or to the External Code Modules folder inside the Cookbook folder on the CD-ROM.

A second form of context check can be implemented using the Apple Guide API. This requires modification to the application, but may provide better results when specific checks have to be made. Thus, a standard external code module to test whether a window with the title "My Document" is open works very well. A context check implemented through a modification to an application is more appropriate when it is necessary to find out if "My Document" contains unsaved changes.

The results of context checks are evaluated in conditions. Panels in a sequence may be presented or not depending on the results. When context checks are part of persistent conditions, Apple Guide can display an Oops sequence.

Oops Sequence

An Oops sequence (usually containing one panel) is displayed when a mistake has been made or when Apple Guide discovers a persistent condition that has become false. (Figure 1.12 shows an Oops sequence that is shown when the user fails to tear off a Tool Palette.)

The Oops sequence usually contains a button that the user clicks when the error has been corrected. Control returns to the original sequence.

Sometimes an Oops sequence has two buttons: one for the user to click when the error has been corrected, the other a "Do It For Me" button to cause the application to take appropriate action.

The panel in an Oops sequence should use the format shown in Figure 1.12, with the word "Oops" in bold.

Continue Sequence

Although structurally the same as an Oops sequence, a continue sequence automatically corrects the problem. The panel of a continue sequence frequently says something like, "Please wait while Apple Guide opens the window." As in an Oops sequence, the user clicks a button (usually named **Continue**) to return to the original sequence. Figure 1.13 shows a continue sequence panel.

Event

The action taken when a button is clicked is called an event. Events are invoked not only when a button is clicked, but they also may be invoked automatically when a panel is created, destroyed, shown, or hidden. (A panel is created and shown when it is the next panel in a sequence. A panel is shown (but not necessarily acreated) when the user expands a previously collapsed panel using the zoom box.) An event is always eventually mapped to an Apple Event.

Apple Guide responds to a number of Apple Events itself, and the Apple Guide author can send events that do things such as running an AppleScript script, playing a sound, going to a specific panel, launching a sequence, or returning from an Oops sequence to the original sequence.

Apple Events can be sent to any other application. For example, a "Do It for Me" button in general sends an Apple Event to an application that causes it to open a document or do some other scriptable activity.

N O T E

Although Apple Events usually are directed to an application for which assistance is being provided, they also can be directed to other applications. This is most common when Apple Guide is being provided for a solution that involves several applications.

SETUP

Apple Guide enables you to set a number of parameters and default values for a guide file.

Signature

Every application on the Macintosh has a four-character signature that the Finder uses to identify it. Developers register their application signatures with Apple, which guarantees their uniqueness. In placing guide files in the Guide menu, Apple Guide can match a signature in the guide file to an application's signature to determine whether that guide file should be listed.

Balloon Help

Introduced in System 7, Balloon Help is a powerful help system that identifies objects on the screen. When the user turns on Balloon Help (by choosing the **Show Balloons** command from the Guide menu), a balloon appears as the mouse is moved over objects on the screen. Balloon Help is very useful for answering "What is this?" questions. If you contrast Balloon Help with Apple Guide, the most obvious difference is that with Balloon Help the user asks for information about something that is shown on the screen. With Apple Guide, the user asks for information about an idea or concept, and Apple Guide shows the user what should be done, identifying screen objects along the way.

Apple Guide is much more powerful than Balloon Help, but it addresses different issues. Balloon Help remains an important tool for identifying screen objects. Applications with tool bars that are loaded with many icons must provide this type of assistance. Because turning Balloon Help on and off is awkward for some users, a section of a status bar is often used to provide information about the tool that the mouse is pointed to. Although the delivery mechanism is different, the service is nevertheless provided to the user.

Gestalt

The Gestalt Manager, introduced in System 7, replaced the earlier Environs procedures and the SysEnvirons function. It is used to let applications query the environment in which they are running—is there a floating-point processor, is QuickTime installed, and so forth. Up to three <Gestalt> commands can be included in a guide file; Apple Guide evaluates them, and if any are true, it places that guide file in the Guide menu (if other criteria are met). (The <Gestalt> commangs are thus evaluated with an OR rather than an AND operator).

Script

The Script Manager is used to manage the input and display of different character sets and languages. The script code identifies a given character set—Roman, Cyrillic, Arabic, Thai, Japanese, and so forth. A given language uses a certain script. The region code identifies a localized version of system software for a given country or area. For example, the French language uses the Roman script, and as implemented by Apple there are region codes representing France, French Swiss, Quebec, and so forth.

This information is used in displaying text, calculating where to split lines, and determining word breaks (so that when a user double-clicks on a word in a word processor the appropriate characters can be highlighted). Apple Guide matches the script code and region code of a guide file to the script code and region code of the script system currently in use on the machine. If they do not match, the guide file is not added to the Guide menu.

MIXINS

Guide Maker allows a guide file to be created from several source files, using an <Include> command when the script is compiled.

Apple Guide itself allows guide files to be formed from several guide files that are combined at run time rather than compilation time. These files are called *mixins*. Commands are provided that allow topic areas, headers, and topics; index headers and topics; and sequences to be combined at run time.

For example, mixin files are used in Macintosh Help to provide assistance for speech or video only if the computer has those capabilities. Similarly, Macintosh Help uses a mixin file for the PowerBook to include assistance specific to the PowerBook.

An alternative would have been to provide separate guide files for speech, video, the PowerBook, and so forth. From the user's standpoint, it is much easier to access a single item in the Guide menu than to switch from one guide file to another.

Figure 2.1 shows some of the Apple Guide files installed in the System folder. The mixin files have a different icon and have the word "addition" in their name.

These files are normally installed in the Extensions folder; they are shown here in another location for clarity.

N O T E

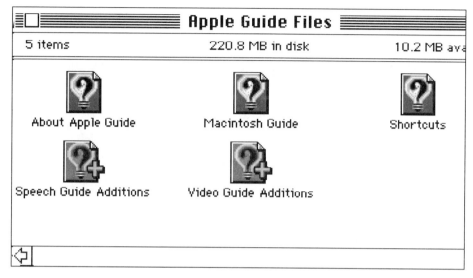

Figure 2.1 Apple Guide files and mixin files.

SUMMARY

It is always a challenge to learn the language of a new tool or technology, and Apple Guide is no exception. The bright side of mastering these terms, however, is that it enables you to actually produce Apple Guide assistance, which relies heavily on coach marks to identify interface elements. For the first time, you and your users can avoid having to describe and learn names for each object seen on the screen: arrows can point to things for users to click, and no one need ever memorize their names. Unfortunately, this benefit is available to only your users: you have to learn the Apple Guide terminology the old-fashioned way.

CHAPTER 3

Accessing Apple Guide

This chapter covers the ways in which users can open Apple Guide files and the distinctions among different kinds of Apple Guide assistance. Before that, however, it is appropriate to ask just where Apple Guide is in the operating system.

WHERE IS APPLE GUIDE?

Apple Guide is a part of System 7.5 and is installed automatically during the installation/update process. When no guide files are open, Apple Guide is said to be sleeping, and it requires very few system resources. When Apple Guide files are open, Apple Guide is active and requires more resources.

Apple Guide consists of the software that displays instructions, draws coach marks, and checks that you have done the right thing. This software is driven by Apple Guide files, which are created and distributed by the application developer, third-party instructional material authors, custom solution providers, and even users who want to use Apple Guide facilities to customize and ease their own lives.

Apple Guide is invoked by choosing an Apple Guide item from the Guide menu, which was shown in Figure 1.16.

N O T E   The Guide menu made its debut as the Help menu in System 7.0. Originally, it was the access point for Balloon Help. Application developers were encouraged to add their help systems to the Help menu as commands. Some did. Others left their help systems where they were—often in the Apple menu either as part of the **About** command or as an additional **Help** command (or commands) beneath the **About** command. Many applications provided entry points to their help systems in both the Apple and Help menus. Because applications can add commands to the Guide menu (as they could to the Help menu), it is not impossible to find a Guide menu that contains Apple Guide files alongside commands that invoke other help systems. Placing all forms of assistance in one place is important because the user who needs assistance doesn't need the added frustration of looking for it.

The Guide menu is also used to get to Balloon Help. Typically, Balloon Help is the third item in the Guide menu (the dashed lines count as dummy items in the numbering scheme). Apple Guide rebuilds the Guide menu whenever you launch an application, placing the names of the appropriate guide files in their appropriate places in the menu.

The Guide menu is available at all times, although its contents change to reflect the current application. When a modal dialog is displayed (such as a Print dialog box or a Save As dialog box) only the **Show Balloons** or **Hide Balloons** command is enabled. Thus, if a user is presented with a dialog box containing items that need explanation, the only assistance available is Balloon Help. Don't waste your time writing Apple Guide assistance for dialog boxes!

N O T E   There are four system menus that may appear in the menu bar in System 7.0 or later. The Apple menu has been part of the interface since the beginning. The Application menu allows rapid switching among applications that are currently running; it also allows you to show or hide windows for the current or all applications. The Keyboard menu allows access to alternative script systems and allows users to switch keyboard layouts easily. The Apple and Application menus are always inserted in the menu bar. If your application's menus require the space, the Guide and Keyboard menus are dropped from the menu bar. For applications that have many menus (or very long menu titles), it may be necessary to provide an alternative to the Guide menu to allow users to access Apple Guide in that application.

TYPES OF GUIDE FILES

There are five types of Apple Guide assistance: about, help, tutorials, shortcuts, and others. Although each type of guide file has a different purpose, the commands and instructions used do not differ from one type of file to another. Thus, neither Apple Guide nor Guide Maker enforces any distinction among the different types of files. You can create a tutorial file that consists of only shortcuts, and no one will be the wiser—except the poor user who will be confused.

When Apple Guide builds the Guide menu automatically, it inserts files into the menu in the following order:

1. About file. If any exist that are co-resident (in the same folder) with the application, the first one is chosen alphabetically based on its title. If no About file is found that is co-resident with the application, a standard Apple Guide About file is used.

2. Tutorial file. Similarly, if any exist, the first one alphabetically is inserted after the **Show Balloons/Hide Balloons** command and the line that is drawn in the menu beneath it.

3. Help file. The same procedure is followed.

4. Shortcuts file. The same procedure is followed

5. Other files. As many as are found co-resident with the application are added at the end of the menu, in alphabetical order.

NOTE

Using the Apple Guide API, an application can build the Guide menu differently. This is discussed in Chapter 17.

Because guide files can contain any commands regardless of the type that they are, it stands to reason that Other guide files can be tutorials, shortcuts, and so forth. The default structure of the Guide menu should be seen as "blessing" specific About, Help, Tutorial, and Shortcuts guide files by placing them at the top of the menu. Guide files that are of type Other—which may be About, Help, Tutorial, and Shortcuts guide files—are placed at the bottom of the menu.

What causes a guide file to deserve to be "blessed"? In the case of Apple Guide assistance provided for an application, these files are the guide files provided by the application developer. The Other guide files listed at the bottom of the Guide menu (which may be Tutorial, Shortcuts, and so forth) often are provided by users, consultants, or solution providers. In some cases, these files may also be provided by the application developer. For example, many word processors are shipped with customized dictionaries for lawyers, doctors, engineers, and so forth, as well as a general dictionary for all users. In the same way, customized guide files can be included by the original application developer as well as by third parties.

Unfortunately, there are other complications when trying to determine whether a given guide file should be blessed or not. If the application developer doesn't provide a tutorial, should a third-party Tutorial guide file be marked as a tutorial, thereby appearing in the Guide menu after a Help guide file and before a Shortcuts guide file (if they exist)? In general, the answer is no, because the application developer may choose to include a Tutorial guide file in a subsequent release of the software. If the third-party tutorial is marked as an Other guide file, it will always appear in the Guide menu. If it is marked as a tutorial and if the application developer adds its own tutorial, only one of those will be blessed and show up in the Guide menu.

The only time when a third-party should definitely identify a guide file as an About, Help, Tutorial, or Shortcuts guide file is when the third-party guide file is intended as a replacement for the application developer's guide file. This may happen when a third party adds Apple Guide assistance to an application and wants the About guide file to reflect not only the original assistance but also the added files. Otherwise, this is an unusual circumstance, most likely occurring only if the application developer's assistance is determined to be unusable for one reason or another.

N O T E   The distinction among different types of guide files causes more confusion among Apple Guide authors and developers than among users. When guide files are properly named (with the words "shortcuts," "tutorial," "about," and "help" in their menu items) users are shielded from this complexity. Whether the differentiation of different types of guide files will have more significance in future versions of the operating system is unclear. Apple Guide authors and developers are best advised to follow the standards and guidelines outlined here and in Apple's interface standards.

About Guide Files

About guide files provide an overview of the assistance currently available in the Guide menu. Usually an About guide file is provided by the application developer. It always resides in the same folder as the application.

NOTE   When the Guide menu is built by the application using the Apple Guide API, there is no routine available to insert an About guide file into the Guide menu. Therefore, only the default behavior—co-residency—can place an About guide file in the Guide menu.

Contents of About Guide Files

An About guide file typically is brief: it may consist only of one panel. It should provide the user with information about what assistance is available from other items in the Guide menu.

Of course, in the case in which third parties add guide files to the menu, this information may be incomplete or misleading. For that reason, if you are adding assistance to an application in the form of additional guide files, you may consider replacing the standard About guide file with one that includes the information from the original and information about the assistance that you have added.

The user is best served if the last person who adds assistance to an application provides the About guide file, thus providing the most comprehensive summary of assistance.

How People Use About Guide Files

Users may look at the About guide file to see what assistance is available. If the other guide files are appropriately named, they may not feel the need to look at this item, however. When they do look at the About guide file, it is often when they are first familiarizing themselves with the application. They tend not to look at the About guide file when they are under pressure (unless all other attempts at getting assistance have failed). For these reasons, don't put critical information in the About guide file that isn't repeated elsewhere.

Tutorial Guide Files

Tutorials guide users through the basic processes and procedures in your application. The word "Tutorial" should always appear in the guide menu name of these files. New users of applications not only do not know how to use them but often don't know what they can do. Can you spell check a spreadsheet with your spreadsheet program?—let the user know in a tutorial. Can you export text as easily from your desktop publishing program as you can import it?—again, a tutorial can let the user know that the functionality is there, even if demonstrating it is beyond the scope of the tutorial.

Of all the questions users ask through Apple Guide assistance, "Can I...?" is one of the least asked. Users form an impression of what a given application can do and then use it for that purpose alone. Examples abound of people who don't know that they can edit graphics in word processing programs, use a communications program to do simple word processing off-line, and so forth. When the user asks "How Do I...?" he or she has already decided that your application can (or should) be able to be used to accomplish the task. By making certain that the application's full range of functionality is demonstrated in a Tutorial guide file (but not, of course, in excruciating detail), you can help your users get the most out of their software investment.

N O T E   People are not stupid. Don't use an Apple Guide file as an opportunity for a commercial (unless you explicitly indicate that). There's nothing wrong with having an Other guide file titled "Other Products from XYZ Software Corp." But if a user settles down to use a Tutorial guide file and encounters half a dozen panels of puffery and promotion, the user will be as irritated as if an instructional video started with five minutes of promotional film clips.

Contents of Tutorial Guide Files

Tutorial guide files help users to develop a basic proficiency in using an application. Like chapters in manuals with titles such as "Quick Start," "Your First Document," or "A Simple Session," a Tutorial guide file not only demonstrates the fundamental tools, commands, and functionality of your application but also gives the user an introduction to the terminology that is relevant to the application (for example, "tool bar," "on-line session," and "screen depth"). Tutorials covering advanced issues may be provided in guide files marked as Other guide files listed at the bottom of the Guide menu (but with the word "Tutorial" in their title).

How People Use Tutorials

Users turn to tutorials to familiarize themselves with an application. New users of an application may explore the tutorials to see the sorts of things that they can do with the application as well as how to do them.

People often turn to tutorials when they are ready to start a process or take some time to learn about an application or solution. Tutorial guide files should be designed with the recognition that people are using them primarily to learn, rather than to assist them in carrying out a specific task at that moment. "Do It for Me" buttons are not used frequently in Tutorial guide files: the point of the tutorial is for the user to learn how to do things. Tutorials often use context checks extensively to make certain that the user has opened the Preferences window, clicked the OK button, or otherwise carried out the step.

Because Tutorial guide files are most often used when the user has the time and attention to devote to learning new tasks, they should be organized carefully with sequences of panels that describe what the topic of the Tutorial guide file will demonstrate and what the user will learn by completing that topic. Typically, the final panels of a topic in a Tutorial guide file recapitulate what the user has learned and make suggestions for further steps in learning to use the application.

Help Guide Files

Although Apple Guide isn't help, it does include help as one of its services.

Contents of Help Guide Files

Help guide files answer users' questions—usually at the moment when they arise. Help guide files should normally use the Full Access window style and keyword searches extensively, and their index screens should be fully loaded. Users should be able to answer their questions very quickly from Help guide files.

While Tutorial guide files are primarily learning assistants, Help guide files are primarily doing assistants. Just as it is not common to see "Do It for Me" buttons in Tutorial guide files, it is very common—and welcome—to see them in Help guide files.

Context checks can be used very effectively in Help guide files. In Tutorial guide files, context checks are most frequently used to check that the user has carried out an action, such as opening a window. In Help guide files, context checks can be used to quickly identify the state that the application and its data are in. For example, if a user chooses a topic area labeled "Emphasizing text," a topic might be "How do I italicize text?" The first panel might use a context check to test whether any text is selected. Another context check might check to see whether selected text is already italicized (in some sizes of some fonts, the appearance is not very different).

When Apple Guide assistance is being developed, the context checks used in Tutorial guide files can often be reused in Help guide files. In this example, a Tutorial guide file might instruct the user to select some text and then check to see whether it has been done. The Help guide file would simply use the same context check to make certain that the user has carried out the commands that were taught in the Tutorial guide file. There is no reason to display a panel in a Help guide file instructing a user to select some text if the text has already been selected.

How People Use Help Guide Files

The user who is opening a Help guide file from the Guide menu is very interesting to observe. In almost all cases, he or she has just hit a roadblock in carrying out a task: either an inexplicable error message has appeared or another obstacle has blocked completion of the task.

In order to write Help guide files properly, you should take a moment to think about the user's state of mind. We don't usually say, "Oh, goody, I want to italicize the next word I type and I can't remember how to do it!" We more often say "s—t" or "f—". Sometimes we blame the damned software for not responding properly to the keyboard equivalent we've typed or for not having the italicize command in a logical place (like in the Preferences menu—after all I prefer to have the following word in italics). Sometimes we blame our boss for wanting the word underlined, sometimes we blame the world.... You get the idea. The user who needs help isn't happy.

Furthermore, the user who needs help has just changed the focus of attention from the task (writing a letter, for example) to the tool (such as italicizing a word). This change of focus has several consequences, all of which the Help guide writer should take into account:

- By changing the focus of attention, the user has been distracted from the primary task. If you think back on the times when this has happened to you, you may remember that when you did finally figure out how to italicize a word you forget what the word was to be. Or what the following word was to be. The faster the user can be helped, the less likely the distraction from the task will have serious effects.

- In providing help, the Help guide file author should at all costs avoid causing the user to change the focus of attention yet again. A help screen that says, "See page 273 of manual volume 2" is dangerous because it not only doesn't answer the question but moves the user's focus (and possibly physical location) yet again. Returning to the scene of the attempted italicization with one's train of thought intact becomes less and less likely.

- Because the user's attention may be focused very intently on a very specific application of the tool (italicization, for example), alternative solutions may not be as obvious as they would be in a calmer moment. In this example, if the user could type the given word in another font or in bold, the immediate problem of emphasis would be solved and the specific problem of italicizing the word could be addressed at a natural breaking point in the task. The Help guide file writer can help restore this perspective by adding comments to the help panels reminding the user of related topics. (Of course, in doing so, the guide file writer must not be so profligate with related topics as to distract the user. No one said creating help was easy!)

From the preceding paragraphs, you may think that users opening Help guide files are foaming at the mouth as they reach for the Guide menu. They (usually) are not. However, by remembering the mental state of someone who is frustrated at not being able to do something and distracted from an important task by a trivial frustration with a tool, you may be able to produce Help guide files that are not only useful and informative but helpful to someone who normally is very calm and nice.

Shortcuts Guide Files

Shortcuts guide files provide the type of quick reference that are provided on end-pages of manuals, reference cards, keyboard templates, and notes stuck to the side of the computer screen.

Contents of Shortcuts Guide Files

Shortcuts guide files often present keyboard equivalents or syntax rules. In general, the information presented in Shortcuts guide files consists of single items. A sequence of commands or keystrokes is usually described in a Help guide file.

How People Use Shortcuts Guide Files

Users turn to Shortcuts guide files for the briefest assistance. One or two mouse clicks should be sufficient to get the information. The Access window for a Shortcuts guide file is usually either a Presentation or a Single List Access window.

If the Shortcuts guide file is designed so that a user must make four or five choices to find the necessary information, it's no longer a shortcut!

Other Guide Files

Other guide files may be Help, Shortcuts, or Tutorial guide files that are provided by third parties or are otherwise not "blessed" as are primary Help, Shortcuts, and Tutorial guide files. They also may be guide files that contain different types of assistance, sometimes combining features of different guide files.

In all cases, the content, purpose, and type of guide file (Tutorial, Help, or Shortcuts) should be obvious from the command listed in the Guide menu. More information about the guide file may be provided in Balloon Help for the menu item, but you should remember that users often do not turn Balloon Help on.

The howdy text on the introductory panel should make the content, purpose, and type of guide file clear.

Contents of Other Guide Files

Users are rarely interested in performing isolated commands in an application: they are interested in solving their problems and performing sequences of commands. Balloon Help is excellent at explaining what an individual button or menu item will do. Apple Guide Other guide files are excellent vehicles for showing how to combine individual commands to accomplish a goal.

For most applications, it is possible to list a number of command sequences that users are likely to want: mail merge in a word processor, totaling a spreadsheet table in two directions and providing percentages and raw totals, or logging onto a communications service. These are ideal candidates for Other guide files provided by the application developer, consultant, third-party solution provider, or value-added retailer.

Solution providers and consultants may also be able to list a number of command sequences that are specific to a given user, such as mail merge using the inactive client mailing list with output going to stock postcard #PC 1234 or updating the investments spreadsheet using yesterday's prices from World, for example.

In each of these cases, the tasks involve a number of commands to be carried out in sequence. Apple Guide is an excellent tool to walk the user through these steps easily.

In the case of a task that is performed regularly, the guide file may be used as a learning tool: after the first few times the user will do the steps manually. The guide file may also be used as a reminder for the user who has been distracted or otherwise can't remember what to do next in the sequence of commands.

In the case of a multistep task that is not done regularly, the guide file may be used every time a user has to perform the task.

In the case of a guide file used as a teaching tool, adding **Huh?** buttons and hot text can provide the information that someone needs to fully understand the process. In the case of a guide file used merely to carry out the task at hand (where the task needn't be learned because it is done relatively infrequently), a "Do It for Me" button for either the entire task or several steps within it can be very helpful.

How People Use Other Guide Files

Guide files that are classified as Other guide files may be Help, Shortcuts, or Tutorial guide files, or they may use the techniques of those files. The behavior of users is accordingly comparable to those other files.

Most important of all is to make certain that the Other guide file (as all guide files) delivers on its promise and the user's expectation. This is done in two ways:

- User Expectations: Make the guide file's techniques clear by including the word "Help," "Shortcuts," or "Tutorial" as appropriate in the Guide menu item. Make its purpose clear by also using the name of the application or guide file subject in the Guide menu. Further clarify these points with the howdy text on the Access window.
- Guide File Delivery: Deliver what you have promised. Don't put shortcuts in a Huh? panel of a Tutorial.

HOW GUIDE FILES ARE MADE AVAILABLE TO USERS

Most of the time, users access Apple Guide through items in the Guide menu. The Guide menu normally is built automatically by Apple Guide. Application programmers who want to change these procedures can customize the process.

Default Guide Menu Behavior

When Apple Guide builds the Guide menu, it relies on several conventions:

- Apple Guide looks for guide files that are co-resident with the application. (*Co-resident* means that they are located in the same folder with the application.)

- Apple Guide places an About guide file as the first menu item. If there is no About guide file co-resident with the application, Apple Guide places a standard "About Apple Guide" item in that location.

- The second through fourth items of the Guide menu are the dummy lines above and below the Balloon Help item, and the Balloon Help item itself.

- If a Tutorial guide file is co-resident with your application, it is placed in the menu as the next item. If more than one Tutorial guide file is co-resident, the first one (alphabetically) is placed in the menu.

- If a Help guide file is co-resident with your application, it is placed next. Again, if more than one Help guide file is co-resident, the first one alphabetically is placed in the menu.

- The same procedure is used to place a Shortcuts guide file in the Guide menu.

- If there are Other guide files co-resident with your application, all of them are then placed at the end of the menu in alphabetical order.

Because of the way in which Apple Guide builds the Guide menu, some user actions can have unintended results. The first action that can cause problems is moving applications without their associated guide files from one folder to another. In the Read Me file distributed with System 7.5, users are cautioned not to do this. But they will, if only to see what happens.

Two things can happen when you move guide files and applications around. The first is that when the application is launched, Apple Guide will find no co-resident guide files, and the Guide menu will have no assistance for that application. The second problem that can occur when files are moved is that the wrong files are associated with an application. In creating a guide file, you can use the <App Creator> command to specify the four-character creator type of the application that you want to open this file. If you always do this, you can be sure that if your guide files are co-resident with your application they will always be opened correctly.

N O T E   If you do not include the <App Creator> command, your guide file may be opened with an application with which it is co-resident but that you know nothing about. Worse, if two guide files of the same type are co-resident with your application and neither has an <App Creator> command, Apple Guide will open the one whose name comes first alphabetically. A special arrangement has been made between Fate and Apple Guide to ensure that nine times out of ten in such a situation the wrong file is opened. (In addition to the <App Creator> command, the <Gestalt> command can be used to select which of several guide files is opened.)

Custom Guide Menu Behavior

In some cases, application developers have chosen to use the Apple Guide API to control the way in which the Guide menu is built. One way of doing this is to place the application's guide files in the Preferences folder (which is located within the System folder). Because many applications already place their own files in the Preferences folder, the rationale is that it is an appropriate centralized place for application guide files to live. If the guide file is properly marked using the <App Creator> command, many guide files can co-exist in the Preferences folder. This allows the user to move the application around at will. (Of course, moving guide files out of the Preferences folder will cause problems, but users seem to have been trained fairly well to leave the Preferences folder alone.)

Unfortunately, using any except the default Guide menu behavior provided by Apple Guide requires making modifications to the application. Fortunately, these modifications are not extensive (and are discussed in Chapter 17.)

N O T E   If this strategy is used, you should be aware of another (though less serious) complication that can occur. If the user somehow places a guide file in the same folder as the application, Apple Guide will automatically place it in the menu. When the application comes along and inserts its guide files from the Preferences folder into the Guide menu, you may have duplicate or irrelevant items.

Another way in which developers have customized the Guide menu is to programmatically pick up guide files that are co-resident with documents that the user is working with. This strategy is particularly relevant to content: if you are using an application to explore five different CD-ROM products, the application-related guide files should appear in all cases. Specific tutorials for each of the different

CD-ROM products should appear for only the relevant title. This can be done programmatically by adding guide files that are co-resident with content documents to the Guide menu when the documents are opened. Again, this requires modifying the application in accordance with the Apple Guide API. Instructions for doing this are given in Chapter 17.

All three of these strategies can be combined, for example:

- You can have an About guide file co-resident with the application to describe the contents of the Guide menu. If this file is moved (or if the application is moved), Apple Guide will not find it and will install a generic **About** item as the first item in the Guide menu. The damage will be minimal.

- You can pick up application-specific guide files from the Preferences folder (or from an application folder within the Preferences folder). Make sure to use the <App Creator> command so that these files are picked up by only your application. This avoids the problem of guide files disappearing and appearing due to disk maintenance by users. Guide files can be placed in the Preferences folder as part of an automatic installation process. A further modification to the application can check that these files are there and post a message if they are not: for example, if the user has copied the application to another machine (using the copy command instead of an installer) but not brought the relevant guide files along.

- In the case of content, make content guide files co-resident with the content document and programmatically insert them in the Guide menu as content documents are opened (and remove them when content documents are closed). Note that these files are still vulnerable to disappearing if users move them away from content documents.

These techniques can be varied and customized further: all of them require modifications to the application, and none is required.

Invoking Apple Guide in Ways Other than from the Guide Menu

For application developers who want to do so, Apple Guide can be invoked programmatically just as any other toolbox call would be made. This means that guide files can be opened in response to menu commands—anywhere in the menu bar, in response to mouse clicks, automatically when an error condition is encountered, or in other ways. Invoking Apple Guide programmatically is discussed in Chapter 17. An example of invoking Apple Guide using a button in a HyperCard stack is given in Chapter 22.

Because the Guide menu can be dropped from the menu bar if there isn't enough room for it, applications with many menus or with long menu names may need to provide other ways of invoking Apple Guide.

Invoking Apple Guide in ways other than from the Guide menu can be very helpful to the user, if this is in addition to Guide menu access. Alternative means of starting Apple Guide should not replace the Guide menu, lest users be confused.

SUMMARY

There are distinctions among the different kinds of guide files—distinctions in their contents, manner of presentation, and user expectations. By considering your purposes in constructing a system of Apple Guide assistance, you should be able to decide which information goes into which kind of file as well as how you want to make these Apple Guide files available to users.

CHAPTER 4

Apple Guide and Other Types of Assistance

The impression that a user forms about your application (or solution or content) is conditioned mostly by expectations of the product derived from reviews and word-of-mouth, external packaging, manuals and assistance; and later by experience with the product. Until the user has successfully used the product, the expectations are critical. Developers know that telling the right "story" about the product is essential to developing expectations that are realistic and that can be fulfilled. No matter how fine a product is, if the user's expectations don't match the product, there will be dissatisfaction. (For example, although you can use a word processing program to do basic calculations in numerical tables, a user who tries to use a word processor as a spreadsheet program will be frustrated and annoyed.)

NOTE   In-house developers may think that their work has no packaging or advertising. Even a HyperCard stack distributed electronically via e-mail with the covering message: "Use this for time sheet data entry" has packaging and advertising.

Apple Guide assistance can be a critical step in moving a user's impression of a product from expectation to experience. The box the software came in may be emblazoned with: "Have your computer name your new pet." It is the job of an Apple Guide tutorial to guide the user—effortlessly—through the steps involved in turning the greyhound rescued from the dog track into "Marco the Magnificent." Having done this, expectations no longer matter: the user's impression of the product is the far more powerful personal experience.

In many cases, the mere existence of Apple Guide assistance is itself a positive feature of the product: it demonstrates an effort by the developer to make the product easy to use. Of course, as with all expectations, if the assistance is not implemented well, this will backfire. (At least one major productivity application that used Apple Guide very early on implemented it poorly, with the result that the assistance was hard to find and often did not answer a user's questions.)

Apple Guide assistance must be coordinated with all other aspects of the product, from the software itself to the packaging. This does not mean that a single font should be used everywhere, for example; it does mean that the "story" should be clear and that there should be a consistent approach to the product's features and functionality. If the product box describes a "tool bar" the manual should not define a "tool strip." (Although this point is obvious, everyone who has dealt with many software products can point to famous—and infamous—examples.)

The most important part of coordinating Apple Guide with other assistance is addressing the issue of printed documentation—manuals. Ideally, both Apple Guide assistance and printed documentation should be complete in and of themselves. For a commuter with a long bus ride, a manual and printed tutorial may be the most convenient introduction to new software. For a user with no commute (or who drives alone to work), reading printed documentation can impose an undue burden compared to just jumping in to the software.

Unfortunately, this ideal world rarely exists. Because the printed medium is totally different from the computer's presentation of information, an excellent written tutorial—even if lavishly illustrated—may be an appallingly bad Apple Guide tutorial. Similarly, the extraordinarily simple coach mark that coaches the File menu in a guide file may need two sentences and an illustration in a printed manual. To provide complete instructions in both printed and on-line form is usually prohibitively expensive.

The best solution available is to choose which aspects of assistance are most appropriate for printed form and which are most appropriate for Apple Guide. A certain subset of the assistance normally will have to be provided in both formats.

As you might expect in a book about Apple Guide, you are strongly encouraged to use Apple Guide as your primary delivery method for assistance. The only things that always need to be provided to a user in printed form are

- product packaging and labeling (even software distributed electronically qsqally has a text file with licensing information)

- instructions on how to install and start the product, as well as instructions that need to be carried out when the application is not running (cabling, modifier keys to hold down when launching the application, and so on)

Duplicating tutorials, help, and shortcuts that are provided in Apple Guide files may be very expensive and not worth the effort. There are two things that often should be provided in printed form:

- shortcuts printed on cards, keyboard overlays, posters, and so on
- a narrative description of the product's capabilities

Apple Guide is excellent at showing how to do something. Showing that the product can even attempt to do a certain task often can best be done in print or with video.

And, of course, there's a (temporary) kicker: Apple Guide works with only System 7.5 or later. Until you can be certain that your users are using System 7.5, you cannot rely on Apple Guide as a primary delivery vehicle for assistance. Actually, this is not as much a complication as it seems. For custom solutions provided to individual clients, the solution provider often has control over the version of the operating system used. New machines have been shipped with System 7.5 since the fall of 1994, and users have been upgrading existing machines to the new software rapidly.

SUMMARY

In this part of the book, you have learned the basics of Apple Guide: what it is (including definitions of its terms and concepts), where the user sees it, types of guide files, how it is provided to users, and how it relates to other forms of assistance.

Unfortunately, a book cannot have a context check. If this were Apple Guide, the right arrow to go to the next chapter would be dimmed until you were comfortable with the contents of this chapter. Using context checks, you can create quizzes in Apple Guide to review the elements of a tutorial (where such a quiz would be most appropriate). Think about how you would do that as you turn to the next part, which covers Guide Maker syntax. In this part you have seen what Apple Guide can do; in the next part, you will do it yourself.

CHAPTER 5

About Guide Script and Guide Maker

Guide Maker is an application from Apple that creates guide files from source files that you create, preferably with a word processor that allows you to enter styled text. The language of Guide Master commands is called Guide Script. Guide Script commands are described in Chapters 6 through 14; Guide Maker is described in Chapter 15. Guide Master itself is provided on the *Real World Apple Guide* CD-ROM.

GUIDE SCRIPT COMMANDS

Guide Script commands are enclosed in angle brackets (<>) and are not case-sensitive. Abbreviations for each command are acceptable to Guide Maker.

NOTE

The syntax for each command is provided in a self-running HyperCard stack on the *Real World Apple Guide* CD-ROM, along with a listing of all abbreviations. The stack and list of abbreviations are located in the folder with Guide Maker.

Guide Script commands often include one or more parameters, which follow the Guide Script keywords. Each Guide Script command is terminated by a return character. Thus, in most word processors, a single Guide Script command corresponds to a paragraph. The keywords and parameters simply wrap around until you insert the return (¶) character.

Examples of Guide Script commands are as follows:

```
<Define Panel> "Panel A"
<End Panel>
```

The <Define Panel> command takes one parameter: the name of the panel. The <End Panel> command has no parameters.

In describing the syntax for commands, the Guide Script keywords are presented in **bold** type; the parameters are presented in *italic*. Optional parameters are shown in square brackets ([]). In the following example, <Standard Button> is the Guide Script command, *buttonTitle*, *buttonLoc*, *buttonEvent*, and *buttonFont* are parameters, and *buttonFont* is an optional parameter.

```
<Standard Button> buttonTitle, buttonLoc, buttonEvent
[, buttonFont]
```

When dealing with optional parameters, you may need to insert commas into the Guide Script command as place holders for missing parameters.. The <Define Format> command provides an example of this:

```
<Define Format> formatName, columnCoords [, txFnt] [, txSize]
[, txStyle], txColor] [, txAlign] [, alignPrompt]
```

If you want to specify a format that uses all default format parameter, you could write:

```
<Define Format> "default values format", Column (0, 0, 300)
```

If you want to specify a color for a format, you must write

```
<Define Format> "red format", Column (0, 0, 300), ,,,RED
```

The commas indicate the absence of the optional parameters *txFnt, txSize,* and *txStyle*. This allows Guide Maker to know that RED is to be interpreted as a value for the *txColor* parameter. The optional parameters following *txColor* don't need to be represented by commas because no other parameter is specified.

PARAMETER TYPES

Parameters can be of various types, but most often they are strings. Wherever a parameter's type is not specified, it is a string enclosed in quotation marks—straight quotes (") not curly or smart quotes ("""). If a parameter is not a string, its type is specified in the text.

Special Characters

Some characters require special treatment.

Return Character

The return character ends a Guide Script command; however, you can use it in a text string that is enclosed with quotation marks. An embedded return is not interpreted as the character that ends the Guide Script command.

Text incorporated into a panel is entered into the panel definition by simply typing it in between the <Define Panel> and <End Panel> commands. In fact, this text is interpreted as a command by Guide Maker, more or less a <Define Text> command. The return character does, in fact, end this command. That is why if you think you have typed a single block of text that happens to contain two paragraphs (separated by a return character), you will find that you have actually defined two panel objects (each a paragraph of text).

Empty Strings

Do not use empty strings: for blanks, use a single space between quotes (" ").

Constants

A number of special values are accepted by Guide Maker for certain parameters. These are always represented in syntax descriptions in CAPITALLETTERS. Constants never contain spaces (hence the peculiar appearance of CAPITALLETTERS); their representation in capital letters is for convenience. As with all Guide Script commands, they are case-insensitive.

Functions and Structures

Sometimes, Guide Script parameters need to represent complex structures. You do this by using a structure or function definition that converts several parameters to the single, complex structure Guide Maker expects.

Guide Maker does not like a space between the structure or function name and the opening parenthesis.

N O T E

Point Structure

This structure specifies a point that consists of two coordinates.

Syntax: **Point**(*xCoordinate, yCoordinate*)

Example: Point(50, 200)

Rect Structure

This structure specifies a rectangle that consists of four coordinates.

Syntax: **Rect**(*top, left, bottom, right*)

Example: Rect(50, 200, 150, 300)

RedArrow Structure

The RedArrow structure specifies the starting and ending points for drawing an arrow. These points represent the midpoints and corners of a rectangle, with 1 representing the upper-left corner and proceeding clockwise to 8, which represents the middle-left point.

Syntax: **RedArrow**(*start,end*)

Example: RedArrow(4, 2)

RGBColor Structure

RGBColor(red, green, blue) specifies a color with the appropriate values.

Syntax: **RGBColor**(*red, green, blue*)

Example: RGBColor(0, 65535, 0)

Column Structure

Column (top, left, right) creates a bottomless column.

> *Syntax:*   **Column**(*top, left, right*)
>
> *Example:*   Column(50,50,50)

BalloonID Function

Given the identifier for an item that has a help balloon associated with it, this function returns the rectangle of the object.

> *Syntax:*   **BalloonID**(*IDnumber*)
>
> *Example:*   BalloonID(4)

DialogID Function

Given the identifier for an item in a dialog, this function returns the rectangle of the object. (Balloon ID and Dialog ID are used in drawing coach marks, and they let you specify a coach mark area by referring to the logical item to be coached, rather than to its physical location.)

> *Syntax:*   **DialogID**(*IDnumber*)
>
> *Example:*   DialogID (1)

Boolean Values

TRUE and FALSE are predefined constants.

REFERENCING FILES AND RESOURCES

Often, you need to include PICT graphics in your guide files. You can do this in either of two ways:

- You can create a PICT resource from the graphic and include that resource in your guide file.
- You can create a PICT file and have Guide Maker automatically produce a resource and include it in the guide file.

Whenever a parameter can accept a PICT graphic, you can supply the resource name or number (if you used the first technique) or the name of the file (if you used the second technique). If you use the first approach, you must create a file with the appropriate resource in it. You load the required resources from that file using the <Resource> command (discussed in Chapter 15). In creating your resources, remember that Apple Guide has a claim to resource IDs from 0 to 2000. Your resources should be numbered with IDs greater than 2000, no matter what type they are.

If you supply the PICT graphic in a file, the file name should be relative to your source code file. If the file is in the same folder as your source code, simply supply its name. If it is in a subfolder, you must supply a partially qualified name, such as subfolder:file.

Other resources are handled in the same way.

SUMMARY

Guide Script commands are straightforward, and their processing by Guide Maker is not different from the processing of many other such languages. The easiest way to become familiar with Guide Maker is to look at samples and try it out yourself. Many of the examples provided in this part of the book are drawn from the Macintosh Guide 1.2 source code. Other examples are provided both as source files and compiled guide files on the *Real World Apple Guide* CD-ROM.

CHAPTER 6

Setting Up Guide Files

In this chapter, you will see how to use Guide Script commands to set default values for many options in Guide Maker, as well as how to set values and controls that are relevant to the guide file as a whole rather than to its parts (such as its name).

COMMENTS IN GUIDE FILES

You should always annotate your guide file source code—just as you annotate any computer code and many other items that cross your desk every day. Guide Maker provides syntax for you to do this in two ways.

Comment Command

The <Comment> command causes Guide Maker to skip all text until a return character is encountered. You can also comment out a line of code with a # symbol. Either method has the same result: the rest of the text *on that line* is ignored.

Within a panel, some special rules apply. The # symbol is interpreted as *text* if it appears in the middle of a line of text. Only a line that starts with a # as the first nonblank character is interpreted as a comment. To start an actual line of panel text with a #, you type ##, and Guide Maker will insert one # into the panel's text.

Syntax:	**<Comment>**
	or
	#
When to Use:	Frequently. Six months from now the hapless and frustrated guide file author who is trying to decipher what in the world you were doing may be *you!*

GUIDE MENU

Usually, your guide file will be listed in the Guide menu—placed there either automatically by Apple Guide or programmatically by an application using the Apple Guide API. Two commands allow you to control the appearance and placement of the guide file in the Guide menu.

Creating a Menu Command Name for a Guide File

As noted in the Introduction, Apple Guide has had several names during its gestation at Apple. Reflecting some earlier terminology, the command to create the Guide menu command for a guide file is <Help Menu>.

Help Menu Command

The text of the menu item in the Guide menu that will invoke this guide file is specified in the parameter *itemString*. As always, certain characters cannot appear in menu items. These items are as follows:

    ; ^ ! < / - ( ) , &

These characters are used by the Menu Manager to control the appearance of menu items—graying them out, adding check marks, and so on.

The <Help Menu> command is where you identify the type of guide file that you have created. You use the *helpType* parameter, which can be set to any of the following constants:

ABOUT

TUTORIAL

HELP

SHORTCUTS

OTHER

(These guide file types were described in Chapter 2.)

You can optionally include a *helpCmdKey*, a one-character string that, with the **Command** key, invokes your guide file. Apple Guide always responds to **Command-?** by opening a Help guide file (if it exists).

The name that appears in the Guide menu should be clear and descriptive of the contents of your guide file, reflecting not only the substance, but also the manner of presentation. Tutorials should contain the word "Tutorial," for example. Remember that guide files not created by the original application developer are normally considered Other guide files.

Syntax:	**<Help Menu>** *itemString, helpType [, helpCmdKey]*
Example:	A tutorial created by a solution provider might use the following <Help Menu> command:
	`<Help Menu> "Invoice Processing Tutorial", OTHER, "I"`
Limitations:	Only one <Help Menu> command is used in a guide file.
Default:	<Help Menu> "Help", HELP, "?"
When to Use:	Almost always, unless you are absolutely certain that your guide file will never be listed in a Guide menu (for example, it will be opened only from a special button or other command within an application). Even in these cases, it doesn't hurt to include this command.

Specifying Balloon Help for Your Guide Menu Items

Balloon Help provides an excellent way for users to identify parts of the interface that they see before them. To quickly find out what a command will do—or what is in a guide file that is listed in the Guide menu—many users turn on Balloon Help. You should always provide Balloon Help for your guide file. Apple Guide will make certain that it is properly displayed as the user moves the mouse over the items in the Guide menu.

Balloon Menu Text Command

Use the *balloonText* parameter to set the string that is displayed. The text of the balloon should be short and to the point. Often, balloons for Guide menu items start with the words "Displays information about...." Resist the temptation to add words that are self-evident to the user ("This menu command displays information about...".)

Syntax:	**<Balloon Menu Text>** *balloonText*
Example:	The tutorial cited above could have the following balloon text:
	`<Balloon Menu Text>` "Displays instructions for completing invoices for customer sales."
Limitations:	Only once in a guide file.
Default:	No balloon will be shown.
When to Use:	Almost always, unless you are certain your guide file will never appear in a Guide menu.

SETTING DEFAULT FORMATS FOR THE GUIDE FILE

By setting appropriate default values, you can avoid having to repeat commands for each sequence in your guide file. More important, when you use global default values, you can quickly make changes everywhere in your guide file.

To set a default value, you must have previously defined the appropriate format, navigation button set, or prompt set using a <Define> command. The definition commands are covered elsewhere.

Each default command can be overridden. Table 6.1 shows the default commands. Common vaules for the default commands are provided in the Guide Maker shells on the *Real World Apple Guide* CD-ROM.

Table 6.1

Default Command	Where Overridden
<Default Format>	Individual panels
<Default Nav Button Set>	Specific sequences
<Default Prompt Set>	Individual panels

Default Format Command

You normally use the **Full** format as a default; Using a font other than Espy Serif for the main portion of the text in your guide file will cause the guide file to have a nonstandard look. Constrain your creativity to making the contents of your guide files clear. Use the standard font.

You use the <Format> command to specify formats other than the default format for individual panels in your guide file.

N O T E

If you frequently use hot text in your panels, you may want to create a new standard default format that does not specify the style of text. In that way, you can use boldface for the hot text. The normal Full format specifies plain style—and thus removes boldface.

Syntax:	**<Default Format>** *formatName*
Example:	<Default Format> "Full"
Limitations:	Once per guide file.
Default:	None.
When to Use:	Always.

Default Nav Button Set Command

You define a set of navigation buttons that appear in the navigation bar for a given sequence. Although you can assign a navigation button set to each sequence in your guide file—and often different sequences have different navigation buttons—it is convenient to have a default set that is applied to each sequence in the guide file unless otherwise specified.

In the Guide Maker shell files on the *Real World Apple Guide* CD-ROM a default set is defined and set as the default. This set includes the **Topics** button and a **Huh?** button. If you are going to create a different default navigation button set, you should remove or comment out that line of code because the <Default Nav Button Set> command can occur only once in your guide file source code.

Syntax:	**<Default Nav Button Set>** *navButtonSetName*
Example:	`<Default Nav Button Set> "Standard Nav Bar"`
Limitations:	Once per guide file.
When to Use:	Always.

Default Prompt Set Command

Prompts appear in most panels as the bottom line of text, such as "Click the right arrow to continue." You can set the prompt set for specific panels. For the sake of consistency, as well as to keep your Guide Maker source files smaller and easier to read, you can set a default prompt set and not have to repeat the command for each panel.

The *promptSetName* parameter is the name that you have associated with a prompt set using the <Define Prompt Set> command.

Different types of guide files may require different default prompts. For example, a Tutorial file might use prompts such as "Do this step, then click the right arrow." A Help file that is not coaching a user step-by-step through a process might more appropriately use default prompts such as "Click the right arrow to continue."

Syntax:	**<Default Prompt Set>** *promptSetName*
Example:	<Default Prompt Set> "my standard prompt set"
Limitations:	Once per guide file.
Default:	None.
When to Use:	Almost always. It makes your guide file source code shorter and easier to read.

Allow Prompts Command

Occasionally, you may not want to use any prompts at all in your guide file. With the <Allow Prompts> command, you can instruct Apple Guide not to leave space for prompts at the bottom of the panels.

The parameter *allow* is either TRUE or FALSE. If you set it to FALSE, you cannot use any prompts on any panels anywhere in your guide file. Such a case is unusual and is most likely to occur in a guide file, the panels of which consist entirely of graphics (pictures or movies).

Syntax:	**<Allow Prompts>** *allow*
Example:	<Allow Prompts> FALSE
Limitations:	Once per guide file.
Default:	TRUE
When to Use:	Rarely.

Setting Maximum and Minimum Heights for Panels

All Apple Guide panels are the same width—currently 341 pixels. Apple Guide automatically sizes the vertical height of the panel to accommodate the contents. Accordingly, under normal circumstances, panels in a guide file are of different heights.

Occasionally, you may want to set maxima and minima for the panels in a guide file. There are two general reasons for doing this:

1. You may want all panels in the guide file to have the same height.

2. You may have a panel with contents that exceed the default maximum height (250 pixels).

In both cases, you should think carefully about what you're doing.

After you have specified a maximum height for the panels in a guide file, it is very easy to return and make a modification that increases the size of one or more panels. With a maximum defined, you may find that you have prevented Apple Guide from showing all the contents of a panel.

When you specify a minimum height, you may well prevent Apple Guide from showing the panel's information in the smallest possible space. Even on computers with multiple large monitors, screen space is limited. Having wasted space in Apple Guide panels may mean obscuring something else.

If you are tempted to specify a maximum height greater than the default (250 pixels), ask yourself whether you are trying to display too much in a panel. If a graphic needs to be more than 250 pixels high, overriding the default maximum height may be necessary; more often, resizing the graphic is the appropriate solution.

The height you specify with these commands is the height of the information panel itself—from the bottom of the title area to the top of the navigation bar.

N O T E

Max Height Command

Use this command to set the maximum height of panels.

Syntax:	**<Max Height>** *height*
Example:	Max Height> 250
Limitations:	Once per guide file.
Default:	250 pixels.
When to Use:	Rarely.

Min Height Command

The companion to the Max Height command is the Min Height command.

Syntax:	**<Min Height>** *height*
Example:	<Min Height> 0
Limitations:	Once per guide file.
Default:	0 pixels.
When to Use:	Rarely.

MODIFYING APPLE GUIDE ASSISTANCE— PROVIDING APPROPRIATE INFORMATION AT ALL TIMES

The Apple Guide designer often has to confront the problem of what to do with a guide file that contains a significant amount of material that is irrelevant under certain known circumstances. (A context check is the appropriate mechanism for handling a small amount of material that is irrelevant, such as assistance for a Preferences window that is not currently open.) This is an issue that is easily dealt with in the regular Mac OS interface: the user is simply not presented with choices that are irrelevant or could fail. Buttons and menu commands are grayed out and disabled when they do not apply.

There is no way of disabling Apple Guide topics. All topics (and headers, topic areas, and index items) are presented in the appropriate Access window. When the user selects a topic, a context check may let Apple Guide select one path or another so that the user can be told why that topic is unavailable or inappropriate at the moment. *But there is no way of preventing the user from choosing the inappropriate topic in advance. Once it is in the Access window, it is available.* Therefore, the Apple Guide designer must consider ways of dynamically modifying the assistance that is available through the Access windows, removing inappropriate material wherever possible.

This is a very different approach from the interface that normally is presented to users through the menu bar and dialog boxes. In that case, it is specifically recommended that the menu commands do not change; the universe of commands is always visible in the same structure, but the disabling of commands from time to time provides the user with a dynamic view of commands that are usable at any given moment.

Another way of providing the dynamic behavior of menus is to use context checks within topics, so that the presentation of information is indeed dependent on transient conditions of the computer. This is discussed in Chapter 12, "Sequences II—Conditions and Context Checks."

There are three ways in which these modifications can be made:

- controlling which guide files appear in the Guide menu,
- including/excluding sections of Guide Script commands when the guide file is compiled by Guide Maker,
- dynamically modifying guide files when they are opened.

CONTROLLING WHETHER A GUIDE FILE IS USED

When Apple Guide builds the Guide menu, it looks for guide files that are co-resident (in the same folder) with the application. Although this often is a simple enough procedure, there are several possible cases in which problems can occur:

- If several applications themselves are co-resident, guide files could be put in the wrong application's Guide menu.
- Because Apple Guide puts only one guide file of types HELP, ABOUT, SHORTCUTS, and TUTORIAL in the Guide menu, there must be a way to determine which guide files to put in the menu when there is more than one of a given type.
- Since Apple Guide can be localized, it is important that guide files written in a language that is foreign to the user not be included in the Guide menu.
- Some guide files should not be included in the Guide menu when certain system environmental features are not present. A guide file that provides

instructions for using speech synthesis is irrelevant when it is not available. Worse, a guide file that relies on QuickTime to present crucial information is useless when QuickTime is not installed.

Fortunately, commands are available to prevent most of these problems and to allow you to customize the Guide menu.

Specifying the Application for a Guide File

The first and most important command allows you to specify that a guide file should only be considered for inclusion in the Guide menu for a specific application. Every application has a signature that is registered with Apple. This *signature* (also called a *creator type*) is a sequence of four characters. Once registered with Apple, the signature is guaranteed to be unique.

App Creator Command

You associate a guide file with an application using the <App Creator> command. The parameter *creator* is the signature of the target application.

N O T E

If you do not know the signature of the application for which you are developing assistance, contact the developer. Alternatively, if you have access to ResEdit, you can check the file information for the application itself. If you do this, be careful not to make any changes to the application. The safest way is to make a copy of the application and to check the creator type on the copy.

If you use the <App Creator> command, you can rest assured that your guide file will never be shown in an inappropriate application's Guide menu.

Syntax:	**<App Creator>** *creator*
Example:	<App Creator> 'PSM1'
Limitations:	Once per guide file.
Default:	None. Your guide file can be added to any application's Guide menu.
When to Use:	Almost always.

Setting the Script for a Guide File

Because the Mac OS is used around the world with many different languages and many different alphabets, it is important to make certain that the guide files are opened in the right script.

World Script Command

Use the <World Script> command to set the script and region codes. Apple Guide will open only those guide files whose script code matches that of the script system currently in use.

Syntax:	**<World Script>** *scriptCode, regionCode*
Example:	<World Script> 0, 0
Limitations:	Once per guide file.
Default:	Roman script (0) and U.S. region (0).
When to Use:	As needed.

Checking the System Environment

The <Gestalt> command enables you to check the environment of the computer where the application is running. The Gestalt function (which is available in all the Macintosh programming languages), allows you to find out the type of processor, the version of system software, and other attributes of interest.

Gestalt Command

The Guide Script <Gestalt> command accesses the system Gestalt routines. The *selector* parameter identifies the particular Gestalt routine that should be invoked; it is a four-character string that is defined in the Gestalt Manager. A long integer value is always returned from the Gestalt function. That value is compared to the *requiredValue* parameter. If they are the same, the <Gestalt> command is considered to have succeeded.

Up to three <Gestalt> commands can be included in a single guide file. If any is true, the guide file can be added to the Guide menu (if other conditions warrant).

The Gestalt function is documented in the *Inside Macintosh* series published by Addison Wesley. See the Resources folder on the *Real World Apple Guide* CD-ROM for further information.

N O T E

Syntax:	**\<Gestalt>** *selector, requiredValue*
Example:	To test whether QuickTime is installed, use:
	`<Gestalt> 'qtim', 0`
Limitations:	Up to three per guide file.
Default:	N/A
When to Use:	As needed.

If All Else Fails...

When Apple Guide is confronted with a number of co-resident guide files, it uses the \<App Creator>, \<World Script>, and \<Gestalt> commands to attempt to winnow them down. However, this may not be sufficient because there is no guarantee that only one ABOUT, HELP, SHORTCUT, or TUTORIAL file will result from the process. (Remember that the Guide menu normally contains only one of each of these guide file types.)

In that case, Apple Guide picks the first eligible guide file of each type—using the alphabetical name of the file. Thus, there is a deterministic route to follow that will yield, at most, one guide file of each of these types. You can rely on the \<App Creator>, \<World Script>, and \<Gestalt> commands, but you should never rely on Apple Guide's alphabetical last-resort choice of guide files.

CONTROLLING WHAT GOES INTO A GUIDE FILE

Using the commands described, you can control whether Apple Guide adds a guide file to the Guide menu, providing some dynamic control over that menu. There are two related ways of dynamically changing guide files: when they are compiled by Guide Maker and when they are actually opened by Apple Guide.

The \<Include> command allows you to include a complete Guide Script file in your source guide. Splitting up your source code has several advantages:

- several people can work on different parts of the source code at the same time,
- some sections that are common to several guide files need not be rewritten each time,
- the structure of the guide file's source code can be clearer.

The <Include> command is discussed in Chapter 15; at this point, it is only necessary to give an example of how it can be used to create a guide file with appropriate contents. In the case where a guide file should contain information about speech synthesis—but only when it is installed—you can create a guide file that uses included files in its structure. You create two make files (the files that assemble the included files). One make file includes the speech synthesis commands (with an <Include> statement), and the other doesn't. You also use the <Gestalt> command in each guide file to check for the presence of speech synthesis. With this simple procedure you let Apple Guide load one or the other guide file into the Guide menu, by relying on the <Gestalt> command. The two guide files are easily maintained, because the difference between them consists only of the <Gestalt> commands and the presence or absence of an <Include> statement.

 The <Include> command can be used in only a make file. It cannot be used in other source code files. Thus, if you use any <Include> files, you must structure your source code as consisting of a make file—with <Include> commands and nothing else—and the included files.

N O T E

In a related way, the <Mixin> command can be used to add (or delete) topics, indices, and topic areas from a guide file when it is opened. The <Mixin> command will be discussed in Chapter 14.

SUMMARY

When you create a guide file, you normally set default values for formats, navigation bars, and prompts. In the case where significant sections of a guide file may be inappropriate, you provide an improved user interface by not showing the user the inappropriate sections. This can be done by eliminating (or adding) specific guide files to the Guide menu, by using <Include> commands to have parallel versions of guide files, and by using the <Mixin> command.

Refer to the Guide Maker shells in the cookbook folder on the *Real World Apple Guide* CD-ROM for examples of the use of default values in setup files.

CHAPTER 7

Access Windows

This chapter covers Guide Script commands for creating Access windows. Access windows provide the user's first look at a guide file. (The exception is for guide files opened programmatically using the Apple Guide API and those opened with AppleScript. Even then, the Access window is often shown first.)

The Access window can provide basic introductory information about the guide file (howdy text). It also provides the means for users to access the information in the guide file—organizing it into topic areas, indexing it, and providing the ability to search for information by keywords.

This chapter includes all the commands used to create and customize Access windows. It is divided into three sections:

1. "Setting Up Access Windows" describes the commands you use to create access windows and customize them.

2. "Creating Topics, Indices, and Headers" covers the commands you use to divide your material into different topics and to organize those topics within headers. The commands for creating topic areas and index headings are also covered here.

3. "Preparing for Keyword Searches" shows how to prepare the information in your guide file so that it can be accessed by users who want to search for individual words or phrases.

SETTING UP ACCESS WINDOWS

Because the Access window is the user's first look at your Apple Guide assistance, you should make an effort to make the window clear and helpful. Fortunately, Apple Guide provides several features that make it easy to let the user know what is in your guide file and how to get to the information quickly.

Defining a Startup Window

Each guide file can use only one type of access window, which is defined with the <Startup Window> command.

Startup Window Command

The parameter *windowType* is one of the following constants:

FULL	for a Full Access window
SINGLE	for a Single Access window
PRESENTATION	for a Presentation Access window (which is actually not a start-up window at all, but merely the first panel of a sequence).

You can specify how the Access window looks the first time it is shown with *accessScreenOptions*. The values are as follows:

HOWDY	To show a special howdy text the first time the Access window is opened
TOPICS	To open the window the first time as it would be if the **Topics** button had been clicked
INDEX	To open a Full Access window as it would be if the **Index** button had been clicked
LOOKFOR	To open a Full Access window as it would be if the **Look For** button had been clicked

Presentation Access windows cannot display howdy text and have no **Topic**, **Index**, or **Look For** buttons. For Presentation Access windows, the *accessScreenOption* must be the name of the sequence to be shown in the window.

Syntax:	**<Startup Window>** *windowType, accessScreenOptions*
Limitations:	Once per guide file.
Default:	A Full Access window, with a howdy text. (If no howdy text has been specified, there will be a blank space on the startup window.)
When to Use:	Always.

Specifying the Howdy Text

Full and Single Access windows provide the option of having howdy text shown the first time they are presented. This text should clearly identify the contents and purpose of the guide file and tell the user what to do next.

Remember that the user of the guide file is focusing on a goal—often solving a problem that is a distraction from the task at hand. The howdy text is not the place for "Hi from the folks who developed this wonderful software" or for a special upgrade offer. It also is not the place to refer the user to other documentation (such as a manual). The howdy text is seen only the first time the guide file is opened. For this reason, make certain that you don't put information in the howdy text that may need to be referred to later (for example, the telephone number to call if all else fails).

You define a block of text and name it; you then use the howdy command to make that text block the howdy text for the guide file. To define a text block, you use the following commands.

Define Text Block and End Text Block Commands

The text for the text block is placed between the <Define Text Block> and <End Text Block> commands. It will be formatted by Apple Guide, so don't waste time adjusting the font and style.

NOTE

By comparison, text specified in a <Define Panel> command is formatted according to formats that you specify, and fonts, sizes, styles, and colors of that text can be modified easily when you create the panel.

Syntax:	**<Define Text Block>** *textBlockName*
	<End Text Block>
When to Use:	Whenever you want to specify a howdy screen.

Howdy Command

Use the <Howdy> command to select the text block that you want to use on the howdy screen.

Syntax:	**<Howdy>** *howdyTextBlockName*
When to Use:	Whenever you want to specify a howdy screen.

N O T E

This two-step process for specifying the howdy text has its roots in the development of Apple Guide itself.

Customizing Instructions on the Access Window

There are five phrases that appear on the Full Access window that assist users in navigating through the guide file. (The phrases were defined and illustrated in Chapter 2.) You can use your own wording for these phrases, but you should do so carefully: remember that one of the virtues of Apple Guide is its consistent interface across applications. All five phrases are customized with similar commands.

Topic Areas Instruction Command

If you want to change the text above the left pane of the Full Access window, use the <Topic Areas Instruction> command.

Syntax:	**<Topic Areas Instruction>** *topicAreasInstruction*
Default:	"1. Click a topic area."
When to Use:	Rarely. The standard instructions provide a consistent look and feel to the Apple Guide Access windows.

Topics Instruction Command

The phrase above the right pane in the Full Access window or above the single pane in the Single Access window is the topics instruction.

Syntax:	**<Topics Instruction>** *topicsInstruction*
Defaults:	"2. Click a phrase, then click OK:" (when Topics or Index button is clicked and a topic area is selected)
	"3. Click a phrase, then click OK:" (when Look For button is clicked);
	"Click a phrase, then click OK:" (in Single Access windows).
When to Use:	Rarely. The standard instructions provide a consistent look and feel to the Apple Guide Access windows.

Index Instruction Command

When the index view of a Full Access window is shown, the Index Instruction is shown over the left pane of the window.

Syntax:	**<Index Instruction>** *indexInstruction*
Default:	"1. Click an index entry:"
When to Use:	Rarely. The standard instructions provide a consistent look and feel to the Apple Guide Access windows.

Look For Instruction Command

This phrase is shown in the left pane of the Full Access window when the **Look For** button is clicked.

Syntax:	**<Look For Instruction>** *lookForInstruction*
Default:	"1. Click the arrow button to begin, then type one or more words to search for:"
When to Use:	Rarely. The standard instructions provide a consistent look and feel to the Apple Guide Access windows.

Look For String Command

When the **Look For** button is clicked, the user is shown a pane with the look for instruction above the box where text can be entered. The look for string (if one is provided) is displayed in the box. A typical look for string is, "Enter a word to search on here."

Syntax:	**<Look For String>** *searchPhrase*
Default:	blank
When to Use:	Rarely.

Placing Your Logo and Name on the Access Window

The area at the upper left of the Full Access and Single Access windows is reserved for a graphic or text identifying the guide file. In Standard Resources, default graphics (both in color and black and white) are provided that generically identify the guide file. Rather than having the area blank, it is a good idea to include those resources. However, it is simple enough to customize your Access window, and you should do so.

You can use either text or a graphic to identify your guide file. Text is the simplest way.

App Text Command

The *string* parameter is limited to 64 characters; it will be displayed in 14-point Espy Sans Bold.

Syntax:	**<App Text>** *string*
Limitation:	Once per guide file. Also, you cannot use the <App Logo> command in addition to the <App Text> command. (If you include all of Standard Resources in your guide file, you will automatically pick up default <App Logo> graphics, so you must explicitly not load PICT graphics numbered 501 and 502 from Standard Resources if you are specifying <App Text>.
When to Use:	To identify your guide file in a Full Access or Single Access window. Text is better than the generic Apple Guide graphic, but not as good as your own graphic.

The <App Logo> command lets you put a graphic onto your Full Access or Single Access window. This graphic should blend the Apple Guide light bulb image with your application's logo. Because the <App Text> command cannot be used in conjunction with the <App Logo> command, the application's name or other identification should appear within the graphic. Because the size of the Access windows is set by Apple Guide, your graphic is limited to 59 by 185 pixels. As always, you should use the standard Macintosh color palette.

N O T E

In point of fact, the <App Logo> and <App Text> commands—if both are present—are processed onto the Access window. You may be able to create a graphic that blends properly with the text you specify in the <App Text> command. However, because this is a nonstandard way of handling the problem of adding text to the graphic, there is no guarantee that it will work in the future. So, even though you may "discover" this trick, it is not something that you want to use in production. Save the knowledge for esoteric bar-room wagers.

Apple Guide uses PICT resources from the compiled guide file for the logo. These PICT resources must be numbered 501 (for a color version) and 502 (for a black-and-white version). You can place these resources in the guide file in one of two ways:

1. You can paste the PICT resources into a file that you include in your guide file using the <Resource> command. The resources must have the correct numbers: 501 for color and 502 for black and white.
2. You can save PICT graphics in a file of type PICT. Use the <App Logo> command to have Guide Maker read in the PICT graphics and convert them to appropriately numbered resources.

The syntax for the <Resource> command is

`<Resource> fileName, resType [, whichResource].`

A sample <Resource> command used to load a color graphic from a file named **resourcefile** is

`<Resource> resourceFile, PICT, 501`

The command is described fully in Chapter 15.

App Logo Command

The parameters *colorLogo* and *B&WLogo* identify files containing the relevant PICT graphics. These files must be co-resident with your Guide Maker source code.

Syntax:	**<App Logo>** *colorLogo [, B&WLogo]*
Limitation:	Once per guide file. (If you include all of Standard Resources in your guide file, you will automatically pick up default <App Logo> graphics, so you must explicitly not load PICT graphics numbered 501 and 502 from Standard Resources if you are specifying your own graphics.) Also, you cannot use the <App Logo> command in addition to the <App Text> command.
When to Use:	If at all possible.

CREATING TOPICS, INDICES, AND HEADERS

Unless you use the Presentation Access window, users will start their navigation of your guide file by selecting a topic from the Access window. In the Full Access window, users locate topics within Topic Areas or from Index or Look For items. Setting up the structure of your guide file's topics, indices, key words, and headers is one of the most important design tasks you confront.

Too often, the temptation is to take the information that you have and want to present and to arrange it in an order that is most sensible to you. You must turn this temptation on its head: your task in organizing the information is to present what the user doesn't know, what the user wants, and to arrange it in an order that is most sensible to the user. These are two totally different ways of organizing information.

N O T E

In order to develop the skill of properly organizing information for the user, get in the habit of watching yourself as you try to learn and understand things. What manuals, guide books, and reference materials do you turn to with relief, knowing that you will quickly find the answer to your question? On the other hand, what searches do you dread, anticipating frustration and wasted time as you struggle with indices that have incorrect page numbers, cross-references to cross-references that never actually get you to the information you want, and other "aids" that seem to hinder you every step of the way? With these observations, you will understand the principles of designing effective assistance. Furthermore, you most likely will retain the knowledge far more effectively than by reading principles of instructional design from a book. Scientists have determined that memories of events that were accompanied by significant emotion—frustration or joy, for example—are more durable than others. It's small consolation, but maybe the anger you felt at a long and fruitless search for information can, in fact, help you learn how not to inflict such misery on others.

Developing an Information Taxonomy for a Guide File

Organizing information in a Full Access window is the most complex challenge for the guide file designer. The Single Access and Presentation Access windows provide subsets of the information design of a Full Access window. Once you have mastered the principles of presenting information in a Full Access window, you will have the skills to design the other types of Access windows. With that in mind, this section addresses Full Access windows.

The organization of information is as much an art as a science. In today's information age, organization and classification of information are done by people in many different professions: librarians, multimedia interface designers, and book indexers, in addition to the graphic designers for newspapers, television, mail-order catalogs, and many others. The term *taxonomy*, which originally referred to the organization of things in accordance with their underlying principles and natural relationships (particularly in botany) is used to describe this process. In the linear world of the great classifiers of the Enlightenment and the Age of Reason, there was a place for everything and everything was in its place. Today, in many scientific disciplines such a static taxonomy is still used.

In today's world of computer interfaces to information, things like hypertext, graphics, and substantial processing power allow dynamic nonlinear information taxonomies to be developed.

Information in a Full Access window can be arranged in three hierarchical levels:

- topic areas or index entries
- headers
- topics

Figure 7.1 shows the Full Access window for Macintosh Guide with the **Topics** button clicked and the Color topic area selected. Headers in the right pane of the window ("How do I", "Why Can't I", "Definitions") can be expanded or contracted when the user clicks the triangles to the left of the headers.

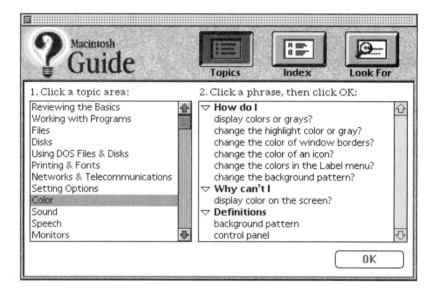

Figure 7.1 Full Access window for Macintosh Guide with the **Topics** button clicked.

In Figure 7.1, the Access window presents information in a manner similar to that of the table of contents of a book. The topic areas correspond to chapters and are arranged in an order that starts with simple issues (such as "Reviewing the Basics") and then proceeds to more complex points that are presented in topic areas (chapters) of their own. Except for the placement of the most basic topic areas at the beginning of the list, there is not an obvious order to the items.

The headers in Figure 7.1 are presented in a set order. If you compare various topic areas in Macintosh Guide, you will see that the headers "How do I," "Why can't I," and "Definitions" recur (usually) in that order. In designing the presentation of information, such consistency is helpful to the user, who comes to know that each chapter (topic area) will have certain standard features.

N O T E

These headers are not obligatory, although many guide file designers use similar ones. WordPerfect, for example, uses "How do I...," "What is...," and "Why..." as its headers. Apple suggests that you use headers of this sort, and adds a "Please" header under which you can group topics that will carry out tasks for the user.

In devising a structure for the information in your guide file, you normally start by developing the taxonomy for the Topics view of the Full Access window. The information as a whole is split into topic areas and is generally not repeated in more than one topic area. The structure of a topic area (its headers) is determined for the guide file as a whole—and usually starts from the "How do I," "Why can't I," and "Definitions" shown in Figure 7.1. Of course, other headers that are relevant to a specific guide file are often added, but it makes it easier for people to use your guide file if you can provide consistent headers—in a consistent order—for all topic areas. (Naturally, not all headers appear in each topic area.)

In Figure 7.2, the Full Access window with the **Index** button clicked is shown with the colors index entry selected.

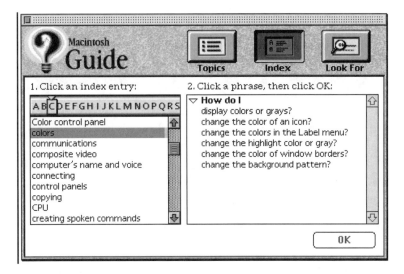

Figure 7.2 Full Access window with **Index** selected.

Compare the two windows. In Figure 7.2, the "How do I.." header and its topics from the Topics view of Figure 7.1 are repeated (but in a different order). The left panel, which now contains index entries rather than topic areas, is organized alphabetically and contains many more items than the Topics view did. (The Index view of a Full Access window is comparable to the index—rather than the table of contents—of a book.)

In comparing the two presentations of information, an additional point becomes clear: in the Index view, information is repeated in different index entries. An Index view is not simply the topic areas of a guide file organized alphabetically!

You will also note in Figure 7.2 that the index entry "colors" contains the "How do I" header from the topic areas "Color," but not the "Why can't I" and "Definitions" headers. Because in a well-designed guide file the headers and topics from a topic area (in the Topics view) may move to very different areas in the Index view, this is not surprising.

In fact, as Figure 7.3 demonstrates, there is a "Troubleshooting" index entry that combines all the "Why can't I" topics from all the topic areas in the guide file.

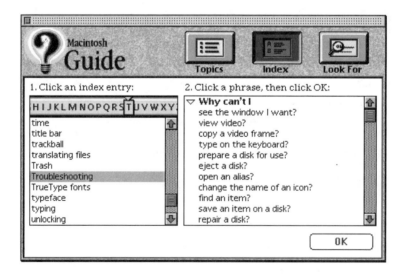

Figure 7.3 Troubleshooting index entry.

And what happened to the topics under the "Definitions" header shown in the Topics view of Figure 7.1? They have been dispersed as well. In Figure 7.4, you see that "background pattern" (which was listed under "Definitions" in the Topics view shown in Figure 7.1) has its own index entry.

Not only is background pattern defined in its own index entry, but related definitions are listed in a Definitions header. And—because it's relevant here, too—the "How do I" header is included, together with the "change the background pattern?" topic.

Thus, the user who wants to change the background pattern can get assistance in any of the following ways:

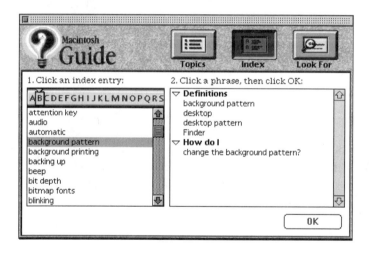

Figure 7.4 Index entry for background pattern.

- In the Topics view, select the topic area **Color**.
- In the Index view, select the index area **colors**.
- In the Index view, select the index area **background pattern**.
- In the Index view, select the index area **screen** (see Figure 7.5).

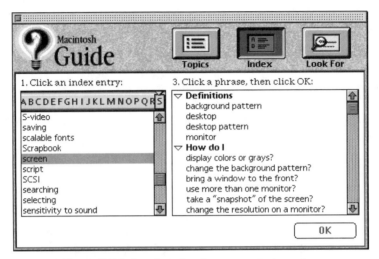

Figure 7.5 Index view showing screen index entry.

The Index view enables you to duplicate topics in many places in the guide file. In reviewing the figures in this chapter, notice that although the headers remain the same ("Definitions," "How do I," "Why can't I"), the topics within those headers change, depending on the topic area or index entry in which they are found. Thus the definition for "background pattern" is adjacent to the definition for "Finder" in the Index view of "background pattern"; in the Index view for "screen," "Finder" is not defined, but "monitor" is added.

Figures 7.6 and 7.7 show the Look For views of the Full Access window for the key words "pattern" and "color." In both cases, the user can find the answer to the questions, "How do I change the background pattern?"
As topics are presented in different order and different contexts in Index views, users may strike out in different directions, particularly when they are exploring the guide file for the first time. Thus, the user who has arrived at Figure 7.7 (Look For "color") sees the "How do I change color of an icon?" topic. That might prompt a search on the word "icon" (see Figure 7.8).

Some of the topics shown in Figure 7.8 have appeared in other contexts. The important point to remember is that in the Topics view of the Full Access window, topics usually are presented in one place. In the Index and Look For views, topics are repeated, reordered, and presented in varying contexts, but in every case there is a logic to the organization of the topics. In organizing Index and Look For views, you should resist the temptation to put topics where you feel they "belong"; you should try to put them wherever people might look for them.

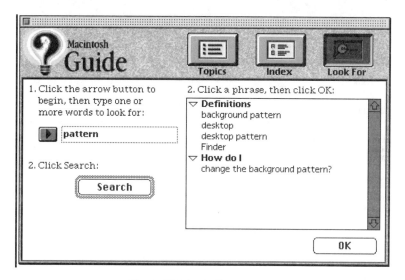

Figure 7.6 Look For: pattern.

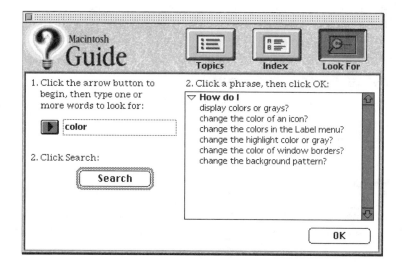

Figure 7.7 Look For: color.

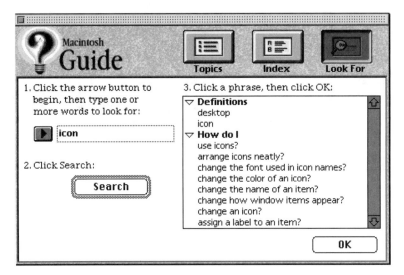

Figure 7.8 Look For: icon.

The logical structure of the Topics view, where topics do in fact belong in certain places, parallels the linear structure of a book in which information is generally not repeated. Thus, although the index of a book might provide many different ways of finding the syntax for the <Topic Area> command, in the organized structure of the book (as reflected in the table of contents), there is only one place where the syntax for the <Topic> command belongs. That place is here.

Specifying Topics and Headers

As you have seen, topics and headers can be shown in Topics, Index, and Look For views of Full Access windows. They also appear in Single Access windows. Topics can be organized under headers.

Topic Command

Topics are defined in Guide Script. Basically, a topic is a sequence of panels (themselves defined with the <Panel> command and the sequence defined with the

<Sequence> command). The mapping of a single topic to a single sequence is the simplest case. A topic may end up invoking more than one sequence—when, for example, a user clicks a control in a panel that launches a new sequence; when an Oops sequence is automatically started; or when other branches are taken as a sequence of panels is shown. Still, each topic starts out being associated with a single sequence with the <Topic> command.

The *topicPhrase* parameter is the name that will appear in the Access window. The *sequenceName* parameter is the name of the sequence that is initially associated with the topic. It is an internal name, and your users will never see it. Accordingly, make certain that your *topicPhrase* is as meaningful as possible for users; make *sequenceName* meaningful for guide file authors.

Although *topicPhrase* can be up to 63 characters long, it will be truncated by Apple Guide if it does not fit in the list of topics in the Access window. (In practice, the visible length of a *topicPhrase* is about half the allowable 63 characters.) Test the string to make certain that it is visible. When the *topicPhrase* completes a phrase that is shown in the header ("How do I") it starts with a lowercase character. In cases where there are no headers, the *topicPhrase* often starts with a number so that the organization of the list is clear.

You are allowed up to 255 characters for a *sequenceName*, so you should have no trouble creating a naming structure for your sequences that allows for easy maintenance of the source code. (The first 63 characters of the *sequenceName* must be unique.)

Sometimes, the structure of a guide file's Access windows will suggest that a single sequence be listed under several different *topicPhrases*. It is crucial that the *topicPhrase* be worded properly. If it is not, the user may not select it, and he or she will miss all the assistance that you have carefully provided for precisely the problem where help is needed. Because using different *topicPhrases* in different contexts is very easy, you can make certain that your assistance is presented in the most effective way in each case.

Syntax:	**<Topic>** *topicPhrase, sequenceName*
Examples:	`<Topic> "name a pet?", "How do I name a pet?"`
	`<Topic> "desktop printer", "Definitions desktop printer"`
	Because the *topicPhrase* parameter is often a truncated phrase that will complete a sentence started by a header, when you have given a sequence a meaningful *sequenceName*, you will be forgiven for sometimes confusing the order of the parameters. This confusion unfortunately is exacerbated by the fact that the <Define Sequence> command presents the *sequenceName* first and the (optional) sequence display title second, the reverse of internal-external names in the <Topic> command. The second example (taken from the Macintosh Guide source code) shows a *sequenceName* that is meaningful and that is clearly an internal name. If you have trouble remembering the order of these parameters, you might want to establish such a naming convention for yourself.
Limitations:	63 characters for *topicPhrase*, but check that the string will be visible in your Access window
	255 characters for *sequenceName* (the first 63 must be unique)
When to Use:	Whenever you need to show a topic in an Access window.

Using headers to arrange topics has several advantages, not the least of which is that because the user can close any headers that are not of immediate interest (by clicking the triangle), a list of topics that otherwise would need to be scrolled to be seen can be seen all at once.

When you structure your guide file, you should decide whether you will use headers. If you use headers at all, you should use them consistently throughout the guide file. Some headers are irrelevant to certain guide files; other guide files cry out for additional headers (a "Where is" header is often appropriate in assistance for multimedia content). Apple's suggested headers are as follows:

- Please, for AppleScript (and other) commands that do the job for the user

- How do I, for step-by-step coaching through a process
- Why can't I, for trouble-shooting assistance
- Definitions

Header Command

The <Header> command immediately precedes the <Topic> commands that are included in the header. Topics can appear in several headers—and often do so in Index views of the Full Access window.

Syntax:	**<Header>** *headerPhrase*
Example:	<Header> "How do I"
	<Topic> "alphabetize a list", "Seq: Alphabetizing a list"
	<Topic> "insert a graphic", "Seq: "Inserting a graphic"
When to Use:	As needed.

Topics (with their optional headers) are displayed in the right pane of the Full Access window. They are grouped into topic areas (shown when the **Topics** button is clicked) or index headers (shown when the **Index** button is clicked).

Specifying Topic Areas

Topic Areas are shown in the Full Access window and are similar to the chapters in a book. When a topic area is selected, the right pane of the window shows its contents: topics grouped under their headers. Just as in a book, the topic areas progress from simple to more complicated. For ease of reading, you can indent headers and topics in your source files.

Topic Area Command

The *topicAreaPhrase* is shown in the left pane. It should be descriptive and simple. Because space is limited to one line for each topic area, the *topicAreaPhrase* should be short.

Topic areas are listed in the order in which you define them in your guide file. In the case where your guide file is assembled dynamically using Mixin files, this order could be ambiguous. For that reason, and to provide you with additional controls over the look of guide files assembled in this way, you can specify a *mixinOrder* parameter that specifically places the topic area in a given place. You have three choices when defining a topic area that will be mixed into an existing guide file:

- you can place it at the beginning of the list by using the constant FIRST,

- you can place it at the end of the list by using the constant LAST,

- you can place it immediately following another topic area by specifying the name of that topic area in the *mixinOrder* parameter.

Syntax:	**<Topic Area>** *topicAreaPhrase [, mixinOrder]*
Example:	This topic area with its header and topics is part of the Macintosh Guide source file. (Some lines are omitted.)
	`<TOPIC AREA> "Reviewing the Basics"`
	`<HEADER> "How do I"`
	`<TOPIC> "review the basics?", "How do I review the basics?"`
	`<TOPIC> "use icons?", "How do I use icons?"`
	`<HEADER> "Definitions"`
	`<TOPIC> "active window", "Definitions active widow"`
	`<TOPIC> "desktop", "Definitions desktop"`
Limitations:	A <Topic Area> command must have at least one header in it.
When to Use:	As needed.

Specifying Index Headers

Topics and headers are grouped into topic areas in the Topics view of the Full Access window; in the Index view, they are grouped into index headers, using the <Index> command. You use the <Index> command to specify the index name; you follow the <Index> command with the <Topic> and <Header> commands that you want it to contain.

Index Command

Like the index of a book, the index is sorted alphabetically. Thus, the order of <Index> commands in your source file is irrelevant. (The order of headers and topics within an index item is precisely as you enter them, however.) The parameter *indexTerm* is the name under which you want the entry to appear in the index. If you are uncertain where to place the information, remember that it is easy to create duplicate index entries, just as happens with the index of a book. Simply copy the entire index entry with its headers and topics, paste it into your source file and change the *indexTerm* to the second entry.

N O T E   Refrain from needlessly duplicating index entries. Providing an Apple Guide file with 50 index entries may make you think that you're providing the user with a great deal of assistance. If those 50 entries actually refer to only five topics, however, you're fooling yourself (and annoying your users). Duplication is appropriate if users may legitimately look under different headings for assistance. When considering a duplicate entry, ask yourself if the second entry should be an exact duplicate or if it should have a different mix of headers and topics, reflecting a different approach to the subject matter.

The **Look For** button lets the user search for information in your guide file. This search is based on the index headers. Because keyword searching is by nature more imprecise than scanning an index, it is necessary to provide additional entry points to the guide file's content. You do this by defining invisible index headers. The optional *visible* parameter can be set to FALSE, creating an index header that is not shown in the list but that is searched when the user uses the **Look For** button. For regular index headers this parameter is omitted and its default value, TRUE, determines that the index header is shown in the list.

Although the <Index> commands are sorted alphabetically, that doesn't mean that you don't have a great deal of control over the order of their presentation. The optional *key* parameter is a string that can be used to sort the index items in a different order than would be the case if the *indexTerm* were used. Because the alphabetical order of an index is its chief organizing characteristic, you should refrain from using the *key* parameter to create an artificial nonalphabetical sequence. Nevertheless, there are cases in which you can use this parameter appropriately.

For example, Guide Script commands are enclosed in brackets: <Index>. If you created an index that included Guide Script commands and other items, a strictly alphabetical sorting would produce the following:

<Default Format>

<Define Format>

<Define Panel>

default values

By using key values and omitting the brackets from the keys, you could produce an index listing like this:

<Default Format>

default values

<Define Format>

<Define Panel>

Another frequent use of keys is to alphabetize numbers (for example, sort "8" with words beginning with the letter "e").

Syntax:	**<Index>** *indexTerm [, visible] [, key]*
Example:	This index header with its header and topics is part of the Macintosh Guide source file. (Some lines are omitted.)
	`<INDEX> "Reviewing the basics"`
	`<HEADER> "How do I"`
	`<TOPIC> "review the basics?", "How do I review the`
	`         basics?"`
	`<TOPIC> "use icons?", "How do I use icons?"`
	`<HEADER> "Definitions"`
	`<TOPIC> "desktop", "Definitions desktop"`
	`<TOPIC> "document", "Definitions document"`
Limitations:	An <Index> command must have at least one header or topic in it. If you use the *key* parameter, you use the <Index Sorting> command in your source file.
Defaults:	*visible—TRUE*
	key—none
When to Use:	As needed.

Controlling the Sort Order

Apple Guide provides two sorting mechanisms for index headers. The default method uses the sorting method appropriate for the script that you specify with the <World Script> command. A faster case-insensitive sorting routine is also available. If you want to use it, you should use the <Sorting> command.

Sorting Command

To use the default sorting mechanism, specify *method* as SCRIPTSORT. The alternative, faster, case-insensitive sort is used if you set *method* to USASCIISORT.

If you use USASCIISORT, you should experiment with your guide file to make certain that the index headers are sorted in the order that you expect. If not, either use SCRIPTSORT or use sort keys to force the sorting to the proper order.

Syntax:	**<Sorting>** *method*
Example:	<Sorting> USASCIISORT
Defaults:	SCRIPTSORT
When to Use:	Rarely.

Sorting on Hidden Keys

If you want to use Apple Guide's capability to sort on keys other than the text of the index headers, you must do so for your entire guide file. The <Index Sorting> command lets you specify how the keys are used.

Index Sorting Command

This command must proceed before any index items are defined in your source code file. There are four possible values for *orderingKey*:

USEDISPLAYEDTERM	The default value, sorting the index items on their names as they appear in the index.
USEHIDDENKEY, USE HIDDENKEYWITH OUTIGNORE	Uses the key value for each index term. If you use this value, you must provide a key value for each <Index> command in your guide file.

NONE	Does no sorting of your index items. They are presented in the order in which they are entered in the source file. This usually does not present a very good index, but can be useful in debugging, for example, when an index item gets lost.

The index items are used for keyword searches with the **Look For** button. When you use keys, you have a choice of how Apple Guide handles the searching. The USEHIDDENKEY value uses the key for both index sorting and searching for key words. The USEHIDDENKEYWITHOUTIGNORE value uses the key for index sorting and lets the keyword search apply to both the key and the index item as it is shown in the index.

Syntax:	**<Index Sorting>** *orderingKey*
Example:	`<Index Sorting>USEHIDDENKEY`
Defaults:	USEDISPLAYEDTERM
When to Use:	Rarely.

Preparing for Keyword Searches

Preparing appropriate usable tables of contents and index items is hard enough, but preparing for keyword searches is a much more daunting task. In the cases of tables of contents and indices, the terms are presented to the user who selects one. In the case of keyword searches, the user enters the word or phrase that will be the subject of the search. Here, you have to imagine how the user will pose a query. There are two general areas of concern in setting up keyword searches:

- the manipulation of the text that the user enters in order to reduce it to searchable items (and as few of them as possible), and
- the creation of appropriate targets for keyword searches.

All software that attempts to manage natural language has to deal with the same general issue: human language is imprecise, redundant, and sloppy. Furthermore, it is often misspelled. These characteristics of natural language, in fact, contribute to its intelligibility—by humans—and to its capability to convey nuances. Although these characteristics are beneficial in human interaction, they can get in the way of a computer's "understanding" of text. The primary goal of a language parser is to remove the imprecision, redundancy, and sloppiness of natural speech. This is accomplished in two ways.

"Noise" Words

First, "noise" words are removed. "Please pass the butter" is polite and acceptable; "Pass butter" is rude and boorish. To a computer, however, "Pass butter" is the preferable phrase. You use the <Ignore> command to specify words and phrases that the Apple Guide language scanner should drop out of its parsing routines.

Ignore Command

In processing Look For commands, the <Ignore> commands are the first step that Apple Guide takes. By specifying a list of words to be ignored, you can let Apple Guide cut the parsing task down substantially. The introductory phrases that you so carefully place in headers ("Why can't I") are noise when it comes to parsing Look For text. In general, it is the nouns that matter in Look For text, not the verbs.

Syntax:	**<Ignore>** *ignoreWord*
Example:	Here are some of the <Ignore> commands from the Macintosh Guide source file:
	`<IGNORE> "damn"`
	`<IGNORE> "did"`
	`<IGNORE> "didn't"`
	`<IGNORE> "didn't"`
	`<IGNORE> "do"`
	`<IGNORE> "does"`
	`<IGNORE> "doesn't"`
	`<IGNORE> "doesn't"`
When to Use:	Often. By letting Apple Guide remove as many noise words as possible, the task of finding index terms is made much simpler and faster.

Stemming and Exceptions

After the noise words have been removed from the search phrase, Apple Guide stems the remaining words. *Stemming* is a commonly used practice in natural language parsers in which suffixes (and, less often, prefixes) are removed. The result of stemming is to produce fewer different words to be processed by Apple Guide. Thus, when "follow" and "following" are stemmed, they both result in "follow," which can be used to match an index term.

There are two potential problems with stemming, both resulting from the creation of a root word that is incorrect. The language parser itself has several built-in safeguards. For example, if the stemmed word contains no vowels, it is backed out. ("Fling" might stem to "fl," but since it contains no vowels, it is unstemmed.)

More serious—but fortunately under the Apple Guide author's control—is the case in which a word stems legitimately to a different word or phrase. An example is DOS. A final "s" is a prime candidate for stemming, and so the "s" is removed, leaving "DO." Not only does "do" have very little to do with "DOS," but in Macintosh Guide "do" is classified as a noise word, and an <Ignore> command for "do" was shown in the previous example.

To prevent this problem, you can use the <Exception> command to prevent the parser from stemming a word or phrase.

Exception Command

Just as using the <Ignore> command increases the speed and efficiency of parsing search phrases, the <Exception> command can decrease that speed and efficiency by preventing stemming, thus causing more words to be passed along to the next step of the process. Nevertheless, if you don't provide exceptions, you will find many unpleasant surprises as Apple Guide parses search phrases, and your users may not find the information they seek.

N O T E   Guide Maker provides a **Test Look For** command that lets you examine how a guide file will be processed. It is almost impossible to create a satisfactory guide file that includes keyword searches without using such a tool. Also, be aware that testing should be done by several people, because individuals vary in their vocabularies and word choices. Regional differences in speech often occur within fairly small geographical areas. For example, the long sandwich that is a *grinder* in Boston is a *hero* in New York City, a *hoagy* in Philadelphia, and a *sub* in Washington, D.C. (and upstate New York).

As if that weren't enough, working with keywords and phrases can blind you to some "obvious" words, particularly when pronunciation changes with stemmed words. The example of DOS stemming to do—with a complete change of meaning, context, and pronunciation—is a case in which the diligent indexer might very well not notice a potential problem.

Syntax:	**<Exception>** *exceptionWord*
Example:	To prevent DOS from being scanned to do (which is ignored in the example), you could use the following command:
	`<Exception>` "DOS"
When to Use:	As often as necessary to prevent confusion. Use Guide Maker's **Test Look For** command to see how phrases are parsed.

Synonyms

The purpose of stemming is to reduce similarly spelled words to a common root, which can then be processed by Apple Guide. The <Synonym> command lets you extend that principle to words and phrases that are not stemmed automatically.

Synonym Command

The word or phrase in the parameter *synonym* will be converted by Apple Guide to the word or phrase in the parameter *indexTerm*. The processing of synonyms occurs after noise words have been removed and after all words (except those identified with the <Exception> command) have been stemmed.

Synonym processing may be done twice. If the search phrase consists of more than one word, Apple Guide looks for a synonym for the whole phrase. If it finds one, it then attempts to locate that *indexTerm* in the guide file. If this fails, Apple Guide returns to the search phrase and checks for a synonym for each individual word in the phrase. Apple Guide then searches for matches for each word (original or replaced synonym) in the phrase. The result is the intersection (common results) of all individual word searches.

Guide Maker's **Test Look For** command shows this process very clearly.

Syntax:	**<Synonym>** *indexTerm, synonym*
Example:	If you decide that each menu command in your application should be able to be the target of a Look For search, you might use synonyms to map several versions of one command to a single index entry. Users might or might not include the ellipsis (…) when entering a command name. The following command eliminates the problem.
	`<Synonym> "Print Preview", "Print Preview…"`
	If a word is commonly misspelled or has alternate spellings, you can use the <Synonym> command to map one spelling to another.
	`<Synonym> "Color", "Colour"`
	`<Synonym> "Gray", "Grey"`
When to Use:	As often as necessary to prevent confusion. Use Guide Maker's **Test Look For** command to see how phrases are parsed.

Making Certain that Searches Succeed

Because so many variables come into play when a user types a search phrase and clicks the **Search** button, only rigorous testing by many different people—including people who are unfamiliar with the application and its terminology—can create a well-functioning keyword search for your guide file. Fortunately, the time is well-spent. If it is not done, users will never use the keyword search. If it is done, users will have a powerful tool to access the information in your guide file.

You should make certain that every topic that appears in the right pane of the Full Access window responds to a search, and that a user who types in any topic name is presented with (at least) that topic. In a basic help file, you should also confirm that all menu commands can be used as search phrases. Other words and phrases that appear prominently in the application's interface ("Setup,"

"Preferences," and so on) but that do not appear in the menu bar also should be tested for inclusion.

Because the Look For interface is so open-ended, it is used in many ways that you may never think about. In one famous example, a word processing program's developers carefully made certain that all of the commands that were specific to their program were available for keyword searches. Someone tried a search and came up empty-handed. Wondering if the problem was the application's, the user tested a keyword search that couldn't possibly fail: "Page Setup." It failed. "Page" failed. "Setup" failed. How many developers would have thought that the guide file should include very basic standard Macintosh assistance (that is duplicated in many other places)? Yet, when you track down bugs and problems, don't you often try the simplest possible case? The effort that would have been entailed in making certain that all menu items were included in the guide file would certainly have been justified—if only to prevent the small firestorm that raged on a computer network.

SUMMARY

No matter how good or plentiful the assistance in your guide file is, it is of no use if users cannot readily know what is available and how to access it. Organizing the information into topics and optional headers and placing it appropriately in topic areas (like chapters of a book) and index entries makes it possible for users to easily take advantage of your work. Apple Guide's Look For mechanism, which is available only in the Full Access window, is a very powerful tool to let users search on phrases that they type in. Developing successful Look For access to your guide file requires testing with a tool, such as Guide Maker's **Test Look For** command, but it can pay off with a very positive user experience.

Once you have provided access to the information in your guide file, you need to present the information in the best possible way. The next two chapters will discuss the techniques for developing the presentation panels of your guide file. Chapters 10 and 11 will cover sequences—the organization of panels.

CHAPTER 8

Panels I: Contents

The heart of your Apple Guide file is the panels that present information to the user. The Access windows play an essential role in getting the user to the information required, but the success or failure of your guide file lies in the material that is presented and the way in which it is shown in presentation panels.

In this chapter, the basics of panels and their information are covered. There are these sections:

- Designing panels and their contents
- Defining panels
- Formatting panels

In Chapter 9, "Panels II—Coach Marks," you will learn how to define and use coach marks in your panels.

In addition to providing information, panels serve as navigation tools. Not only can the user click left and right arrows to move through the information, but also buttons and hot items in the panel—and buttons in the navigation bar. These features of panels are covered in Chapter 10, "Panels III—Controls."

DESIGNING PANELS AND THEIR CONTENTS

Although the syntax for defining a panel is straightforward, designing the panel's content requires careful design. Keep the following design points in mind:

- A panel should contain one thought or instruction. In addition to making it easy for a user to read and understand the panel, limiting a panel to one thought or instruction makes it easier for you to reuse the panel in another context.

- All panels in a sequence should be more or less the same length, which means that the individual thoughts and instructions should be of approximately the same complexity.

- The language of the panel should be simple, straightforward, and phrased in the active voice.

A consistency in the panels in your guide file is a big help to the user and makes for a more pleasing appearance. The consistency should extend to overall design, formatting, and language. Just as you would with any written document, set up a style sheet (so that you consistently spell, punctuate, and capitalize the terms that are specific to your subject area and application) and rely on common standards for spelling, punctuation, capitalization, and the like. (The *Apple Publications Style Guide*, together with a good up-to-date dictionary, Strunk and White's *The Elements of Style*, and *The Chicago Manual of Style* should be your constant companions.)

How Users See the Panels

There is no question about *what* users are doing when they look at your panels— they are looking for assistance of one sort or another. By examining *how* they look at the panels, you can learn a great deal about designing effective Apple Guide assistance. The most important aspects of how users see the panels are as follows:

- They usually see the panel once, so you should not hesitate to make the information explicit, clear, and complete.

- They often see the panels in orders or sequences you have not envisioned, so you should make each panel as self-contained as possible, not relying on information or instructions from other panels.

- They look at the panels quickly—often with a single glance. Careful formatting of the panel and appropriate use of graphics can make that glance most effective.

Users May See Your Panels Only Once

Although you may think of Apple Guide as an interface element (indeed, often as an additional interface laid on top of your application's standard interface), the panels in your guide file differ in one crucial way from your other interface elements, such as dialog boxes, palettes, and menus, which become very familiar to users. Your Save dialog box is seen repeatedly by users and is most likely very similar to other Save dialog boxes that they see in other programs. The ubiquity and similarity of Save dialog boxes means that users often don't notice nuances, particularly the "fine print" of special messages and the placement of buttons.

Your Apple Guide panels, however, are usually seen once, and the user often attends closely to the content; if it were familiar, there would be no point in looking at it. (The exception to this is Apple Guide files, which are routinely used to carry out automated tasks.) This behavioral aspect of the user's interaction with your guide file panels should have consequences in your design; some of these consequences are also related to the next aspect of how users see your guide file panels: they see them in orders and sequences that you have not planned for.

Users See Panels in Their Own Sequences

In a linear medium, such as print, film, or music, the sequence in which people come across the information is usually known to the author, and it can be manipulated for best effect. (Agatha Christie is a past master at the manipulation of the sequence in which information is delivered.) The presentation of Apple Guide assistance is not linear, despite the left and right arrows on each panel. Users can close windows, return to the Access window, click **Huh?** buttons, and use panel controls to jump to other areas of assistance and move to other tasks.

The techniques that you use in linear media to improve the flow of information can become obstacles in a nonlinear medium. The last phrase of the previous section ("some of these consequences are also related to the next aspect of how users see your guide file panels: they see them in orders and sequences that you have not planned for") is an example of a transition that is appropriate only in a linear medium.

Because users may see panels only once and in an order other than that which you have in mind, each panel must be as self-contained as possible. This means eliminating references to other panels, except where those references are implemented in functional terms, such as hot text. It also means not relying on information or instructions from a "previous" panel—what is previous in your scenario may not be previous in the user's exploration.

Users May See Your Panels at a Single Glance

Although you are carefully planning your panels, you must remember that users sometimes will only briefly glance at your handiwork. The close box and right arrow sit there tempting the user to move on to something else. A large **Continue** button may beckon, letting the user continue on to something else without reading the contents of the panel. Careful formatting of the panel can let the user's glance work most effectively to see what is on the panel (thus pausing to read it instead of immediately moving on) and to understand the information or instructions provided.

Reconciling Conflicting Advice

If you review the three aspects of how users interact with your guide file panels, you will see conflicts and inconsistencies. On the one hand, users may see your panels only once and attend to them closely; on the other, they may view them in a random order and only glance at them. The truth is that different users at different times do different things.

The design of a panel should convey one idea or instruction clearly, it should look and behave like other Apple Guide panels, and any special instructions for its use should be provided—but not to the extent that these instructions obscure the purpose of the panel. All of these decisions require judgment, experimentation (on yourself and others), and experience. Learning how to design Apple Guide panels is a subjective process that involves reconciling often-conflicting elements of design.

There are two things that you can do to help yourself provide the most effective service to the user. First, you should put yourself in the user's place as much as possible. This may involve formal research in a lab equipped with two-way mirrors and video cameras, or it may involve your simply using a program (your own or another) and observing your problems and successes. You must learn not to watch with the proprietary air of the developer who wants to see things go well. You are looking for problems, difficulties, and hesitations.

The second thing you can do is to learn how to talk about the user experience, assistance, and Apple Guide in particular. Perhaps because the computer age is so young and many of the basics are still being developed, there is a very scant vocabulary available to talk about the nature of software. When the quality of software is discussed, the conversation usually starts—and ends—with "ease of use" (whatever that may be). Almost anyone can compare two chairs and speak for several minutes about the differences between them. One might be appropriate for a living room, one might be a dining chair; one could stand up to the heavy use of a schoolroom, the other might be better placed in a rarely used formal parlor. It doesn't take a cabinetmaker to make these observations.

Discussing and comparing software, however, is a different matter. The concepts and vocabulary to use are not widely known, even within the industry, in large part because the notion of teaching "comparative software" is not part of the standard computer science curriculum the way in which "comparative literature" is part of the English major's studies. Just as you make a conscious effort to watch yourself as you use software, you should make a special attempt to analyze and discuss the services that are provided to users with Apple Guide assistance, traditional on-line help, Windows Help, and other tools.

Learning to Talk about Panels

This section provides the sort of analysis of Apple Guide assistance that should become second nature to you. The point of the analysis process is to learn what the issues are and how to deal with them. Sometimes choices that have been made are obviously good; other times you may question them.

Consider the panels from Macintosh Guide that explain "How do I change items in the Apple (🍎) menu." (Like most of the Apple Guide assistance that is shipped with the Mac OS, this sequence is very good. The fact that it stands up to detailed analysis and questioning demonstrates the care that went into its development. Fortunately, standards and guidelines appear to have been bent and broken in a few places, which makes the discussion all the more interesting.)

Figure 8.1 is the first panel in the sequence.

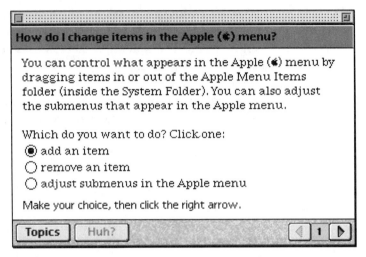

Figure 8.1 How do I change items in the Apple (🍎) menu?—panel 1.

How many things does the user need to know in order to use this panel?

1. To close the window or end assistance, click the close box.
2. To expand or contract the window, click the zoom box.
3. To move the window, use the drag bar.
4. To look at other topics, click the **Topics** button.
5. Click one of the radio buttons to select which type of change you want to accomplish in the Apple menu.
6. Click the right arrow to go to the next panel.

The first three items are basic Macintosh principles and are not elucidated on this panel.

The fourth point, clicking the **Topics** button to see other topics, relies on the user's knowledge that the thing in the lower left of the panel is a button and can be clicked on, as well as what topics are in the context of Apple Guide.

The fifth and sixth points are explicitly explained on this panel.

This division of information about how to use the panel is appropriate and serves as a good model. Three levels of expertise are assumed here:

- The panel assumes a basic knowledge of Macintosh techniques—close boxes, zoom boxes, and window dragging. These techniques are so basic that you can reasonably assume that all users are familiar with them (with the exception of people using a very basic introductory tutorial). To add explicit instructions for such basic techniques makes it harder for the user to find the information that is important in the panel.

- The panel also assumes a basic familiarity with the interface design of Apple Guide—at least so far as knowing what a topic is and recognizing the **Topics** button in the lower left of the panel. Because this button is a standard feature of most navigation bars (although it now has a different graphical representation, the Apple Guide light bulb), you can assume that a user who has used Apple Guide knows what it is.

- The final two interface elements are basic Macintosh interface components, but they are used in different ways in different places in the interface and in different ways on different Apple Guide panels. Because of the variation in their use, it is appropriate and necessary to instruct the user to click one of the radio buttons and to prompt the user to click the right arrow.

The next panel in the sequence is shown in Figure 8.2.

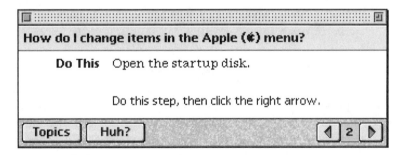

Figure 8.2 How do I change items in the Apple (🍎) menu?—panel 2.

Once again, consider what other assumptions are made about the user's knowledge of Apple Guide and how to use it.

In this case, two additional assumptions are made about the user's familiarity with the interface. Here, the **Huh?** button is enabled. In its interface guidelines for Apple Guide, Apple suggests explaining in the panel's content what the **Huh?** button will do. Sometimes, however, the Apple Guide designer thinks that the

Huh? button's meaning is so clear from the context that no additional explanation is necessary. In this case, it is pretty difficult to imagine that the **Huh?** button would do anything except explain what the startup disk is.

The other assumption made here is that the user is prompted to continue by clicking the right arrow; the fact that the left arrow will back up to the previous screen is not explicitly stated. Once again, this may be a justified assumption. In the first place, you really don't want the user to go backward; in the second, the user will rarely go backward.

If the user clicks the **Huh?** button, the panel shown in Figure 8.3 appears.

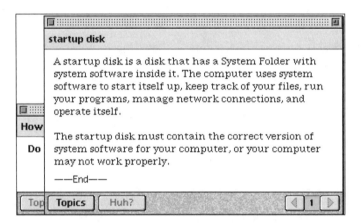

Figure 8.3 Huh? panel for "startup disk."

No new assumption is made, but one assumption of the user's knowledge that has been in effect from the start of the sequence takes on greater importance here. The user can close this panel by using the close box or drag it out of the way with the drag bar. The user also can click on a partially obscured window that is behind this one in the Apple Guide layer to bring it forward. Because this panel partially obscures the previous panel, the user must take some action to return to Figure 8.2—closing this window, moving it, or clicking on the part of Figure 8.2 that is visible.

The judgment here is that these are all such basic techniques that the user can continue with the sequence without additional instructions. Nevertheless, some users who are using Apple Guide for the first time will click the **Topics** button and return to the Access window when they actually want to return to Figure 8.2.

If the user does not open the startup disk as requested in Figure 8.2, but simply clicks the right arrow, Apple Guide opens the window for the user, displaying the panel shown in Figure 8.4.

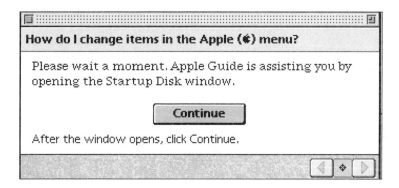

Figure 8.4 Continue panel shown while AppleScript is executing.

The prompt for the user to click the **Continue** button is appropriate here: although many users will see a **Continue** button and know that it should be clicked, this element of the design of Apple Guide files is not as ubiquitous as the close boxes and drag bars in the Huh? window. An explicit instruction of what to do wastes space when the action is very basic and widely known; when it is not, the space is well-used to prevent users' confusion.

Bearing in mind the design issues involved, you are ready to start defining Apple Guide panels.

DEFINING PANELS

For all the power and flexibility that Apple Guide provides in the display of information, there are only five commands that you use to define a panel:

- <Define Panel> introduces a panel definition
- <End Panel> closes the definition
- <Format> lets you apply a predefined format to all or part of the text in a panel
- <PICT> inserts a PICT graphic into a panel at a specified location

- <QuickTime> inserts a QuickTime movie into a panel at a specified location and lets you choose the type of controller used

It really is remarkably simple. (Of course, should you choose to add hot text, buttons, navigation bar buttons, or other goodies, a few additional commands are required, ten of them in fact. But they're covered in the next chapter.)

Creating a Panel

A panel consists of all the text and commands between the <Define Panel> and <End Panel> commands.

Define Panel and End Panel Commands

The text for the panel can be formatted in various ways. A format command (either specific to the panel or the default format for the guide file) can set the font, font size, color, and style of the text. Any attributes that are set in a governing format command are set by Guide Maker. Any attributes that have not been set in the <Format> command are taken from the text that you type in. See the <Define Format> command for examples of the interplay of format commands and text styles.

The *panelName* parameter should be meaningful not only in describing the panel's contents, but also in identifying the panel in the scheme of things. Because guide files tend to contain many panels, some naming convention is needed. Following are some examples:

- Preface panel names with "Def:" for panels containing definitions.
- If panels are always used in a sequence, add a numeral at the beginning of the name, as "Def: 1/Italics," "Def: 2/Italics."
- Use the preface "Tip:" for panels containing a tip.
- If a panel is always used in a certain context or sequence (usually a bad thing), include a reference in the name, as "Tip: Tutorial-Italics."

There are no hard and fast rules because the way in which you organize your panels and their names is solely for the convenience of guide file authors. What is certain is that panels with names such as "A1" and "A2" are not easy to maintain over time.

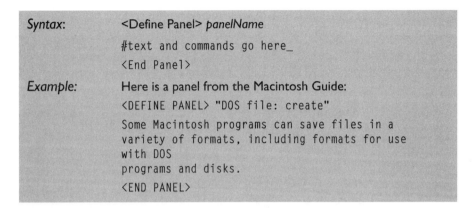

Syntax: <Define Panel> *panelName*

#text and commands go here_

<End Panel>

Example: Here is a panel from the Macintosh Guide:

<DEFINE PANEL> "DOS file: create"

Some Macintosh programs can save files in a variety of formats, including formats for use with DOS
programs and disks.

<END PANEL>

Specifying a Format for a Panel

If you have specified a <Default Format> command, that format will be used for all panels in your source files. You can override that format with one or more formats in a given panel, using the <Format> command. The <Format> command applies to everything that follows it until either the end of the panel or the next <Format> command.

Format Command

Apple Guide formats specify the familiar font, size, style (bold, italic, and so on), color, and alignment for an area in the panel. This area is a bottomless column whose top, left, and right coordinates are specified in the <Format> command. (The column is "bottomless" because Apple Guide extends it to whatever length is necessary to accommodate its contents.) This makes it very easy to create formats, such as the **Tag** and **Body** formats used in Figure 8.5.

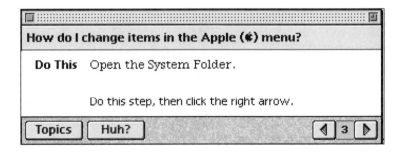

Figure 8.5 How do I change items in the Apple () menu?—panel 3.

Because the <Format> command specifies a location in the panel, it can be used to position objects other than text, such as PICT graphics and QuickTime movies. All of the text and other objects that appear after a <Format> command in a panel (and before the next <Format> command or the end of the panel) are placed sequentially in the column specified by the panel.

Syntax:	**<Format>** *formatName*
Example:	<Format> "Tag"
	Do This
	<Format> "Body"
	Open the System Folder.
Default:	If a <Default Format> command has been specified, that format is used; otherwise Apple Guide's standard full-panel format is applied.
When to Use:	As needed, but limit the total number of different formats that you use in a guide file so that there is a consistent look. It is appropriate to use different formats for different purposes, for example, panels with a "Do It" or "Oops" tag should look different from descriptive and definition panels.

Placing a PICT Graphic in a Panel

There are a number of reasons to use a PICT graphic in a panel:

- Use a diagram to illustrate a concept (such as the relationship of a spreadsheet to two windows—one of which displays the data, the other of which displays a chart based on the data).

- Use a screen shot with call-outs (labels, lines, and arrows in common language) to quickly identify a number of items in the interface at once. If you do not use call-outs or identify several items in the graphic at once, use a coach mark on the actual object. Never use a picture of a dialog box or window without clearly showing that it is a picture and not the object itself. Call-outs or a picture with a jagged edge indicating that the object is incomplete will prevent the user from attempting to click in the graphic rather than the object itself.

- Use a corporate or application logo on a panel of a Simple Access window for your About guide file.

There are many reasons not to use a PICT graphic in a panel, but they all boil down to one: Do not use PICT graphics as decoration.

As always when you use graphics on a computer monitor, you must make certain that the graphic reproduces well with different color settings. You also should make certain that color is never used as the sole differentiating characteristic of two otherwise-identical objects.

Pict Command

Pictures that are to be placed in panels are incorporated into your guide file by Guide Maker from either a resource file or a PICT file.

Including a PICT Graphic from a Resource File

The graphic can be stored as a resource in a file that is included in your guide file with the <Resource> command. In this case, *pictGraphic* is the ID or name of the resource.

To place the graphic in a resource file, you must have a tool such as ResEdit. The graphic's resource ID should be greater than 2000, and it should be marked "purgeable." (If you don't understand this paragraph, you must include your PICT graphic from a PICT file as described next.)

Including a PICT Graphic from a PICT File

Your graphic can be saved as a file of type PICT, and that file can be referenced from the <PICT> command. In this case, *pictGraphic* is the name of the file. The file should be in the same folder as your source file; if it is in a subfolder, the *pictGraphic* file name should include the path relative to the source file. For example, if the file is in a folder called *Graphics* that is co-resident with your source file, the *pictGraphic* parameter would be Graphics:Pict1.

Specifying a Black-and-White Picture

The optional parameters *b&wPict* has the same syntax as *pictGraphic*—that is, it is a resource name or ID or the name of a PICT file. This PICT graphic is displayed on monitors with a bit depth of four or less. By providing your substitute picture, you can exercise greater control over the appearance of the graphic in different environments.

Locating the Picture

Three constants can be used for the *location* parameter:

LEFT

CENTER

RIGHT

These align the picture horizontally, placing it by default immediately after the last line of text (or other object) that was automatically placed by Apple Guide.

Formats in Apple Guide specify not only text attributes, but also columns on a panel. The alignment of a picture is relative to the current format. Thus, if you were using the **Body** format shown in Figure 8.5, aligning a PICT graphic to the left would place it under the word "Open." If you were using the **Tag** format, aligning a PICT graphic to the left would place it under the words "Do This." Using the standard format **Full**, aligning a PICT with the CENTER constant would center it in the panel. The next object (including text) that is placed in the panel is placed immediately underneath the PICT graphic unless an intervening <Format> command is encountered.

You also can locate a graphic explicitly by using the Point function in Guide Maker for the *location* parameter. The Point function has two arguments: a horizontal offset and a vertical offset. Following is an example:

```
Point(15, 25)
```

When you use this syntax, you specify a location for the graphic *relative to the last position where Apple Guide placed an object*. This is not an absolute location in the panel. Furthermore, when you place a graphic with the Point function, Apple Guide places the next object (including text) immediately after the preceding object—not after the PICT graphic. In other words, locating a graphic with the Point function temporarily interrupts Apple Guide's normal flowing of objects into a panel, and that normal flowing resumes with the next object.

Syntax:	**<PICT>** *pictGraphic, location [, b&wPict]*
Example:	`<PICT> "Graphics:Pict 1", LEFT, "Graphics:B&W:Pict 1"`
When to Use:	Whenever the graphic will enhance the information in the panel. Do not use as decoration or to identify parts of the interface that can be identified with coach marks.

Placing a QuickTime Movie in a Panel

QuickTime movies can be very effective in Apple Guide files, but the same cautions apply as with pictures. Do not use movies as decoration, and do not use them to replace coach marks. For example, if you want the user to choose the **Save** command from the File menu, use a coach mark. Do not use a movie showing the mouse moving to the File menu and pulling it down to select the **Save** command.

QuickTime Command

The *QTMovie* parameter is the name of the file containing your movie. As with all files referenced from your source code, the name must be relative to your source file. If the movie is in the same folder as your source code, its name is sufficient. If it is in a subfolder, the name must be qualified with the subfolder name (for example, Movies:Movie1 if the Movie1 file is in the folder "Movies," which is in the same folder as your source code).

The *location* parameter is the same as the corresponding parameter in the <PICT> command. It can take the values

    LEFT

    CENTER

    RIGHT

or the function Point, which specifies a point relative to the position of the last item that Apple Guide placed in the panel. Alignment is within the column specified by the currently applied format.

Apple Guide can place two different types of controllers on your movie—or none. The *QTController* parameter can have the following values:

CONTROL   Places the standard QuickTime controller beneath the movie.

BADGE   Places a small movie icon on the movie image when it is not playing. Double-clicking the badge opens the standard QuickTime controller beneath the movie.

PLAIN   No controller is shown.

Whether or not a controller is shown, double-clicking the movie starts it and a single click stops it.

If Apple Guide cannot find the movie file or if QuickTime is not available when the guide file is opened, a PICT graphic can be displayed in the space the movie would have used. Use the optional *moviePict* parameter to specify such a PICT graphic. As with the <PICT> command, the parameter may be a resource ID or name or a file name. (If it is a resource, that resource must be included with the <Resource> command.)

Syntax:	**<QuickTime>** *QTMovie, location, QTcontroller [, moviePict]*
Example:	`<QuickTime> "Movies:Opening Toner Cartridge Door", LEFT, CONTROL, "Graphics:Toner Cartridge Door"`
Limitations:	Only one QuickTime movie per panel is allowed. Because of the memory required to run movies, check to see that large movies play properly in your Apple Guide panels.
When to Use:	As appropriate.

FORMATTING PANELS

Apple Guide formats much of its windows for you, but the layout of the contents of the presentation panel is up to you. There are three groups of tools available:

- You can format the text of your panels with your word processor using standard formatting instructions, such as boldface type.
- You can define formats that can be applied to text (or other panel objects).

- You can modify the text and placement of the prompt at the bottom of each panel.

Formatting Text with a Word Processor

Guide Maker lets you use your favorite word processing application to prepare the source guide files, complete with the appropriate text styling commands (fonts, size, color, and so on). Guide Maker uses XTND translators to read this formatted text, and the format commands are saved when the final guide file is written by Guide Maker.

N O T E

In order for this process to work, you must have an XTND translator installed in your System folder that converts your word processor's files to a standard format that Guide Maker can read. XTND translators are provided with many applications (see the "Resources" appendix). Because they are commonly used to provide interapplication file reading and writing, you may have some XTND translators installed without even knowing it. The basic XTND system is included on the *Real World Apple Guide* CD-ROM.

Defining Formats

Guide Maker format commands are used to override your styling commands, as well as to place text and other objects properly on the panel.

An Apple Guide format consists of the usual formatting instructions (font, font size, style, color, and alignment) and a location on the panel. A format defines a bottomless column on the panel. You specify the top, left, and right coordinates; Apple Guide flows the text (and buttons, PICT graphics, and QuickTime movies) into the column, applying the formatting elements as needed.

You define a format with the <Define Format> command and use it by placing the <Format> command in your panel before the text and objects that you want to be affected by the format.

Define Format Command

If you use formats other than those provided in The shell files are on the *Real World Apple Guide* CD-ROM, they should be declared together in your Guide Maker source file and should be given meaningful names with the *formatName* parameters.

The *columnCoords* parameter describes the three values for the bottomless column in which Guide Maker places text and other objects. The Column function is used to specify the three values: top, left, and right. These values are relative to the upper-left corner of the panel's data, that is, below the title area.

All of the other parameters to the <Define Format> command are optional. If a parameter is not included, Guide Maker applies the appropriate value from your source code file if it is available. (If you save your source file as a TEXT file, formatting information is not available. If you save it in a format that Guide Maker can read, the font, size, and other attributes are available.) If no value is specified in the format and none is available from your source file, Guide Maker uses its defaults: Espy Serif, 10-point size, plain style, black color, and aligned left.

txFnt is the name of the font that you want to use for this format. As always when specifying a font, make certain it is one that will be installed on your users' machines. The Espy fonts that are Apple Guide's defaults have been designed for readability and to provide a standard "look" for Apple Guide text. Depart from the standard at your own risk. You can create an assistance window that is so far removed from those that the user normally sees that you will hear, "Oh, is *that* an Apple Guide window? I never would have known."

The *txSize* parameter—if present—specifies the font size.

If you want to provide a *txStyle* parameter, you can set the style of the text in your format using one of the following constants:

PLAIN

BOLD

ITALIC

UNDERLINE

OUTLINE

SHADOW

CONDENSE

EXTEND

Remember that this parameter is optional: PLAIN is not the same as omitting the parameter. Because only one of these constants can be used, you cannot create a format that combines two or more styles—underlined and condensed text, for example. If you absolutely must do so, omit the parameter and set the styles in your word processor.

N O T E   Italicized text and text that is underlined often is hard to read on the screen. Use these styles carefully. Test any styling parameters you choose on the font that you have selected: some fonts display very little difference on the screen between bold and plain styles. Or use the standard styles. They didn't drop out of thin air: they evolved out of a lot of careful work on the part of developers and designers.

You can specify the color for the text affected by a format command by using either the RGBColor function (which takes three parameters: the red, green, and blue values of the color) or one of the predefined constants:

> BLACK
>
> YELLOW
>
> MAGENTA
>
> RED
>
> CYAN
>
> GREEN
>
> BLUE
>
> WHITE

Think carefully before specifying a color other than black. Remember that not every user has a color monitor and that colored text can be very difficult to read under some circumstances.

The standard four values for alignment are provided in constants for the *txAlign* parameters:

> LEFT
>
> CENTER
>
> RIGHT
>
> SYSTEM

Finally, the *alignPrompt* parameter allows you to specify that the prompt at the bottom of the panel should be aligned with the left edge of this format's column. It can take the values TRUE and FALSE. Like the preceding parameters, it can be omitted. In Figure 8.5, *alignPrompt* is TRUE for the **Body** format, so the prompt is placed at the left of that format—underneath the word "Open."

Four formats are provided in the Guide Maker shell files—**Full**, **Tag**, **Body**, and **ResetPen**. The **Full** format was used in Figure 8.3 for the entire panel. The

Tag format was used in Figure 8.5 for the words "Do This." The **Body** format (normally used with the **Tag** format) was applied to the rest of the words in Figure 8.5. The **ResetPen** format is used to restore the default format values.

Syntax:	**<Define Format>** *formatName, columnCoords [, txFnt] [, txSize] [, txStyle], txColor] [, txAlign] [, alignPrompt]*

Example:	`<DEFINE FORMAT> "Full", Column(6,11,330),`
	`   "Espy Serif", 10, Plain, Black,Left, false`
	`<DEFINE FORMAT> "Full No Style", Column(6,11,330),`
	`   "Espy Serif", 10, , Black,Left, false`
	
	In the Full No Style format, there is no value supplied for the *txStyle* parameter. This means that whatever style was applied in the word processor file is used for the panel. If you use hot text in your panels and want to have the hot text shown in boldface type, use the Full No Style format. If you use the Full format (which includes the value Plain for the *txStyle* parameter), Guide Maker will force your carefully bolded words to plain text.

Default:	The format specified by a <Default Format> command (if present). Otherwise the Apple Guide defaults of Espy Serif, 10 point, black, aligned left, and plain style.
When to Use:	As needed. To keep your assistance consistent with itself and other Apple Guide files, try to use the formats from the shell files as much as possible. For your own purposes, design a limited number of additional formats that you use for your guide files.

Layering Text over Graphics

The text and other objects that are placed in a panel in accordance with a format command are placed on a white background. Accordingly, if you have carefully placed a picture on your panel and then have just as carefully placed text on top of it (by specifying the same column coordinates in both formats), the picture will disappear. Use the <Define Transparent Format> to create a format that uses as its background whatever is behind it on the panel.

Define Transparent Format Command

The syntax and parameters are the same as for the <Define Format> command.

Syntax:	**<Define Transparent Format>** *formatName, columnCoords [, txFnt] [, txSize] [, txStyle] [, txColor] [, txAlign] [, alignPrompt]*
Example:	<Define Transparent Format> "Caption", Column (6, 11, 330), "Geneva", 12, , CENTER, FALSE
	The *txColor* parameter is omitted in this format definition, so the color of the text from the word processing file will be used. The designer has specified (in a style sheet for the guide file) that the picture captions should be either white or black, depending on the color of the picture on which they appear.
When to Use:	As needed. Most frequently you use the <Define Transparent Format> command to put text on top of images.

Prompts

The last part of your formatting options for an Apple Guide panel concerns the prompt that is usually shown at the bottom of the panel. You use the <Default Prompt Set> command to select a set of prompts that appears on all panels in the guide file, but you can use the <Sequence Prompt Set> command to select an alternate prompt set for a given sequence, and you can use the <Panel Prompt> command to install a different prompt for a single panel.

N O T E   Prompt sets consist of prompts that Apple Guide uses for the first, last, and intermediate panels of a sequence, as well as a separate prompt used on panels with controls, such as buttons. Prompt sets are defined with the <Define Prompt Set> command, which is described in Chapter 12.

When you design your guide file, you should decide how to handle prompts. You will normally have at least two sets of prompts:

- For sequences that are primarily informative, prompts should be of the form: "Click the right arrow to continue."

- For tutorial sequences, prompts should be of the form: "Do this, then click the right arrow to continue."

Sometimes, guide file designers use panel prompts to let users see what lurks beyond the right arrow. Such prompts are of the form, "To see a Tip, click the right arrow" or "To learn about the Colors palette, click the right arrow." In other cases, the panel prompt is used to alert the user not to continue. When Apple Guide sends an event that causes something to happen, the user may need to wait before clicking a **Continue** button or a right arrow. In these cases, a prompt such as "When the Colors palette is open, click the Continue button" is used.

Part of your guide file's design process should be devoted to deciding how to use prompts. A needless variety of prompts makes the guide files harder to maintain and does nothing for the user. A consistent use of prompts—even if it is a consistent use of different prompts—helps the user.

Review the panels that are presented in the figures in this chapter. Notice how the prompts differ and how the sequence default prompt ("Do this step, then click the right arrow") is used.

When you assemble your source files, you should place all the <Define Prompt Set> commands together. In that way you can avoid needlessly defining new prompt sets with text that is identical to that used in other prompt sets.

N O T E

Panel Prompt Command

If you choose to override the global and sequence-level default prompt sets, you use the <Panel Prompt> command.

Syntax:	**<Panel Prompt>** *promptName*
Example:	<Panel Prompt> "Right arrow for tip"
Limitations:	Only one <Panel Prompt> command is used in a panel.
Default:	The prompt set defined for the sequence; if none, the default set for the guide file.
When to Use:	As needed.

Although the prompt at the bottom of each panel is very useful, there are some cases where you want no prompt to appear. Use the constant NONE for the *promptName* parameter when you want no prompt to appear on a panel.

SUMMARY

This chapter has covered the basics of creating and formatting panels and including text, PICT graphics, and QuickTime movies. The following panel definition (taken from the Macintosh Guide) uses many of the commands discussed in this chapter. You should be able to understand the syntax and, most important, you should be able to visualize the panel that it creates and to discuss the design decisions that come into play here.

```
# Panels for the sequence "How do I use windows?"
<DEFINE PANEL> "window: def with prompt"
<FORMAT> "Full"
A window is a rectangle on the screen that displays the contents
of a disk, folder, or document. Some windows display messages or
offer choices.
    <PICT> 1028, Center
    <PANEL PROMPT> "Prompt Overridden: 4"
<END PANEL>
```

CHAPTER 9

Panels II: Coach Marks

Coach marks are the most visible difference between Apple Guide and traditional on-line help systems. (The use of Apple Events is arguably the most significant difference of all, but coach marks are much more visible.)

If you compare Apple Guide assistance to help files developed for use with help systems of other sorts, you may be struck by the fact that Apple Guide files often have fewer graphics than the other files do. The reason is quite simple: other systems often need to reproduce some of the interface elements so that they can be identified and described. Apple Guide authors simply specify a coach mark. The words and diagrams used to describe interface elements have been replaced.

COACH MARKS AND NONVERBAL BEHAVIOR

Coach marks are significant not only because they make it easy to follow instructions, but also because they eliminate a layer of complexity for the user who is trying to use software. In traditional help systems (both on-line and printed documentation), the user must read a description of what must be done. Having read these instructions, the user must understand them and then translate them into actions. The entire process is based on words.

The Problem of Understanding Words

Processing verbal instructions in our brains is more complicated and slower than processing physical and spatial instructions. Sometimes, in fact, it is almost impossible to describe in words the physical actions that we undertake in order to carry out a task. For example, you would be hard-pressed to learn how to ride a bicycle or to drive a car with a standard transmission by reading a book.

Using the clutch in a car involves a rather tricky maneuver in that you feel the point at which the gears have started to engage—with your left foot—while applying gas with your right foot. Most people do not have a name for the point at which they feel the gears engage; finding it is one of the hardest parts of learning to drive a stick shift. There are no visual clues, and the physical feedback from your left foot is hard to learn. You are moving your foot in an arc with your heel resting on the floor of the car. Although you can easily remember a left-right position (the difference between the clutch and the brake pedal, for example) or a vertical position (the height of the steps in your house), it is very hard to remember a point on an arc. The process of learning to use the clutch is unlikely to be made easier by words: doing it (and stalling when you don't do it right) is the only way to learn.

The Problem of Naming Things

In addition to the complexity that can be introduced to a task when it is described in words (as opposed to visualizing or experiencing it), the use of words requires that every part involved in the process be named. Although this may seem an obvious point, it is far from trivial. We deal with many things in our daily lives (and on our computers) that are not named or for which we do not know the names.

For example, there is no need to name things that are not used. The * and # keys on push-button phones are often called the "star" and "pound" keys, but this nomenclature is far from universal. For many years, this did not matter at all, which is why alternate names such as "asterisk" and "number key" arose. Only with the advent of voice mail and automated phone services, when instructions needed to be given verbally over the phone with no visual reference as backup, was it necessary to name these keys. Even now, some automated systems refer to the "pound sign, which is located below the 9 on your telephone" (which, of course, it isn't on some phones).

The burden of naming things (including learning and remembering the names) is significant. Not only does it take time, but it involves higher levels of processing in the brain. When you learn how to resize a window on your computer, you learn to recognize a symbol that is found in the lower-right corner of a window, and you drag it. In order to write those instructions in a manual, the size box (that is the official name for that thing in the lower-right corner) has to be identified and named. You can try an interesting experiment by asking colleagues to identify the size box in a standard Mac OS window. You will find that a significant number of people who can resize a window without thinking twice about it have to pause and think for a moment what the size box is. Some may call it a "resize box" and others may identify the zoom box in the upper right of the window as the size box. Compare this to the simplicity of the illustration with a coach mark in Figure 9.1.

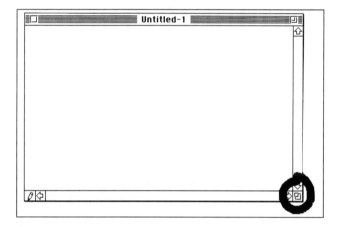

Figure 9.1 Window with coach mark on size box.

N O T E   The extent of the difficulty of properly naming the size box (and getting people to use the proper name) is reflected in the Guide Script syntax for defining a window coach. The constant that is used to specify a coach mark for the size box is GROWBOX.

With coach marks, you can show the user what should be clicked without naming it. Because this bypasses verbal reasoning in the brain and sidesteps the need to name and define the object in question, it is much more straightforward than verbally describing the process.

This may seem obvious, but it has important implications for an author of Apple Guide assistance. Coach marks and graphics (including movies) placed in Apple Guide assistance are not used for decoration. Even the application logo that you can place in the upper-left corner of an Access window is not decoration. The Apple Guide window is recognizable as an Apple Guide window because of its unique font, special drag bar, and layout, which is constant for all applications that use it. Your custom application logo immediately identifies that Apple Guide window as belonging to your application, which is important as users switch from the Finder to one application or another. (Users who are doing this repeatedly with Apple Guide windows open are likely to be new users of the machine and, as such, need every assistance and subliminal clue that can be devised.)

HOW COACH MARKS ARE DRAWN

In order to draw a coach mark, Apple Guide calculates a region of the screen that will be behind the coach mark. It then copies that region to an invisible window that floats in front of all other windows, displays the region (that is at this moment a duplicate of what is beneath it), and then draws the coach mark onto this duplicated region. When the coach mark disappears, these graphics are removed from the invisible window, leaving behind the original image before the coach mark was drawn.

The region that Apple Guide copies to the invisible window and that it uses to draw the coach mark on is calculated based on the parameters you provide to the coach mark definition. Normally, this is a rectangle, and Apple Guide can calculate the area needed to be copied based on the rectangle and the type of coach mark. Circle coach marks surround the target rectangle, never intruding on it. In this case, the region is a "hollow" rectangle slightly larger than the target itself, where the hole is precisely the size of the target.

Underline, arrow, and x-mark coaches use different regions, but all are calculated in the same manner: by getting the target rectangle and creating a region based on it and the type of coach mark.

This process is important to you only in a few special circumstances. For example, if you want to use a coach mark to identify an area of the screen that contains something that moves—for example, a clock, a movie, or an animation—you must make certain that the coach mark rectangle completely surrounds the moving area, and you must choose a coach mark that does not cause Apple Guide to copy the pixels from the area that moves. (The red circle coach mark is safe in this case.) If you do not take these precautions, Apple Guide will copy some pixels from the screen image as it is when the coach mark is first drawn, and those pixels will remain in front of your moving image, blocking its view.

In another case, the mouse tracking mechanism will send mouse moving events to the invisible system window when the mouse is in the area of the copied region. If your application is tracking the mouse for the purpose of changing the cursor, that code will break when the mouse is moved into the region where the coach mark is drawn.

Under normal circumstances, you need not worry about the implementation of Apple Guide's coach marks. Being aware of the basic procedure that is used to draw the coach marks may come in handy when you are debugging apparently abnormal behavior. If you are attempting to explain and fix aberrant behavior, change the type of coach mark and its target rectangle several times until you get a feel for exactly what region Apple Guide is using in its invisible window.

STYLES OF COACH MARKS

There are four styles of coach marks that Apple Guide can draw: circles, arrows, x-marks, and underlines. In addition, menu commands are coached by modifying the color or style of the item in the menu.

Circle Coach Marks

The most common coach mark is the circle (see Figure 9.1). It is most appropriate for identifying an object on the screen, usually indicating where the user should click the mouse. On color or gray-scale monitors, the circle is red (or gray), and the underlying screen image can be seen through it. On black-and-white monitors, the circle is narrow and black; the underlying screen image cannot be seen through it, so it is designed to obscure as little as possible.

Arrow Coach Marks

The arrow coach mark has a direction in which it points; it is often used to indicate movement, such as dragging with the mouse. As with circle coach marks, the arrow coach mark is drawn in red (or gray) on a color or gray-scale monitor, and in black on a black-and-white monitor.

An arrow coach mark can show the user how to enlarge a window in both directions by dragging the size box (see Figure 9.2).

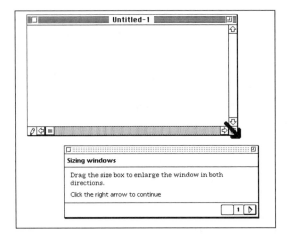

Figure 9.2 Arrow coach mark showing how to expand a window in two dimensions.

In Figure 9.3, the user is coached in the procedure used to reduce the size of the window in both directions.

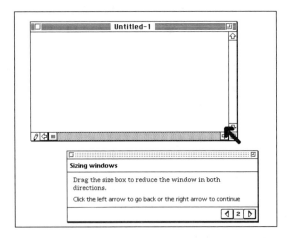

Figure 9.3 Arrow coach mark showing how to reduce a window in two dimensions.

Just as you specify a rectangle around which the circle coach mark is drawn, you specify a rectangle for an arrow coach mark—and tell Apple Guide the direction of the arrow to be drawn. You can use the corners or midpoints of each size of the rectangle. In Figure 9.4, the midpoints of the sides of the rectangle are used, instructing the user how to resize the window horizontally.

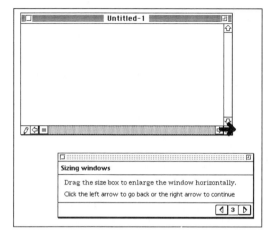

Figure 9.4 Arrow coach mark showing how to expand a window horizontally.

Underline Coach Marks

In addition to identifying a location and suggesting movement, coach marks can be used specifically to direct a user to type information. The underline coach mark (see Figure 9.5) is used to direct the user to click the mouse in the field underlined and to type information there.

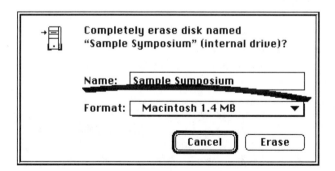

Figure 9.5 Red underline coach mark on text entry field.

The underline coach mark is red (or gray) on color or gray-scale monitors, and black on black-and-white monitors.

X-Mark Coach Marks

A green x (gray on gray-scale monitors, black on black-and-white monitors) is also available to indicate to a user where to type information. Use the x-mark instead of the underline coach mark when the underline coach mark would be too large or misleading. For example, when a user is coached to enter a multiline address, use the x-mark coach mark to indicate where the first line of information is to be typed.

Menu Command Coach Marks

When you provide a coach mark for a menu, the menu title is circled. When the user pulls down the menu, a specific menu command may also be highlighted with a color or underlined. The menu coach mark includes both the circle for the menu title and the emphasis for the menu command. Until the user pulls down the menu, only the circle around the menu title is visible.

ADDING A COACH MARK TO A PANEL

To use a coach mark with a panel, you use the <Coach Mark> command, specifying a coach mark that you have defined elsewhere in your guide file.

Coach Mark Command

Coach marks are included in your panel definition (between the <Define Panel> and <End Panel> commands). They are drawn after the panel is displayed and remain on the screen until a user event (such as mouse moving or key pressing) has occurred.

Syntax:	**<Coach Mark>** *coachMarkName*
Example:	<Coach Mark> "Coach Preferences Command"
Limitations:	Only one <Coach Mark> command is used in a panel. If you have more than one, Guide Maker uses the last one.
When to Use:	Frequently.

DEFINING COACH MARKS

There are five types of coach marks that can be defined for Apple Guide. They are used to coach

- menus and menu commands,
- windows and their contents,
- dialog boxes and their contents,
- objects defined by an application, and
- locations described by an AppleScript script.

Do not confuse the five types of coach marks with the five styles (circles, underlines, x-marks, arrows, and menu coaches) of coach marks. The styles reflect how the coach mark is drawn and what the user sees. The type of coach mark reflects how the Apple Guide author specifies the coach mark.

N O T E

Basic Coach Mark Parameters

Several parameters are common to all the coach mark definitions. They are described here for the sake of simplicity and are not redefined as they are used in the following syntax discussion.

Naming the Coach Mark

The parameter *coachMarkName* is the name of each coach mark. The name should be meaningful both in and of itself and in the context of other coach marks. In a guide file of any length, you will have several coach mark definitions. They should all be placed in one location and should be named so that it is clear what they are.

Specifying Target Application

You use the *targetApp* parameter in coach mark definitions (except <Define AppleScript>, where the target is the Mac OS that processes AppleScript commands) to specify the application that should receive the coach mark instruction. The application is identified by its four-character signature. You can also use the constant FRONT to have Apple Guide apply the coach mark to the front-most (active) application. Because of the ease with which users can switch from one application to another (intentionally or not), it is far better to use the application's signature for this parameter. *targetApp* is an optional parameter; its default value is FRONT.

Selecting a Coach Style

The different coach mark styles are specified in the *coachStyle* parameter. The constants REDCIRCLE and REDUNDERLINE can be used in any coach mark definition. GREENX or the RedArrow specifier are available for all coach marks except <Define Menu Coach>, where they would be meaningless. REDCIRCLE is the default value in all cases.

The RedArrow specifier takes two arguments that give the start and end location for the arrow that is drawn. The values represent the corners and midpoints of the rectangle on which the coach mark is based and have the following values:

1 top left

2 top center

3 top right

4 right center

5 bottom right

6 bottom center

7 bottom left

8 left center

The arrow shown in Figure 9.4 uses RedArrow (8, 4); Figure 9.3 uses RedArrow (5, 1); and Figure 9.2 illustrates RedArrow (1, 5).

Coaching a Menu or Menu Item

Coaching the user to select a command from a menu is a two-step process: the menu title is coached (with a circle or underline) in the menu bar, and after the user has pulled down the menu, the relevant menu item is then highlighted in one way or another. The <Define Menu Coach> command enables you to specify both parts of the coaching process; you also can use it only to coach the menu title.

Specifying the Menu to be Coached

The menu title you want coached is specified in the *targetMenu* parameter. You can either specify the exact menu title as it appears in the menu bar or use the menu number. (Menus are numbered sequentially: the Apple menu is 1, the File menu is 2, and so forth.) It is preferable to use the menu title. In the course of developing and enhancing an application, sometimes the menu bar is rearranged. Using the menu title rather than the number often prevents incorrectly placed coach marks as this process occurs.

In addition, when an application has several menu bars (generally based on the type of window or tool selected), a single menu may appear in different locations on different menu bars. Using the menu title will ensure that your coach mark functions properly in all cases. (For example, many applications have a Window menu at the end of their menu bar. As a user switches from a text window to a graphics window, the Window menu—always at the end of the menu bar—may change numbers.)

Coaching a Menu Command

In addition to highlighting the menu title, you can highlight a specific menu command. If you do so, use the *targetItem* to identify a menu item by either number (starting at 1 for the first item in the menu) or name. The same cautions with regard to using numbers rather than names apply here as for the *targetMenu* parameter.

If you do not specify a *targetItem*, there is no secondary coach mark beyond that drawn on the menu title.

If you have specified a *targetItem*, then you can select a highlighting color and style for it. (This color is used for the secondary coach applied to the menu command—it does not affect the color of the circle or underline used to highlight the menu title.) Use the *itemCoachColor* command to select one of these constants that will be used to highlight the command:

> BLACK
>
> BLUE
>
> CYAN
>
> GREEN
>
> MAGENTA
>
> RED

WHITE

YELLOW

The default value is RED.

You can use the *itemCoachStyle* parameter to modify the style of the menu command so that it is further highlighted for the users. The following constants are available:

PLAIN

BOLD

CONDENSE

EXTEND

ITALIC

OUTLINE

SHADOW

UNDERLINE

The default value is PLAIN.

N O T E   In designing your guide file, you should use a common method of highlighting menus and their commands. As a result, you may immediately have to remove some of these values from consideration. For example, a word processing program with a Style menu may already display menu commands that are condensed, extended, italic, and so forth. In such a case, a user may not be able to distinguish between your highlighting and the normal menu item appearance. A common form of menu item highlighting is the combination of RED and UNDERLINE. This prevents confusion with a menu that displays colors (in which the menu item "Red" might normally be displayed in red) and a menu that displays styles (in which the menu item "Underline" might normally be underlined). It is unlikely that a menu item would be both red and underlined.

As you experiment with menu coaches, you may learn how appearances can deceive. The "menu bar" that spreads across the top of the screen in some applications is not a menu bar. (This is the case in 4th Dimension and in several custom solutions written in HyperCard.) When an application does not use the Mac OS Menu Manager routines, it can draw a "menu bar" in the appropriate location and intercept mouse clicks appropriately. There are many reasons for doing this, but the result is that menu coaches from Apple Guide will not work.

In such a case, there is a work-around available to you. Instead of using a menu bar coach, you can coach the primary coach mark (the emphasis on the menu title) by specifying a coach mark that is identified by a location on the desktop—a location that you calculate to be precisely the location where the "menu's" title appears. The <Define Window Coach> command that is normally used to coach windows and their components is used for this.

Define Menu Coach Command

Use the <Define Menu Coach> command to coach menu titles and commands within them.

Syntax:	**<Define Menu Coach>** *coachMarkName [, targetApp] [, coachStyle] , targetMenu [, targetItem] [, itemCoachColor] [, itemCoachStyle]*
Example:	<Define Menu Coach> "quitting", 'PSM1', REDCIRCLE, "File", "Quit", RED, UNDERLINE
Limitations:	Coach marks are not drawn for menus if the application is in the background; they are also not drawn for menus not created under the aegis of the Menu Manager.
When to Use:	Often.

Coaching a Window

The <Define Window Coach> command is similar to the <Define Menu Coach> command, but where the menu coach specifies coaching locations by reference to menu titles and menu command, the <Define Window Coach> command specifies the locations with either constants representing parts of the standard window or rectangles.

Specifying the Window for the Coach Mark

The window coach mark is drawn relative to an item in a window, but often it is drawn beyond the bounds of the window. In order for Apple Guide to create the necessary region in which the coach mark is drawn, it needs to identify the window in question. You specify the window with the *targetWindow* parameter.

You can use the constant FRONTWINDOW to specify the front-most window. There are, however, several problems with this approach. Many applications use floating windows and palettes that float in front of the basic application windows (but still behind the layer in which the Apple Guide windows float). In some cases, the front-most window in an application is the front-most floating window; in other cases, the front-most window is the front-most nonfloating window (a window that is behind other application windows). It is easy enough to test how the application you are coaching manages this problem. In a simple application, FRONTWINDOW is a very easy way to coach the intuitively and actually front-most window. Even when there are no floating windows, if the user can open more than one window at a time (a preferences window, for example), the front-most window may not be what you expect it to be.

The safest way of specifying a window is with its title—the title that appears in the title bar. This works very well in many cases but is a total failure when you are coaching a user through the process of creating a new document. You very carefully coach the user to choose **New** from the File menu, but then what is the title of the window that has been created? "Untitled-1"? "Untitled-17"? In such a case, you must use the FRONTWINDOW constant for *targetWindow* (or use the <Define Object Coach> command, described later).

Another constant for the *targetWindow* parameter is DESKTOP. This specifies that the location you are specifying is relative to the desktop itself. When coaching pseudo-menu bars, you set *targetWindow* to DESKTOP and specify the exact location of the menu title in the *windowRectangle* parameter.

Specifying the Coach Mark Location Relative to the Window

After you have identified the target window, you need to help Apple Guide construct the rectangle it will use in drawing the coach mark. You do this with the *windowRectangle* parameter. The Rect function lets you define that rectangle. Its arguments are normally the values for the top, left, bottom, and right coordinates of the rectangle. *These values are relative to the window's origin.* Thus, wherever the window is on the screen, the values you specify will identify the same rectangle in the window.

There are also four constants that can be used for the *windowRectangle* parameter. They identify predefined areas in most windows:

GROWBOX

ZOOMBOX

CLOSEBOX

TITLEBAR

If you set *targetWindow* to DESKTOP and set *targetApp* to the Finder ("MACS"), you can also use the constant BOOTDISK to specify the startup disk on the desktop.

Occasionally, you may want to specify the values for the rectangle's coordinates in a different order. The optional parameter *rectOrigin* identifies the first point in a Rect function with one of the following constants:

TOPLEFT

TOPRIGHT

BOTTOMLEFT

BOTTOMRIGHT

If you use the *rectOrigin* parameter to identify the first point in the Rect function, the subsequent points are assumed to follow from that location in clockwise order.

Specifying a rectangle in an order other than the standard top, left, bottom, right sequence may make your source code hard to maintain.

N O T E

Define Window Coach Command

Use the <Define Window Coach> command to coach windows, fixed locations within them, and items on the desktop.

Syntax:	**<Define Window Coach>** *coachMarkName [, targetApp]* *[, coachStyle] [, targetWindow], windowRectangle [, rectOrigin]*
Example:	This is the command used to specify the coach mark shown in Figure 9.5. Because this window is a new unsaved (hence untitled) window, the FRONTWINDOW constant is used:
	`<Define Window Coach> "enlarge h", FRONT,` `    RedArrow(8, 4), FRONTWINDOW, GROWBOX`
When to Use:	Often.

Coaching an Item in a Dialog Box

Just as with the <Define Window Coach> command, the <Define Item Coach> command is used to specify a rectangle for a coach mark relative to a given window. In the case of dialog boxes, they contain elements that are structured more than the text or graphics that often appear in application windows. These elements are specified in a dialog item list ('DITL') created in ResEdit or by the application at run time. These elements have unique numbers. These elements may also have help balloons attached to them. Because of this, you can identify the rectangle of an element in a dialog box by identifying that element and letting Apple Guide find its location.

You can use a <Define Window Coach> command to coach items in a dialog box, but except for the constants known to the <Define Window Coach> command, you will have to specify the location of each button, field, and other interface element in the dialog box by supplying its coordinates. With the <Define Item Coach> command, you can specify these interface elements by their identifiers: Apple Guide will calculate the appropriate rectangles. Although you may think that items in dialog boxes will not move once an application's design is finalized, you should be aware that substantial interface changes can occur during user testing. In addition, when applications are localized for languages and scripts other than those of their origin, the sizes and locations of these interface elements almost always change. Their identifiers do not.

Specifying the Window for the Coach Mark

You identify the window for the coach mark using the same syntax described in the <Define Window Coach> command section earlier.

Specifying the Coach Mark Location Relative to the Window

With the <Define Item Coach> command, you need only identify the interface element in the dialog box—Apple Guide will find its location. To reference an element of a dialog box for Apple Guide, you use either its ID number from the DITL or its Balloon Help identifier. (You can obtain these from the application's documentation or API or by using a resource editor, such as ResEdit.) The *targetItem* parameter uses either the DialogID function or the BalloonID function. The DialogID function takes as its single parameter the identifier of the element wanted; the BalloonID function takes as its single parameter the identifier of the balloon associated with the element.

In some cases, you want to specify a rectangle to be coached that is smaller than the rectangle of an interface element. If you do so, you use the optional *itemRectangle* parameter to specify a rectangle that is relative to the upper-left corner of the item's rectangle.

Clearly identifying a subrectangle on an interface object, such as a button, is unlikely; in the case of an interface element that allows multiple lines of text to be entered, you might want to specify a subrectangle, such as Rect (0, 0, 14, 14), so that an x-mark coach mark can be drawn at the upper left of the text entry box—where the first line of text would be entered. In such a case, if you do not specify a subrectangle, a much larger x-mark will be drawn to the left of the entire multiline text box, vertically centered between the top and the bottom.

Define Item Coach Command

Use the <Define Item Coach> command to coach items in dialog boxes.

Syntax:	**<Define Item Coach>** *coachMarkName[, targetApp]* *[, coachStyle] [, targetWindow] ,targetItem [, itemRectangle]*
Example:	Dialog item 1 in most dialog boxes is the OK button. You would coach the OK button with the following: `><Define Item Coach> "OK button coach", 'PSM1', REDCIRCLE, "Preferences", DialogID(1)`
When to Use:	Often. When coaching a dialog box and its elements, the <Define Item Coach> command is more robust than the <Define Window Coach> command. Either can be used, but you must explicitly describe item locations in the <Define Window Coach> command, leading to potential problems with maintenance and localization.

Coaching an Item Dynamically Using AppleScript

To draw a coach mark, Apple Guide needs to know only the style of the coach mark and the basic rectangle that is to be coached. The preceding commands specify that rectangle in more or less direct ways. The <Define Menu Coach> command uses the menu name (and optionally the command name) to find the rectangle. The <Define Window Coach> uses predefined constants or your own painstakingly counted pixel locations to identify the rectangle. The <Define Item Coach> relies on the identification of interface elements in dialog boxes to find their locations.

In all of these cases, Apple Guide is simply trying to find the rectangle to use. You can take a more flexible (and often easier) approach by using AppleScript to provide that rectangle. To do so, you need an AppleScript that returns a rectangle, and you invoke it with the <Define AppleScript Coach> command.

The parameter *AppleScriptID* contains either an AppleScript's resource ID or the name of a script file (relative to the location of your source code). If you use a resource ID, you must add that resource to your guide file with the <Resource Command>.

Using AppleScript coaches can be very effective. The business of determining the coach mark rectangle is pushed off on AppleScript and the script writer—often to the application itself. AppleScript coaches are particularly robust, appearing in the correct locations even after substantial modifications are made in the course of development and localization. In Figure 9.6, you see part of the Apple Guide Command Stack, a HyperCard stack that is provided on the CD-ROM accompanying this book. Apple Guide assistance is (of course) provided for the Apple Guide Command Stack, and the source code for all of the guide files is also provided on the CD-ROM.

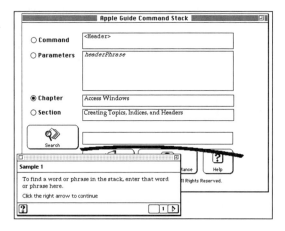

Figure 9.6 Red underline coach mark for background field "Search."

A brief AppleScript is provided that returns the rectangle of the background field **Search**:

```
tell application "HyperCard"
    copy (bounds of background field "Search") to fieldLoc
    copy (loc of window "Apple Guide Command Stack") to windowLoc
    set item 1 of fieldLoc to (item 1 of fieldLoc) + (item 1 of
windowLoc)
    set item 2 of fieldLoc to (item 2 of fieldLoc) + (item 2 of
windowLoc)
    set item 3 of fieldLoc to (item 3 of fieldLoc) + (item 1 of
windowLoc)
    set item 4 of fieldLoc to (item 4 of fieldLoc) + (item 2 of
windowLoc)
    return x
end tell
```

NOTE   A recipe in the Cookbook on the CD-ROM provides further details of the AppleScript syntax used here. Briefly, the script queries HyperCard to find the rectangle representing the bounds (borders) of the field in question. Because HyperCard returns this rectangle relative to the window's location, the script then finds the location of the window and adds its horizontal and vertical offsets from the origin to the bounding rectangle of the field.

If you install the Apple Guide Command Stack on your computer and open it with HyperCard, you will be able to prove that no matter where you move the buttons and fields, the AppleScript-driven coach marks are always in the correct locations.

Coach marks based on AppleScript-derived rectangles can be extremely robust. There are, however, two reasons why you may not want to use them:

1. Because the AppleScript commands have to be sent to the target application and the rectangle returned and interpreted, they are noticeably slower than other coach marks.

2. Not all applications are scriptable. Even among those that are scriptable, you will often find that the application can easily return the location of objects related to its content but that its interface elements are not avail-

able in its AppleScript dictionary. These issues are discussed at length in Part 4: Adding Apple Guide to Custom Solutions and Content.

Despite these occasional drawbacks, AppleScript-based coach marks are very popular. Remember that as long as the script returns a rectangle, Apple Guide does not care what else it does. On the way to returning the coaching rectangle, the script might cause a window to scroll, launch a new application, or perform many other tasks that are appropriate as the user steps through your assistance.

Define AppleScript Coach Command

Use the <Define AppleScript Coach> command to associate an AppleScript script that you have included with a <Resource> command with a coach mark.

Syntax:	**<Define AppleScript Coach>** *coachMarkName [, coachStyle], AppleScriptID*
Example:	This is the definition of the coach mark illustrated in Figure 9.6 using the script just presented:
	`<Define AppleScript Coach> "Search Field Coach", REDUNDERLINE, ":Scripts:Search Field Coach"`
Limitations:	Watch out for performance problems.
When to Use:	Often. AppleScript-based coach marks are particularly useful in providing assistance to custom solutions based on tools, such as HyperCard and QuarkXPress.

Coaching an Item Dynamically Using the Apple Guide API

The final command you can use to define a coach mark relies on the application being coached to return the coaching rectangle. Whereas the AppleScript coach relies on you (or a script-writer) to derive the necessary rectangle using whatever AppleScript commands an application supports, the <Define Object Coach> command requires the application to explicitly support Apple Guide.

Fortunately, this support is very easy to implement. Chapter 17, "The Apple Guide API" explains the full syntax an application may use to support Apple Guide. In simplified form, to provide custom coaching, the application installs a call-back routine using the **AGInstallCoachHandler** function. This routine is called whenever Apple Guide requests an object coach from the application.

The call-back routine receives the name of a coach mark and returns the rectangle Apple Guide should use in drawing the coach mark. As with AppleScript-based coach marks, it is up to the application to do any other processing while it has control. This additional processing can include scrolling an object into view in a window, opening a new window, and providing a coach mark location in the new window.

The notion of modifying an application to support Apple Guide strikes fear into some people. In fact, the process need not be particularly complicated or time-consuming. In Chapter 19, "MacApp and Apple Guide," a strategy is spelled out that allows for Apple Guide object coaching to be added in a few hours—certainly less than a day—regardless of the size of the application. Because of the ease with which applications can be modified for Apple Guide object coaches, and because object coaches are the most robust and efficient of all coaching methods, you should look carefully at the (minimal) resources required to modify your application for Apple Guide coach marks.

Define Object Coach Command

Use the <Define Object Coach> command to associate an external code module or a call-back routine in the coached application with a coach mark.

Syntax:	**<Define Object Coach>** *coachMarkName, targetApp [, coachStyle] [, objectName]*
Example:	`<Define Object Coach> "Play Button", 'PSM3', REDCIRCLE, "controller-play button"`
Limitations:	The application being coached normally requires modifications to use object coaches.
When to Use:	Often, when modifying the application is a possibility.

SUMMARY

Coach marks, which are the most visible manifestation of Apple Guide, provide assistance to users that goes far beyond the tools that have been available in the past. In this chapter, the five styles of coach marks and the five types of coach mark definitions were covered. You should feel comfortable with the uses of coach marks and the ways in which the different styles are used. If you also have a passing familiarity with the different types of coach mark definitions (enough so that you can return to this chapter for reference as needed), you can move on to the next chapter.

CHAPTER 10

Panels III: Controls

Panels can contain display objects, such as text, QuickTime movies, and PICT graphics. You format and locate these panel objects using format commands and the styled text commands from your word processor. By placing a <Coach Mark> command in your panel definition, you can cause Apple Guide to draw a coach mark to help illustrate the information in the panel.

Panels can also contain controls of various sorts. Controls differ from all other panel objects in that they are active. They are also an integral part of the interface that we now know as the Mac OS. In the *Macintosh Human Interface Guidelines*, a control is defined as:

An object in a window on the Macintosh screen with which the user, by using the mouse, can cause instant action with visible results, or change settings to modify a future action.

In this chapter, you will learn about the controls that you can place on Apple Guide panels. In keeping with the definition, the chapter is divided into two parts:

- Controls that cause immediate actions
- Controls that store information to affect future actions

The actions that controls cause and effect often involve navigation through the panels of an Apple Guide sequence. There are three types of navigation the designer should consider:

- relative navigation: next/previous panel
- absolute navigation: returning to the Access window or displaying a Huh? panel
- specific navigation: going to a certain panel or sequence

N O T E   Huh? panels are considered absolute navigation rather than specific naviga- tion, even though they differ from panel to panel. Because a Huh? panel always has the same purpose and characteristics, its use is as constant as returning to the Access window. Specific navigation involves going to a panel or sequence in the form of a jump to some other information or task. The commonality of purpose of **Huh?** buttons makes them absolute rather than specific navigation tools.

Most controls cause a predefined event to occur. Events are defined using the <Define Event> and <Define Event List> commands, which are described in Chapter 12, "Sequences II—Events."

CONTROLS THAT CAUSE IMMEDIATE ACTIONS

Three types of controls for Apple Guide panels cause immediate actions:

- navigation bar buttons
- hot items
- buttons

Navigation Bar Controls

You associate a particular set of buttons on the navigation bar with a sequence using either the <Seq Nav Button Set> command (discussed in Chapter 12, "Sequences II—Events") or the <Default Nav Button Set> (discussed in Chapter 6, "Setting Up Guide Files"). The navigation bar button set cannot be specified at a level below the sequence—that is, you cannot specify a navigation bar button set for an individual panel.

One button in a navigation bar button set can be marked as DIMMABLE. This button is dimmed and disabled on all panels unless you specifically enable it with the <Dimmable Button Data> command. The <Dimmable Button Data> command allows you to associate a given sequence with the dimmable button—possibly a different sequence on each panel. The most frequent use of this feature is the **Huh?** button. On a panel where the **Huh?** button is enabled, clicking on it opens a new sequence in its own window in front of the current Apple Guide window. Either window (or both) can be closed with its close box.

Compare the behavior of a **Huh?** button with that of the **GoStart** or **Guide** button often placed in the lower-left corner of an Apple Guide panel. This button has the same effect on every panel in the sequence—it returns you to the Access window. When you want to give the user the ability to do different things of the same sort on many panels in a sequence, you use a DIMMABLE button.

N O T E   Because you are allowed only one DIMMABLE button in a navigation bar set, its use must be generalized. If you find that you need more than one, or that you need a dimmable button only on one or two panels in the sequence, use a button placed directly into the relevant panels. This technique is discussed in the next section.

Dimmable Button Data Command

The name of the dimmable button, provided in the parameter *buttonName*, must match the name of a button defined in the current navigation bar button set.

The *sequenceName* parameter identifies a sequence you define with the <Define Sequence> command. That sequence is launched in its own Apple Guide window. The user can close either or both of these windows, continuing on an alternate path through the information in your guide file. In the case of **Huh?** buttons (the most frequently used dimmable buttons) most designers limit the sequence invoked by the **Huh?** button to one panel.

Syntax:	**<Dimmable Button Data>** *buttonName, sequenceName*
Example:	`<Dimmable Button Data> "Huh button", "Definition:` `what is a window?"`
Limitations:	Only one dimmable button is allowed in a navigation bar button set.
Default:	If a button is defined as dimmable in a navigation bar button set, it is always dimmed and disabled unless the <Dimmable Button Data> command exists on the panel being shown.
When to Use:	As needed.

Buttons

Buttons cause immediate actions that, in the case of Apple Guide, are not reversible. They are associated with events that are defined elsewhere in your guide file. Most often these events cause an AppleEvent to be sent to the target application so that a command is carried out (such as creating a document), or they cause an immediate jump to another location in your guide file.

You can place more than one button in a panel, but before doing so you should consider your design carefully. Because buttons have immediate effects, whichever button is clicked will cause something to happen. When alternatives are possible, a preferred design is to use check boxes or radio buttons. These controls store information that is used later when the user clicks the right arrow.

Standard Buttons

You use the <Standard Button> command to create a standard two-dimensional button in a panel. Apple Guide takes responsibility for drawing the button's title and the border surrounding it—both when it is at rest and when the user clicks on it. The <3D Button> command allows you to place a button that you have drawn with color and shading in a panel. You provide alternative images for different button states. In the case of the 3D button, Apple Guide does no drawing, but merely places your images in the appropriate place on the panel.

Standard Button Command

The parameter *buttonTitle* specifies the title of the button that Apple Guide will draw for you. As always, the title should be short and meaningful. You should provide text that precedes the button to tell the user what to do with the button. For example, when your Apple Guide file is performing a task for the user, do not create a button with the title, "Click here when the window has opened." Place the text, "When the window has opened, click the Continue button" in your panel, and then place a button with the simple title "Continue" below it.

Like other panel objects, buttons are placed in the panel within the bottomless column specified by the current format, after whatever objects have been previously placed. The *buttonLoc* parameter allows you to align the button within the format using the following constants:

LEFT

CENTER

RIGHT

As with PICT graphics and QuickTime movies, you can also use the *buttonLoc* parameter to explicitly place the button with the Point function. The Point function specifies a horizontal and vertical offset at which the button is placed: the starting position for these offsets is the location at which the previous object in this column was placed. Because of the danger of inadvertently overlapping buttons and other panel objects, most designers do not use the explicit placement option.

If you do decide to explicitly place your buttons, you should know that they are 20 pixels high and at least 59 pixels wide (wider if necessary to accommodate the title).

The most important parameter of the <Standard Button> command is the name of an event or event list, which is placed in *buttonEvent*. Events can consist of Apple Events that are sent to various applications and a number of built-in events to jump to specific panels, launch new sequences, and so on (these are described in Chapter 13, "Sequences II—Events.") When the user releases the mouse button, the specified event is processed.

Finally, you can specify the *buttonFont* parameter. If omitted, Apple Guide uses 10-point Espy serif for the button title, or you can specify the constant APPLEGUIDE. The other allowable value—SYSTEM—uses the system font for the button title.

Syntax:	**\<Standard Button\>** *buttonTitle, buttonLoc, buttonEvent [, buttonFont]*
Example:	\<Standard Button\> "OK", CENTER, LaunchNewSequence("StyleWriter cartridge replacement", APPLEGUIDE
When to Use:	As needed.

3D Buttons

Although Apple Guide takes full responsibility for drawing and highlighting your standard buttons, you are responsible for providing graphics for a **3D** button. **3D** buttons can improve the appearance of your panels, although they require more preparation on your part.

3D Button Command

If you compare the \<3D Button\> command with the \<Standard Button\> command, you will notice that there is no *buttonTitle* parameter for **3D** buttons: the title of the button is provided as part of your PICT graphic for the button. For this reason, if you want a button that contains only a graphic and no words, you must use a **3D** button.

You supply at least two PICT graphics for the **3D** button. One is displayed when the button is up; the other is displayed while the user holds the mouse button down on the button. Each can be either a PICT file or a PICT resource. If the graphic is in a file, the *buttonUpPict* and/or *buttonDownPict* parameters contain the name of the file (relative to your source code file). If the graphic is a resource, these parameters contain the ID number of the PICT resource, which you must include with a \<Resource\> command.

Rather than let Apple Guide do its best to display your carefully designed color graphics on a black-and-white monitor, you can provide your own black-and-white PICT graphics for use when displayed on a black-and-white monitor using the parameters *b&wUp* and *b&wDown*. As with the color graphics, these can be either PICT files or resources. The black-and-white version of your graphics is optional.

The *buttonLoc* and *buttonEvent* parameters are identical to the parameters in the \<Standard Button\> command.

Syntax:	**<3D Button>** *buttonUpPict, button DownPict, buttonLoc, buttonEvent, [b&wUp], [b&wDown]*
Example:	`<3D Button> "Continue btn up", "Continue btn down", CENTER, GoStart(), "Continue btn up bw", "Continue btn down bw"`
When to Use:	As needed.

Hot Items

With the advent of hypertext, users have become used to clicking on more than buttons: everything from text to graphics to movies can be "hot" and can respond to a mouse click by launching an event for Apple Guide to process. Apple Guide events can do a wide range of things, from displaying other panels and launching new sequences to sending Apple Events to applications that, in turn, do still more.

Some designers are hesitant to use hot items in Apple Guide panels. Their caution stems from these concerns:

- Added to the buttons in the navigation bar and the controls (buttons, radio buttons, and check boxes) that normally appear in the content area of panels, hot items may simply provide too many different ways of navigating through a help file. The user may become confused.

- Because hot items do not normally present themselves as clickable—in the way that buttons do—they must be highlighted in some way so that the user knows they can be clicked on. This highlighting may clutter the panel.

- In some cases, hot items can actually hide information from the user. The interface elements most often used in Apple Guide (buttons, topics, etc.) show the user what the choices are; with hypertext and hot items, the user may only discover what the information choices are after having navigating through several levels.

These concerns are valid but should not discourage you from using hot items. On the contrary, when you use hot items, you should be aware of the potential pitfalls and plan around them.

Windows Help relies very heavily on hot items. The Windows Help designer does not have the range of tools available to the Apple Guide designer. As a result, hypertext jumps account for much of the navigation provided for a Windows Help user. When developers design assistance that can function not only as Windows Help but also as Apple Guide, hot items are a necessary part of the interface. Hot items are used not only to launch new sequences but also to provide pop-up definitions of terms on the current panel.

On the other hand, some demonstrations of Apple Guide eschew the use of hot items to deliberately differentiate Apple Guide from Windows Help, highlighting its greater powers.

The fact that Windows Help uses hot items should not discourage you from its use. Similarly, the fact that you must use hot items if you want to keep a Windows Help system more or less in synch with an Apple Guide version should not make you throw up your hands and use none of the other Apple Guide navigation tools. Chapter 26, "Apple Guide and Windows Help," covers these issues in more detail.

Complexity of Navigation with Hot Items

The secret to using hot items successfully alongside navigation bar buttons and check boxes, radio buttons, and other buttons on your panels is to think through the different uses you want to make of each control. These uses may well differ in different guide files, but a common strategy might be outlined as follows:

- navigation bar buttons: relative navigation (left and right arrows) as well as constant, absolute navigation (return to Access window and **Huh?** for further explanation of the current panel's information)

- panel buttons: specific navigation (**Do It for Me** to start an Apple Event, **OK** to return from an Oops sequence, **Printer setup** to start a new sequence, and so on)

- radio buttons and check boxes: store choices to be used for relative navigation

- hot text to define the word or phrase highlighted with an Oops sequence of no more than one panel that returns to this panel with an **OK** button

With such a strategy in hand, when you design your guide file there is little question which control you use for which purpose. The use of hot items is limited to hot text and is further constrained by the convention that it will be a one-panel definition that returns to the current panel. The branching to other sequences that hypertext jumps accomplish in Windows would be done according to this strategy with buttons that perform specific navigation.

Confusion sets in when different interface objects have different functions.

Preventing Clutter with Hot Items

To let the user know that an item is hot in the panel, it must be highlighted in some way. In some help systems, a solid underline and a certain color (such as brown) indicate that text is hot and that clicking it will move you to a sequence of panels providing information about it. Further, dotted underlining and green text may provide a definition of the text without moving from the current panel. Unfortunately, such a variety of highlighting can become distracting to the user; in addition, remembering the difference between the two forms of highlighting puts an added burden on the poor user, who only wants to know how to change a laser printer toner cartridge.

When hot text is used to provide definitions of terms, the text can be presented in bold type. (Remember to use a format definition that omits the *txStyle* parameter or your bold type will be converted to plain text.) This is a simple convention and does not distract much from the user's reading of the text. Furthermore, the convention is consistent with the paper publishing convention of presenting new terms in bold type the first time they are encountered. Italicizing and underlining of any text in panels is discouraged: it can be hard to read and in some cases does not appear different from other text.

When objects other than text are hot, different interface issues arise—for example, you can't make a PICT graphic bold. In these cases, the most appropriate interface approach is to include text that instructs the user to click on a graphic. The most likely use of such an interface is for an Apple Guide file that is helping a user with a piece of hardware, such as a printer. Instead of asking the user whether the printer is a StyleWriter or a LaserWriter, the panel could display several PICT graphics showing printers, each of which is hot. The instruction on the panel would say, "Click the printer you have."

Making an Object Hot

The easiest way to make an object hot is to use the <Hot Object> command.

Hot Object Command

This command is placed in your panel definition immediately before the object you want to make hot. Thus it may appear before a <PICT> or a <QuickTime> command, making the PICT graphic or QuickTime movie hot. If it precedes a paragraph of text, that paragraph becomes hot.

When the mouse is clicked on the object, the event specified in *eventFunction* is processed.

N O T E

QuickTime movies handle mouse events themselves— a double-click to start, and a single-click to stop. Thus, making a QuickTime movie hot has meaning only in the case where the movie is not found and the QuickTime object is displayed as a PICT.

Syntax:	**<Hot Object>** *eventFunction*
Example:	<Hot Object> LaunchNewSequence("StyleWriter cartridge replacement"
Limitations:	Because the <Hot Object> command applies to the next object in the panel definition, you must remember to move it if you rearrange the objects in the panel.
When to Use:	Use for PICT graphics that are hot. Use <Hot Text> for text that is hot.

Making a Rectangle Hot

Sometimes you want to make a specific area of the panel hot. The <Hot Rectangle> command allows you to make a part of an included graphic hot, whereas preceding the <PICT> command with a <Hot Object> command would make the entire graphic hot. Remember to make clear to the user what can be clicked on and what the effect will be.

Hot Rectangle Command

The *hotRect* parameter uses the Rect function to specify a rectangle relative to the bottom of the last object that was placed in the panel.

Syntax:	**<Hot Rectangle>** *hotRect, eventFunction*
Example:	Here is an example of how assistance can be provided for users of a LaserWriter printer. A picture of the printer is displayed on the panel; parts of it are made hot so that the user can look at the printer and point to the source of confusion or exasperation:

```
<PICT> "LaserWriter graphic", CENTER
```
```
Click the part of the printer about which you want
information.
```
```
<Hot Rectangle> Rect (71, 158, 116, 225,
LaunchNewSequence("LW:Paper tray")
```
```
<Hot Rectangle> Rect (71, 158, 116, 225,
LaunchNewSequence("LW:AppleTalk connector")
```

When to Use:	As needed.

Using Hot Text

The most frequent hot item in a panel is hot text. Hot text normally is distinguished from other text by being shown in bold type.

Hot Text Command

The text that you want to make hot is specified in the *hotText* parameter. Remember that it is your responsibility to indicate to the user that the text is hot—usually by using bold type. The <Hot Text> command controls only the mouse events in the text; it has no effect on the representation of the text on the screen.

You use the *whichOccurrence* parameter to specify one of the following constants to determine which of several occurrences of the specified text is hot:

> FIRST
>
> LAST
>
> ALL

Finally, the *eventFunction* parameter specifies the predefined event that is launched when the text is clicked.

The <Hot Text> command applies to the next paragraph in the panel, not to the entire panel's text. Thus, if you want a word or phrase to be hot in each of several paragraphs in a panel, you must repeat the <Hot Text> command. Normally, only the first occurrence of a word or phrase is hot.

Syntax:	**<Hot Text>** *hotText, whichOccurrence, eventFunction*
Example:	<Hot Text> "boldface", FIRST, LaunchOopsSequence("Styling Text") You can use boldface to indicate that words or phrases in a panel are hot.
Limitations:	Applies to the next paragraph (not the entire panel).
When to Use:	As needed.

CONTROLS THAT STORE INFORMATION TO AFFECT FUTURE ACTIONS

Buttons and hot text cause events to be launched immediately when they are clicked. Check boxes and radio buttons are highlighted when the user clicks them. When the right arrow is clicked, the condition of these controls is checked (either automatically by Apple Guide or explicitly in your Guide Script commands) and a new sequence is displayed. This delayed action lets the user reconsider the choice before proceeding.

Check Boxes

Check boxes are used when a user can select one or more choices. Radio buttons are used when a user must select only one choice from several possibilities. Use the <Checkbox> command to have Apple Guide insert a check box in the panel. To prevent any confusion, you should either precede the check boxes on your panel with an instruction or use a panel prompt that instructs the user to click a check box before proceeding.

Checkbox Command

The *checkBoxTitle* is displayed to the right of the check box itself.

Use the parameter *checkBoxState* to indicate how the check box should first appear to the user. The two values are TRUE and FALSE, representing whether the box is checked or not.

You can use the conditions and context checks described in Chapter 12 to determine whether the check box is checked and modify your presentation of panels accordingly. You can also let Apple Guide handle this for you. If you provide the name of a sequence in the *seqTrue* parameter, that sequence will be launched when the user clicks the right arrow, provided that the check box is checked. Similarly, a sequence whose name is provided in *seqFalse* will automatically be launched if the check box is not checked.

The check box is placed on the panel immediately below the previous object that was placed in the bottomless column of the current format. If you want to modify this placement, use the Point function to specify an offset from the bottom of the last flowed object. The *checkBoxAnchor* parameter is used for this purpose.

Finally, you can select either APPLEGUIDE or SYSTEM for the *checkBoxFont* parameter. APPLEGUIDE is the default and the recommended choice for this parameter.

Syntax:	**\<Checkbox\>** *checkBoxTitle, checkBoxState [, seqTrue] [, seqFalse], checkBoxAnchor] [, checkBoxFont]*
Example:	This is a text version of the example given above to provide assistance for a LaserWriter printer. In comparing the two, note that the \<Hot Rectangle\> version provides a jump to whichever part of the picture is clicked. This structure enables the user to select several parts that will be described in turn.

```
Click the part(s) of the LaserWriter printer about
which you would like information.
<Checkbox> "Paper Tray", FALSE, "LW:Paper tray"
<Checkbox> "AppleTalk connector", FALSE,
    "LW:AppleTalk connector"
```

When to Use:	As needed.

Radio Buttons

Radio buttons are used when only one choice from several must be made by the user. A radio button cannot appear by itself, it must have at least one other. In addition, normally one radio button is always set to TRUE. (In the case of check boxes, you can easily have several check boxes on a panel and have none of them set to TRUE.)

Radio Button Command

Use the <Radio Button> command to place a radio button on a panel.

The radio button is drawn by Apple Guide, which places the *buttonTitle* next to the button itself. The *buttonFont* (either SYSTEM or APPLEGUIDE) is used to draw the text. Specify TRUE or FALSE for each radio button on a panel, but be certain to have one button set to TRUE.

As with check boxes, you can provide the names of sequences to automatically launch when the user clicks the right arrow. If the radio button is on, the sequence in the *seqTrue* parameter will be started, and if it is not on, the sequence in the *seqFalse* parameter will be started. These parameters are optional, and you can test the value of the radio buttons in your panel to handle your own processing. This is particularly necessary when the radio buttons are not used for controlling navigation, which happens frequently when Apple Guide is used as a front end to a custom solution (i.e, the action to be taken is not launching a new sequence).

When the <Radio Button> command starts a sequence that was specified in the *seqTrue* or *seqFalse* parameter, that sequence is inserted into the current sequence: the user clicks the right arrow and goes to the first panel of the new sequence in the same window as the current sequence. Clicking the left arrow returns to the first sequence.

As with check boxes, the *buttonAnchor* parameter allows you to use the Point function to place the radio button precisely in relation to the bottom of the last object that was flowed. The parameter is optional: normally you accept Apple Guide's sequential placement of the radio button.

Syntax:	**<Radio Button>** *buttonTitle, buttonState [, seqTrue] [, seqFalse] [, buttonAnchor] [, buttonFont]*
Example:	Using the same example of LaserWriter printer assistance, note that the behavior of a radio button implementation behaves similarly to the hot item implementation: only one choice can be made:
| | ```
Click the part of the LaserWriter printer about which
you would like information.
<Radio Button> "Paper Tray", TRUE, "LW:Paper tray"
<Radio Button> "AppleTalk connector", FALSE,
    "LW:AppleTalk connector"
``` |
| *Limitations:* | If you use radio button,s you must have at least two radio buttons on a panel, and one of them must be set to TRUE. |
| *When to Use:* | As needed. |

Radio Button Launch New Seq Command

The <Radio Button Launch New Seq> command differs from the <Radio Button> command only in that the sequence that can be automatically launched using the *seqTrue* or *seqFalse* parameter is severed from the first sequence. The user cannot use the left arrow to return to the first sequence. All other parameters and syntax are identical to the <Radio Button> command.

Syntax:	**<Radio Button Launch New Seq>** *buttonTitle, buttonState [, seqTrue] [, seqFalse] [, buttonAnchor] [, buttonFont]*
| *Example:* | ```
<Radio Button Launch New Seq> "Paper Tray", TRUE,
    "LW:Paper tray"
``` |
| *When to Use:* | As needed. |

SUMMARY

With this chapter, you have covered all of the commands that relate to panels. Chapter 8 covered their contents (text, graphics, and movies). Chapter 9 covered coach marks, and this chapter covered controls (hot items, buttons, check boxes, and radio buttons).

The following panel definition, taken from the Macintosh Guide, incorporates a number of these commands. It should look familiar to you. If it does, it's time to move on to sequences, which is the way in which you combine panels.

```
<DEFINE PANEL>"initialize: troubleshooting"
<FORMAT> "Full"
If you can't initialize or erase a disk, the disk may be locked,
or it may be damaged. Or there may be a problem with the disk
drive.

If you want to prepare a disk in DOS or Apple II (ProDOS) format
but the format menu doesn't include the choice you want, you may
need to turn on the PC Exchange control panel.

Which do you want to do? Click one:
    <RADIO BUTTON> "unlock a floppy disk", true,,, ,APPLEGUIDE
    <RADIO BUTTON> "test and repair a disk", false,,, ,APPLEGUIDE
    . <RADIO BUTTON> "prepare a disk in DOS or Apple II format",
false,,, ,APPLEGUIDE
<END PANEL>
```

Sequences I: Definitions and Controls

In Chapter 7 you saw how to design the Access windows that enable users to get to the information in your guide files. That information is displayed on individual panels, which were covered in Chapter 8, "Contents," Chapter 9, "Coach Marks," and Chapter 10, "Controls."

In the next three chapters, you will see how to put panels together into sequences and control the display of these panels. This chapter focuses on the basic definition of sequences and their controls. The information in this chapter enables you to put together a help system that is comparable to most on-line help systems today; they basically present information in response to user requests and do not have the "intelligence" to query the environment in any meaningful way.

In Chapter 12, you will go beyond this to see how to use conditions and context checks to query the environment—to see what hardware and software is installed, where in a process the user is, and whether the user has correctly carried out instructions. Chapter 13, focusing on events, provides the information you need to initiate tasks that are carried out by Apple Guide, the operating system, and the applications that you are coaching. These tasks can be as simple as displaying a new panel and as complex as launching an application.

This chapter is divided into three sections:

- Defining a sequence
- Defining prompts and navigation buttons
- Starting new sequences

DEFINING A SEQUENCE

A sequence consists of between 1 and 32 panels on a related topic. Each panel presents one concept or action, and the entire sequence should make up a logical whole. Although users can use controls and other buttons to jump from one panel to another (or to another sequence), each sequence should have a unity to it.

A long sequence may need special panels to introduce the subject area and to summarize the information at the end. When providing such panels, make certain that they are not mere decoration. Often, dividing a long sequence into shorter sequences eliminates the need for introductory and closing panels, providing more concise information delivery and more specific control from the Access window.

Define Sequence and End Sequence Command

You define a sequence in your source code with the <Define Sequence> and <End Sequence> commands. All commands between the two are part of the sequence.

The *sequenceName* parameter matches the *sequenceName* parameter in a <Topic> command:

```
<Topic> topicPhrase, sequenceName
```

The *topicPhrase* parameter is what is shown to the user in a topic list. If the user selects it, the sequence named in the *sequenceName* parameter is launched. The title bar of a presentation window contains the name of the sequence. If you do not provide the optional *seqDisplayTitle* parameter, the *sequenceName* parameter is used in the title bar. It is generally preferable to use the *seqDisplayTitle* parameter. In that way, you can provide meaningful names for users (*seqDisplayTitle*) and for guide file developers (*sequenceName*).

Syntax:	**\<Define Sequence>** *sequenceName [, seqDisplayTitle]*
	\<End Sequence>
Example:	**\<Define Sequence>** `"sequence1", "Introduction to`
	`    Sequences"`
	`#contents of sequence`
	\<End Sequence> `#you can place a comment after the`
	`                    end`
Limitations:	A sequence must have at least one panel in it and cannot have more than 32.
When to Use:	As needed.

Placing Panels in a Sequence

You place panels in a sequence either by defining them as you want them using the \<Define Panel> command or by referring to a previously defined panel with the \<Panel> command. You can use either technique (or both). Defining panels in-line makes it easier to read the sequence; defining panels separately makes it easier to reuse them.

Panel Command

Use the \<Panel> command to insert a previously defined panel into a sequence.

Syntax:	**\<Panel>** *panelName*
Example:	`<Panel> "panel 1"`
When to Use:	As needed.

Setting Sequence Defaults

You can set defaults for the prompts that are used in all sequences and for the navigation button set for all sequences. You can also specify prompts and navigation button sets for an individual sequence.

Sequence Prompt Set Command

Use the <Sequence Prompt Set> command to set the default prompt for panels in a sequence. Individual panels can override the defaults.

Syntax:	**<Sequence Prompt Set>** *promptSetName*
Example:	<Sequence Prompt Set> "standard prompts"
Limitations:	One per sequence.
Default:	The prompt that is the default for the guide file—set with <Default Prompt Set>.
When to Use:	As needed.

Seq Nav Button Set Command

Use the <Seq Nav Button Set> command to specify the navigation bar button set for the sequence. Unlike the <Sequence Prompt Set> command, this command cannot be overridden on individual panels within the sequence.

Syntax:	**<Seq Nav Button Set>** *navButtonSetName*
Example:	<Seq Nav Button Set> "Standard Nav Bar"
Limitations:	One per sequence.
Default:	The navigation button set defined in <Default Nav Button Set>
When to Use:	As needed.

DEFINING PROMPTS AND NAVIGATION BUTTONS

A prompt generally appears at the bottom of the content area of each panel, advising the user what to do next. This prompt usually includes a general instruction regarding the panel contents ("Read this, then…," "Do this, then…") and then provides a suggestion about what to do next. That action usually involves a button in the navigation bar ("…click the right arrow to continue," "That's it—you're done.").

Defining Prompt Sets

Except in very rare circumstances (such as full-panel graphics that are totally self-explanatory), a prompt should appear on each panel. Prompts always come in sets of four:

- a prompt for the first panel in a sequence (a panel with the left arrow disabled)

- a prompt for middle panels in a sequence (a prompt with both arrows enabled)

- a prompt for the last panel in a sequence (a panel with the right arrow disabled)

- a prompt for any panel in a sequence that has a control (button, check box, and so forth) on it

N O T E   Sometimes when you use the <Panel Prompt> command to associate a prompt set with an individual panel, you will wish for the ability to have a prompt set with only one prompt in it. Unfortunately, you cannot have it. You must define all four prompts. You may choose to make three of the prompts consist of a blank space or all four of them the same text in the case where the prompt set will be used on only one panel.

Having defined a prompt set, you can make it a default for all sequences in a guide file using the <Default Prompt Set> command; you can override that default for a given sequence by using the <Sequence Prompt Set> command; and you can further override even that default for an individual panel using the <Panel Prompt> command. The <Default Prompt Set> and <Panel Prompt> commands have already been discussed, and you have had to take the definition of the prompt set on faith. Here, at last, is the <Define Prompt Set> command.

Define Prompt Set Command

As with most Guide Maker objects, you assign a name to the prompt set, in this case using the *promptSetName* parameter. As with other objects that can be reused, all prompts should be defined together in your source code, and they should be given meaningful names. From the user's point of view, the prompts should have a similar tone and style. For example, the last panel in a sequence might have the prompt "—End—," "That's it: you're done," or some other closing remark. Your guide file design style sheet should specify what this closing prompt is and all of your prompts should match it.

The strings for your four prompts are specified with the parameters *promptFirstPanel*, *promptMiddlePanel*, *promptLastPanel*, and *promptForPanelsWithControls*. Your prompts should be short and consistent. Remember that users will see many of them repeatedly. None of the four prompts is optional, but any (or all) of them can be identical or blank (""). (A blank prompt consists of a space between two quotation marks.)

Apple Guide defines a prompt set with the name NONE. Using this in a <Default Prompt Set>, <Sequence Prompt Set>, or <Panel Prompt> command causes Apple Guide to omit the space for a prompt at the bottom of the appropriate panels.

Syntax:	**<Define Prompt Set>** *promptSetName, promptFirstPanel, promptMiddlePanel,promptLastPanel, promptForPanelsWithControls*
Example:	`<Define Prompt Set> "standard prompts", "Click the right arrow to continue", "Click the right arrow to continue or the left arrow to review", "End", "Make your choice, then click the right arrow to continue."`
When to Use:	As needed.

Defining Navigation Buttons and Navigation Button Sets

The navigation bar appears at the bottom of all Apple Guide presentation windows. Apple Guide manages the dimming and enabling of the left and right arrows as necessary; they are always shown in the navigation bar. You can define additional navigation buttons and assemble them into navigation button sets. Navigation button sets can be assigned to individual sequences; you also set a default navigation button set for your guide file, which is used unless individual sequences override it.

Navigation buttons and navigation button sets are defined in the Guide Maker shell file on the *Real World Apple Guide* CD-ROM. Many Apple Guide authors never need to create their own buttons and button sets.

N O T E

Up to three navigation buttons can be used in a navigation button set. Each button can have an event associated with it. For example, the GoStart event defined in Apple Guide closes the presentation window and reopens the Access window. This button and its event are available and enabled on all panels where it appears.

One of the three buttons can be defined as DIMMABLE. A dimmable navigation button is dimmed in all cases except when a panel includes the <Dimmable Button Data> command. The presence of that command causes Apple Guide to enable the button. The command also associates a sequence (not an event) with that button for that panel.

Navigation buttons are designed to be used as a group consistently across the panels of a sequence. Special buttons with special events should be placed in the content area of presentation panels.

Define Nav Button Command

The name that you specify in *buttonName* is used when you want to associate navigation buttons into a navigation button set. The user does not see this name, so it should be meaningful to you and your colleagues who write and maintain the source code.

You must provide at least three PICT graphics for a navigation button; these represent the image of the button when it is up (unclicked), when it is down, and when it is dimmed. These graphics can be provided either as PICT resources or as PICT files. You provide either a resource ID or name or a file name (relative to your source code) in the parameters *buttonUpPict, buttonDownPict,* and *dimmedButtonPict.* These PICT graphics should use the Apple Guide font (10-point Espy serif) and should be 18 pixels high. Because the graphic is placed on the navigation bar, which does not have a white background, make certain that no stray white pixels are copied to the PICT graphic when you create it.

You can optionally provide a parallel set of black-and-white PICT graphics for use on black-and-white monitors. If you provide them, their resource IDs, names, or file names are specified in the *b&wUp*, *b&wDown*, and *b&wDimmed* parameters.

If you use resources for any of the button graphics, you must include the appropriate resources with the <Resource> command.

In the *buttonEvent* parameter, you supply the name of an event or event list that will be initiated when the button is clicked. Alternatively, you can provide the constant DIMMABLE, which allows you to associate a sequence with this button for an individual panel.

Syntax:	**<Define Nav Button>** *buttonName, buttonUpPict, button-DownPict, dimmedButtonPict, buttonEvent [, b&wUp] [, b&wDown] [, b&wDimmed]*
Example:	These two navigation buttons are defined in the shell files on the CD-ROM. The button PICT graphics are resources that are provided in the Standard Resources file.
	`<Define Nav Button>  "Huh?",1101,1111,1121,DIMMABLE` `<Define Nav Button> "GoStart",1103,1113,1123,GoStart()`
Limitations:	Only three per navigation button set; only one in a set can be dimmable.
When to Use:	As needed. The **GoStart** button is a part of the standard Apple Guide interface and should be used on all panels. Use the **Huh?** button as appropriate.

Define Nav Button Set Command

After you have defined one or more navigation buttons, you can assemble them into a navigation button set. The navigation button set can be associated with an individual sequence, or it can be made the default for all sequences in a guide file.

The *navButtonSetName* parameter is only used internally and so should be meaningful to you and those who will maintain your guide file in the future.

You place navigation buttons in the navigation button set by specifying their names in the parameters *leftNavButton*, *midNavButton*, and *rightNavButton*. All navigation buttons appear in the navigation bar to the left of the arrows, but you can control the placement of the buttons within that area.

Syntax:	**\<Define Nav Button Set\>** *navButtonSetName [, leftNavButton]* *[, midNavButton][, rightNavButton]*

Example:	These navigation button sets are provided in the Shell files on the CD-ROM:
	`<Define Nav Button Set> "Standard Nav`
	`    Bar","GoStart","Huh?"`
	`<Define Nav Button Set> "GoStart Only","GoStart"`
	`<Define Nav Button Set> "Huh? Only","Huh?"`

Limitations:	One dimmable button per set.
When to Use:	As needed.

STARTING NEW SEQUENCES

Three commands let you combine sequences in various ways. These commands are discussed in the following sections.

Insert Sequence Command

The \<Insert Sequence\> command inserts another sequence into the first sequence as if its panels were defined in the first sequence. Its main use is to allow you to reuse small sequences that are appropriately used within the context of several sequences.

Syntax:	**\<Insert Sequence\>** *sequenceName*
Example:	`<Insert Sequence> "Using styled text"`
Limitations:	There cannot be more than 32 panels in the combined sequence.
When to Use:	As needed to reuse small utility sequences.

Jump Sequence Command

The <Jump Sequence> command transfers control to another sequence. At the end of that sequence, control returns to the first sequence. It is commonly used to transfer control conditionally to a sequence based on a context check or panel control value (such as a check box).

Syntax:	**<Jump Sequence>** *sequenceName*
Example:	This example uses a context check, DocumentIsEmpty, which checks to see whether the application's current document is empty. Context checks are defined in the next chapter.
| | ```
<Panel> "Enter some text"
<IF> DocumentIsEmpty()
<Jump Sequence> "How to enter text"
<ENDIF>
<Panel> "Paginating Text"
``` |
| *Limitations:* | A panel must be shown in a sequence before a <Jump Sequence> command is allowed. In other words, you cannot create a condition in which a sequence has nothing to display until it jumps to another sequence. |
| *When to Use:* | As needed to reuse utility sequences and to handle exceptions; sequences that are jumped to do not count against a sequence's limit of 32 panels. |

Launch New Sequence Command

The <Launch New Sequence> command transfers control to another sequence, which is shown in the first sequence's window. Control cannot return to the first sequence, however. This command is primarily used in the case in which a sequence exceeds 32 panels: it is broken in two, and the second one is started with the <Launch New Sequence> command.
```

Syntax:	**<Launch New Sequence>** *sequenceName*
Example:	`<Launch New Sequence> "Another sequence"`
Limitations:	The user cannot use the left arrow to return to the first sequence once the second sequence is launched.
When to Use:	As needed, usually only when a sequence exceeds 32 panels.

SUMMARY

This chapter covers the basics of putting panels together to create a sequence. You should feel comfortable reading the following sequence definition from Macintosh Guide:

```
<DEFINE SEQUENCE> "How do I manage Power Macintosh memory?" , "How
do I manage Power Macintosh memory?"
<SEQUENCE PROMPT SET> "Standard Prompts"
<PANEL> "Power Mac: memory intro"
<PANEL> "Power Mac: VM tips1"
<PANEL> "Power Mac: tips2"
<END SEQUENCE>
```

CHAPTER 12

Sequences II: Conditions and Context Checks

As personal computers became common in the early 1980s, an increasing number of people had the dubious pleasure of being unable to use them to do what they considered to be simple things. With the impressive processing power of the chips that were then common, developers began to add on-line help to their applications so that users could press a single key and be presented with a vast amount of textual information which might (or might not) contain a clue as to what was wrong. Some innovative applications even provided context-sensitive help. This was the same old help system as before, but it magically opened up to the area of help text that was most likely what you wanted. Or at least to an area that was possibly relevant in some way to what you would want if you were using the program properly (which you probably weren't because you couldn't print or do some other supposedly simple task).

Context-sensitive help, which still is a major selling point for many programs on the market today, usually refers to a help system that provides information about the dialog box or window currently open. Although this is better than nothing and certainly better than a help system that always opens with an index of terms from A-Z, it is usually a far cry from what the user wants. (Balloon Help is an ideal delivery tool for information about what each button and entry field in a dialog box is for.) The user who wants serious assistance often wants it at a higher, more abstract level than help with using a dialog box. The most frustrating problems are often conceptual: why does the printer always restart before printing a document (different printer drivers are installed on different machines on the network), what is the key combination to send output to the fax modem rather

193

than the printer, and so forth. Moreover, many times the user's question or problem is not related to the specific task currently being done. It's the next task—be it printing, indexing, or calculating—that often poses the problem.

With the traditional sort of context-sensitive help, the application decides what information to present to the user based on what dialog boxes or windows are open, where the cursor is, or some other criteria defined in the application. Apple Guide employs a different model to handle context sensitivity. The application, if it is involved at all, responds to Apple Guide's queries about the context or state of the application. Apple Guide, following the instructions in its guide file, decides what action to take. Thus, it is the designer of the guide file rather than the application developer who decides what assistance is delivered in different circumstances.

With this model of context sensitivity, there are two areas of responsibility:

- Context checks must be defined and evaluated by the application or operating system when Apple Guide requests them to be.
- Apple Guide (not the application) must be able to evaluate the results of the context checks and to act accordingly.

Because it is the responsibility of the context check only to answer the query (letting Apple Guide decide what action to take based on the response), it is easy to use context checking not only to determine what panels and sequences to show, but also to provide the step-by-step coaching and assistance that is a hallmark of Apple Guide.

The two main sections of this chapter deal in turn with context checks and their definitions in guide files and with the conditions that you can create in guide files that allow Apple Guide to take the necessary actions based on the results of context checks.

N O T E   For some reason, context checks make many guide file designers feel nervous. In fact, context checking is very easy to do, and the Standard Resources file includes a number of powerful context—checking routines that you can use. Context-checking routines are written in code-usually C— but using them requires no programming knowledge. The code is discussed in Chapter 17, "The Apple Guide API." If it will make you queasy, skip that chapter, but don't skip this one!

CONTEXT CHECKS

Although each application and solution is different, you can make some general assumptions about the sorts of things you would like to be able to accomplish with context checks:

- If you are about to coach the user to do something, you should be certain that it can be done.

- If you have coached the user to do something, you should be able to verify that it has been done.

- If you are coaching or describing a multistep process, you should be able to determine where the user is in that process when you start the guide file topic. Has the user started performing the task and gotten stuck part way through? Does the user not have the most remote clue about how to even begin the process? Has the user actually done the task and accomplished the goal but now wonders if there couldn't be an easier way? (In fact, you need to perform this sort of checking constantly: sometimes the user will get ahead of the guide file, by doing several steps that are self-evident. A well-written guide file should be able to jump over intermediate steps that have been accomplished by the user.)

- If the user is concentrating on a specific goal, your guide file should not have to interject an irrelevant question. For example, if you are carefully coaching a user through the steps involved in adding a graphic to a spreadsheet, it is a distraction to ask whether the monitor is color or black and white.

In order to develop the appropriate context checks, you should consider issues related both to their design and implementation.

Designing Context Checks

In an ideal world, the application and Apple Guide designers would sit down together at the beginning of a project, planning the interaction of the application and Apple Guide. Throughout the development process, both parties would be on the alert for changes in their own areas that might (or should) affect the other's design. Because this is often not the case (and in fact is never the case when a consultant is adding Apple Guide assistance to a custom solution or an existing application), both application and Apple Guide designers should think about specifying and providing context checks that will most likely best serve the needs of the user in the absence of complete specifications.

In designing context checks, you may be amazed to learn how productive a few context checks can be and how few context checks are needed to provide powerful assistance to a user. This is fortunate, because many times the context checks must be limited to those available in the external modules in Standard Resources. When you are able to specify your own context checks, they often need to be specified before the Apple Guide files are designed.

The design of context checks can be looked at in many ways. Two of the most important distinctions to make are

- logical versus physical context checks
- direct versus indirect context checks

In addition, when you are able to design new context checks, you should consider the possibility of adding additional functionality to the context check itself so that it actually performs part of a task.

Logical Versus Physical Context Checks

Context checks tell you something about the state of an application or process. The physical aspects of an application—what windows are open, what type of processor is being used, whether a color monitor or floating point unit is available—are easily checked because they correspond to interface objects or system components, both of which are visible to the operating system. The logical aspects of an application (is entered data valid?, is there unsaved data?) often have no visual representation on the screen and may need to be checked by application code. Sometimes, a context check combines aspects of both physical and logical attributes (is a window open with unsaved data in it?).

Physical context checks often can be handled by generic context checks, such as the external modules provided in Standard Resources. After all, a window titled "Find" and belonging to a specific word processing application either is or isn't open and the operating system knows about it. Usually.

The Mac OS is renowned for its power, consistency, and ease-of-use. To a large extent this is made possible by the many toolbox routines made available to application developers. Since most applications use common routines to do common tasks, windows, menus, check boxes, and other interface elements of the Mac OS appear and behave the same way no matter where they appear. Occasionally, this causes a problem for application developers. Sometimes they need to provide a functionality or appearance feature that differs from the standard Mac OS. Although most toolbox routines can be customized in many ways, sometimes developers have gone their own way, bypassing the standard routines. As a result, there are applications around that have menu bars that are drawn and processed independent of the Menu Manager toolbox routines. Windows (particularly floating windows and palettes) have sometimes been implemented behind the back of the Window Manager.

Although some of these cases amount simply to "hacks" by people who don't have the patience or temperament to use standard code, other cases reflect particular needs of applications and their data. It is often a requirement that an application have a standard look on different platforms. Compounding the problem is that some of these interface features are in fact improvements. And they wind up being implemented in subsequent releases of the operating system itself. This produces the anomalous case where the innovator becomes the nonstandard implementation and later adopters of the technology are able to use standard toolbox calls. This is a fact of life in a field where (fortunately) innovation is rapid and abundant.

In the case of applications that have bent or modified interface standards and implementations, you may find that generic context checks fail or produce unexpected results. Fortunately, the number of these applications is small, but several major applications do from time to time take this approach to parts of their interface.

For the most part, however, physical context checks can be handled in a straightforward manner, often with the generic context checks in Standard Resources. Logical context checks may not be quite so simple.

A logical context check reflects the state of the application and its data, not the state of the interface. Logical context checks would appear to be application-specific and to require custom programming, which is often the case. Fortunately, the sensitivity of the Macintosh interface to user actions can be used to convert logical context checks into physical ones that can be performed more easily. For example, the apparently logical context check to determine whether a window has unsaved data in it can be seen as a physical context check: is the **Save** command enabled in the File menu. (It is normally disabled as soon as a document is saved.)

By casting context checks in generic and physical terms as often as possible, you will most likely be able to use and reuse context checks from other applications. The specific context checks that you do require to be custom-written will be fewer in number. That increases the likelihood of them being done: not only is the cost lower, but the programming staff is likely to be interested and enthusiastic about adding two or three context checks to an application. The prospect of adding 50 or 100 context checks is likely to be greeted with groans. (This applies even if you yourself are the programming staff.)

Direct Versus Indirect Context Checks

Recasting the example application-specific logical context check (is there unsaved data?) to a generic physical context check (is the **Save** command enabled?) is an example of the use of an indirect context check. We use indirect context checks all the time in our daily lives. In the village of Philmont, people have two ways of telling if the public library is open. If you are on upper Main Street, you look down the street to see whether the lights are on. If you are by the post office on Maple Avenue, you look to see whether the librarian's car with the Support American Farms bumper sticker is parked by the bank. Both checks are indirect and, thus, may provide erroneous information: the custodian could be cleaning the carpet and have the lights on or librarian Cindy Tipple could have walked to work. But while realizing their limitations, people rely on these indirect context checks because they are easier than walking up to the front door and seeing whether the library is open.

Indirect context checks abound on the Macintosh. Did the user choose **New** from the File menu? You could check to see what the most recent menu command was, or you could check to see whether there is an open, unsaved document. Sometimes indirect context checks can be circuitous: did the user select an item in a certain window? If that window is not open, it is either impossible or a moot point. Furthermore, if that window is not the active window, it's unlikely that the user has just clicked in it. (Of course, it is not impossible: the user could have selected the item, and then clicked on another window. The more indirect and circuitous a context check is, the more likely it will provide misleading information.)

The reason for performing these contortions is simple: there never are enough context checks to do precisely what you want. As a result, you start from the context checks you have: those in Standard Resources, as well as any other external modules that you have, together with any context checks that the application has already provided. Can you use those context checks to answer the questions that you need to answer? (Being able to check for an open or active window with a specific name covers a great many of your context checking needs.)

Collateral Actions

Werner Heisenberg, the physicist who developed the theory of quantum mechanics, propounded the famous uncertainty principle in 1927: it is impossible to measure both the location and velocity of a subatomic particle at the same time. The possibility that the process of measurement itself could affect the thing that was to be measured had profound implications for 20th-century physics.

That possibility also has significant effects on Apple Guide authors and designers, in a somewhat different manner. The code written to perform a context check is not limited in any way. The routine invoked should ultimately return a result (a one-byte Boolean), but what else the routine does along the way is its business. Thus, you can design a context check that pays homage to Heisenberg and affects the context itself by performing a collateral action while it carries out the context check. An example of such a case is a context check that returns true if the scroll bar of a window is scrolled all the way to the top. You can design a context check that simply checks this and returns the appropriate result. Alternatively, you could design a context check that checks the position of the scroll bar and if it is not at the top, scrolls the window to the top, and then returns the result, which might be reinterpreted to mean that the window was already scrolled to the top (true) or that it was not scrolled to the top but had been adjusted by the context check (false).

Before adding additional functionality to a context check, you should consider whether that is the right place to do it. Generally this is the case when:

- the action can be accomplished very quickly
- the action is trivial
- the action is closely tied to the context check

As you will see in the second part of this chapter, context checks are repeatedly processed by Apple Guide, even while the machine is "at rest" and the user may be doing nothing (or at least nothing involved with Apple Guide and its assistance). This is to ensure that when the user finally does click the right arrow, the context check will reflect the state of the application and computer at that moment. As with any routine that is called frequently, you want to minimize the processing requirements of the context check so that other tasks and processes on the computer (including background printing and network services) get their chance to work.

In identifying a "trivial" action, you should take into account both the appearance of the interface and the user's actions. Because context checks are processed in advance of the user clicking on the right arrow to go to the next panel, the user may not realize that a context check is being handled by the computer. If that context check causes something on the monitor to change or move, the user can be distracted or irritated. In this example, the context check with the collateral action of scrolling the window could cause the user to get into a battle with the window—the user scrolling the window to the bottom and the repeatedly invoked context check scrolling it to the top. This is certainly not a trivial action, and because it can entail the user's loss of control over the computer as well as bewilderment at what is happening it is a dubious strategy.

Adding collateral actions to context checks can also make them harder to reuse. The entire division of labor in Apple Guide's implementation of context sensitivity puts the checking squarely in the lap of the application or external code modules, and puts the actions in the lap of the guide file. Putting collateral actions into context checks blurs this distinction.

Why, then, even mention collateral actions? They can (even in the scenario given here) be valuable to both users and designers. The key to successful use of these collateral actions is to allow the user control over them. You can provide different levels of assistance in either in the same guide file or in separate guide files targeted for different purposes and levels of expertise. The sophisticated user might welcome an "express" tutorial that skips over window resizing and scrolling steps in order to focus on three significant actions that are required to correct a misspelled word. Other users might want to be coached through every step, including scrolling the window so the misspelled word is visible. As with everything in a well-designed system, if you provide the user with control and a reason why things happen the way they do, you provide a welcome and useful service.

So how do you provide a context check that sometimes performs a collateral action and sometimes doesn't? When you specify the context check to the programmer, make certain to include a parameter that controls the context check's behavior.

NOTE   Adding collateral actions to coach marks ensures that they are evaluated only once when a panel is shown, rather than repeatedly as with a context check. You can also package such an action into an event that is performed once when a panel is shown, hidden, created, or destroyed. Each of these strategies causes the action to be performed once.

In the case where you sometimes want to accompany the context check with a collateral action, it may be appropriate to parameterize the context check, even at the cost of repeated execution.

Implementing Context Checks

There are two ways for context checks to be carried out. If the application can be created or modified to respond to Apple Guide context check queries, it can do so directly. The application installs a handler for context check queries; this routine is called in response to a context check request from Apple Guide, and its result is returned to Apple Guide. If the application cannot be created or modified to respond to Apple Guide context check queries, or if the query itself is related more to the total hardware or software environment than to a specific application, context check queries can be processed using external modules. These are code resources that are compiled and attached as resources to the Apple Guide file (not to the application, which remains untouched). When the query is to be processed, the code resource is automatically executed by Apple Guide.

The eight external modules provided in Standard Resources enable you to do a number of significant context checks without writing any code, either in your application or in custom-written external modules. As a result, you will be able to use context checking at some level in most of your guide files. Whether using these context checks or ones developed specifically for your application, you should plan on an overall strategy for the use of context checking in your guide files. With the possible exception of Shortcuts guide files, it is hard to conceive of an Apple Guide file that does not use context checking or that could not be improved by its use. The coach marks get the "oohs" and "aahs," but the context checks provide the user with a sense of confidence and assurance—not only that Apple Guide is watching to make certain that nothing goes wrong but also that the assistance provided will be relevant.

Choosing between External Code Modules and Application Context Checks

It is rare that you can freely choose between creating an external module and modifying an application to perform a context check solely on design considerations. The decision is made for you automatically in several cases:

- If you cannot modify the application, you must use external resources.
- If the context check relates more to the logical state of an application and its data than to its physical state, an external code resource will likely be more complicated and time-consuming to write and debug than a context check performed directly by the application.

Parameterized Context Checks

Context checks—whether external modules or application codec—an receive parameters that are sent from Apple Guide. This makes it possible to achieve a great deal with a few carefully designed context checks. For example, you are best advised not to create a context check that returns TRUE if the Preferences window of your application is open. You more likely would devise a context check that takes the window title ("Preferences") and returns TRUE if it is open. That same context check with different parameters can check for any window that your application might open and for which you know the title. If you add a context check within your application, you can extend this context check further. Your application's context check might take as a parameter a window characteristic rather than a title. Some application-specific characteristics for which you might want to check are

- a window that has never been saved ("Untitled-n")
- a window that contains unsaved data but that has previously been saved
- a window that contains no unsaved data but that has been modified while the application is running
- a window that has not been printed since the last modification
- and many more.

If you assign constants to each of these application-specific conditions, you can create a single context check that uses a single incoming parameter to determine what response to give.

Although the programmer who implements the code for your context checks may well find a way to combine several checks into a single parameterized context check, you should think ahead on your own and suggest possible parameters to use so that code can be reused.

Application-Based Context Checks

Using a context check in an application program is a two step-process:

1. You write a context check that is called in response to requests from Apple Guide.
2. You install the context check, usually when your application starts up. See the AGInstallContextHandler function in Chapter 17, "The Apple Guide API," for details of this process.

The context check in your application is associated with a context check definition in your guide file by an Apple Event ID (a four-character string) which both share. The AGInstallContextHandler function establishes this connection on the application's side; the *codeResSpec* in the context check definition establishes the connection in the guide file.

 You can do almost anything in an application context check, but you must do it in the way in which Apple Guide wants it. If you are going to write a context check in an application, you must read this section. Otherwise, feel free to skip it.

N O T E

When you use a context check that is implemented in an application program, the basic shell of the context check is fairly standard. Within it, you can do almost any thing that you want. The context check is a ContextReplyProc, and has the following syntax:

ContextReplyProc function

The result of the ContextReplyProc (type OSErr) indicates whether the context check has been able to be processed; it is not the result of the context check itself. Apple Guide looks only to see whether the result is 0 (constant: noErr). If it is not, it assumes that something untoward has occurred, and treats the context check result as false. There are no Apple Guide-specific values defined for this result; it's noErr or nothing as far as Apple Guide is concerned.

When you define a context check in a guide file, you can specify a number of parameters that will be passed to the context check. The context check specifies the type of each parameter (string, integer, and so on). Apple Guide packs them sequentially into a pointer, *pInputData*, of size *inputDataSize*. Your context check is responsible for unpacking and parsing these parameters. The simplest way of doing this is to declare a **struct**, the elements of which correspond to the input parameters. Coerce the *pInputData* pointer to a pointer to your struct, and you will be able to reference the elements directly. (Many context checks have either one or no parameters.)

When you have evaluated the context check, you return either a 0 (FALSE) or a 1 (TRUE). This value is returned as a Boolean in the pointer *ppOutputData*, which is *pOutputDataSize* bytes long.

The final parameter, *hAppInfo*, is a handle that points to a structure defined by Apple Guide:

```
struct AGAppInfo {
AEEventID eventId;
long      refCon;
void      *contextObj; /* private system field*/
};
```

The *refCon* is a reference constant that you assign to the context check when you install it in your application. You most commonly set it to a pointer to your application or another object whose data structures you want to reference in the context check. *eventID* is an Apple Event ID that you assign in your context check definition in your guide file.

eventID is the link between the specific context check definition in your guide file and the context check in your application. When you install a context handler, you specify the event to which it will respond. Because a single context check can be used to respond to several events, you can use *eventID* in the context check to see which event has, in fact, triggered the context check. In the case where a context check responds only to one event (that is, AGInstallContextHandler establishes a one-to-one relationship between an event and a context check), you need not use *eventID* in your context check.

Because the ContextReplyProc is called as a callback routine, all of the rules for callback routines apply. Specifically:

- The function should be in a locked unpurgeable segment.
- You should save and restore the A5 register.

Syntax: **pascal OSErr ContextReplyProc (Ptr pInputData, Size inputDataSize, Ptr *ppOutputData, Size *pOutputDataSize, AGAppInfoHdl hAppInfo)**

Example:
```
pascal OSErr ReplyToContext (Ptr pInput, Size
inputDataSize, Ptr *ppOutput, Size *pOutputDataSize,
AGAppInfoHdl hAppInfo)
{
// set default values for the error and result
//did the context check encounter an error in
//executing
OSErr    err = noErr;
//result of the context check
Boolean  result = false;
// save A5 world to restore on exit
long     theA5=SetA5(*(long*)CurrentA5);
// if you have used hAppInfo.eventID — as you would
if this
// code is used to process several context checks —
// branch on the value of eventID here


// if you have used hAppInfo.refCon to store a
// reference to
// an application object, dereference it here


// if parameters are passed in pInput, parse them and
// place in local variables


// perform context check, set result variable
```

```
        // place result in ppOutput
        ppOutput = NewPtr (sizeof(Boolean));
        if (*ppOutput)
            {
            *ppOutput = result;
            *pOutputDataSize = sizeof (Boolean);
            };
        //restore the A5 world to what it was on entry
        SetA5 (theA5);


        return err; //will return noErr, unless it has been
        changed during the function call
        }
```

When to Use: As needed.

External Code Modules

External code modules are attached to your guide file rather than to an application. Although the code involved may be similar, using external code modules differs from using application context checks in two ways:

- There is no installation process. The association of a given external code module with a specific context check definition in a guide file is very simple: the name of the external code module is the same as the *codeResSpec* in the context check definition.

- The final parameter of the ContextReplyProc, *hAppInfo*, is not available to external code modules. Thus, there is no *refCon* or *eventID* value available to the external code module.

Other than that, the procedure for writing an external code module is much the same as for writing an application-based context check.

Syntax: **pascal OSErr main (Ptr pInput, Size inputDataSize, Ptr *ppOutput, Size *pOutputDataSize, Handle ignoreHandle)**

Example:

```
pascal OSErr main (Ptr pInput, Size inputDataSize,
Ptr *ppOutput, Size *pOutputDataSize, Handle
ignoreHandle)
{
// set default values for the error and result
//did the context check encounter an error in
//executing
OSErr     err = noErr;
//result of the context check
Boolean   result = false;


// if parameters are passed in pInput, parse them
and place in local variables


// perform context check, set result variable


// place result in ppOutput
ppOutput = NewPtr (sizeof(short));
if (*ppOutput)
    {
    *ppOutput = result;
    *pOutputDataSize = sizeof (Boolean);
    };


return err; //will return noErr, unless it has
been changed during the function call
}
```

While an application-based context check is compiled as part of your application, you must compile and link the external code module by itself. If you are using MPW, the following make file will properly compile and link an external code module "myModule" with the ID "myMd".

```
myModule ƒƒ myModule.make myModule.c.o
    Link -sn myModule=myMd -mf -t extm -c reno -rt ∂
        extm=1200 -m MAIN -sg myModule ∂
        myModule.c.o ∂
        "{Libraries}"Interface.o ∂
        -o myModule
myModule.c.o. ƒ myModule.make myModule.c
    C -r -b myModule.c
```

You add the external code module to your guide file with the <Resource> command.

Standard Resources External Modules

The two previous sections showed intrepid programmers how to write context checks either as external code modules or within applications. For the nonprogrammer, context checks are still available. In Standard Resources, Apple provides eight external modules that can be used in an Apple Guide file. Although some of these are mostly of use to Macintosh Guide itself, many are of use to other Apple Guide designers.

These modules have a number of parameters. The first is a long integer that specifies which of several context checks in each module is referred to. Additional parameters pass necessary information from Apple Guide to the external code module. The Table 12.1 lists the basic context checks that can be performed with each external code module. The value of the long integer parameter is shown in the Selector column. A self-running stack on the *Real World Apple Guide* CD-ROM provides complete syntax for all context checks in command resources.

Table 12.1 Standard Resources Context Checks

External Module	Selector	Description
SYST	0	general Gestalt test (often used for processor type)
	1	does a menu item exist
	2	does a menu item exist and is it checked
	3	does a menu item exist and is it enabled
	4	does a menu item exist and is it disabled
	5	background printing on or off
	6	file sharing on or off
	7	video hardware bit depth
	8	monitor bit depth
	9	does the computer have a name
	10	Guest Access on or off
	11	number of monitors
FILE	0	active window is the startup disk window
	1	startup disk window is open and visible
	2	startup disk is the current directory
	3	PrintMonitor installed
	4	AppleShare software installed
	5	EtherTalk software installed
	6	TokenTalk software installed
	7	check that a specific control panel is installed
	9	check that a specific file is within a system-defined folder (extensions, Apple menu, control panels, and so forth)
WIND	0	specified window is active
	1	specified window is open
	2	specified window is invisible
	3	Sharing window is open

(continued)

Table 12.1 Standard Resources Context Checks **(continued)**

External Module	Selector	Description
	4	Sharing window is active
	5	specified window is collapsed (with WindowShade)
	6	Find dialog box is active
	7	"More Choices" Find dialog is active
	8	any dialog active
CHSR	0	printer directly connected to this computer
	I	number of network printers in this zone (can compare to a given value with =, <, >, >=, <=)
	2	serial printer connected to this computer
	3	printer connected through a SCSI port
	4	selected printer has specified name
	5	AppleTalk on or off
	6	number of zones on the network
	7	modem or printer port selected
	8	modem or printer port in use
	9	any zones on the network
PCSS	0	specified application is active
	I	specified application is open

With just a few of these context checks (for example, those that test for the active window, for specific menu items and for the active application), you can produce a very powerful guide file that "stays with" the user on every step of a complex process.

Defining a Context Check

Once you have your hands on the context checks you need (whether as standard context checks, custom-written external code modules, or application-based context checks), you must define them in your guide file.

Define Context Check Command

Once you have defined a context check, you use it in your guide file as if it were a function:

```
OpenWindow("Preferences")
```

Thus, the *contextCheckName* (which will be used as if it were a function name, not enclosed in quotation marks) cannot have embedded spaces.

The second parameter of the <Define Context Check> command, *codeResSpec*, has different meanings for external code modules and application-defined context checks. For external code modules, it is the name of the code resource; for application-based context checks, it is the Apple Event ID associated with the context check. In both cases, it is a four-character identifier enclosed in single quotation marks.

The *targetApp* parameter is the four-character identifier of the application to which the context check should be sent. The default value for this optional parameter is the front-most application. You can also explicitly specify the constant FRONT for this parameter (which may make for better code readability).

The remaining parameters are the parameters that will be passed to the context check itself. The context check definition specifies the type and order of these parameters, and they must match the type and order of parameters that the context check itself expects.

For example, to use the standard context check shown in Table 12.1 to test whether the startup disk window is active, you could define a context check as follows:

```
<Define Context Check> "StartUpDiskWindowActive", 'FILE', 'MACS',
LONG
```

This associates the StartUpDiskWindowActive context check with the external module named FILE. The target application is MACS (the Finder), and the context check takes one parameter: a long integer, which is the selector shown in the second column of the table.

You could use this context check in a guide file as follows:

```
<If> StartUpDiskWindowActive(0)
```

In this case, the parameter is always 0 for this context check. You can specify a default value in your context check definition by following the parameter's type with a colon and a value, as follows:

```
<Define Context Check> "StartUpDiskWindowActive", 'FILE', 'MACS',
LONG:0
```

With this definition, your use of the context check becomes:

```
<If> StartUpDiskWindowActive()
```

Another way of approaching this context check would be to define it as follows:

```
<Define Context Check> "StartUpDiskStatus", 'FILE', 'MACS', LONG
```

By using a parameter when you invoke the context check, you can check for the startup disk window being either open or active:

```
#checks for the startup disk window being active
<If> StartUpDiskStatus(0)
#checks for the startup disk window being open
<If> StartUpDiskStatus(1)
```

Most people find that using default values in context check definitions makes for clearer code than using parameters in the context check invocation.

The data types that can be specified in a context check definition are as follows:

SHORT

LONG

PSTRING

LPSTRING

OSTYPE

Numbers are assumed to be decimal unless prefixed with 0x, indicating that the number that follows is hexadecimal.

The PSTRING and LPSTRING types are identical in their use in a context check. The LPSTRING type is used for a string, which you will want to localize using Guide Maker. Strings of type LPSTRING are extracted by the Localize function; strings of type PSTRING are not.

Syntax:	**<Define Context Check>** *contextCheckName, codeResSpec [, targetApp] [,additionalParam] [, additionalParam] [, ...]*

Example:	`<Define Context Check> "OpenWindow", 'WIND', FRONT,`
	`    LONG:1, LONG:10, LPSTRING`
	
	This context check uses the WIND standard context check to test if a certain window is open. You would use it as follows:
	
	`<If> OpenWindow("Preferences")`
	
	The first two parameters (the long integers 1 and 10) are given default values in the context check definition. The 1 is the selector shown above, the 10 specifies the type of comparison to be made between the parameter and the window titlein this case a match. (Values for this comparison type are given in in the extended code modules stack on the CD-ROM).
	
	`<Define Context Check> "SubPartsButton", 'cntT',`
	`    'PSM3', OSTYPE:'Bsub'`
	
	This context check uses an application-based context check to test whether a certain button on the application's controller is clicked. Because it has only one parameter and a default value is provided for it, you would invoke it as follows:
	
	`<If> SubPartsButton()`

When to Use:	As needed. And you need it a lot! Context checks can mean the difference between the unobtrusive, customized service that you want to provide and a guide file that is the butt of jokes (or worse) as it blithely coaches users through actions that can't be performed because the wrong window is open, the application isn't running, and so on.

CONDITIONS AND BRANCHING

After finding or writing the code for context checks and after defining them in your guide file, the time comes to actually put them to use. Apple Guide is designed to evaluate simple and persistent conditions. Simple condition tests are evaluated and an action is taken (or not taken) based on the result. Persistent condition tests are evaluated repeatedly while a section of a guide file is active. If the condition becomes false, an Oops sequence is launched and control does not return to the main sequence until the condition is true.

Evaluating Conditions

The conditions that are tested in all of the commands in this section consist of one or more context checks. If more than one context check is given, they are joined by the operators AND and OR. The compound condition is TRUE when both context checks evaluate to TRUE and are joined with AND. If either of two context checks evaluates to TRUE and they are joined with OR, the compound condition is also TRUE. Conversely, with AND, the compound condition is FALSE if either context check is FALSE; with OR, the compound condition is FALSE only if both context checks evaluate to FALSE.

The unary operator NOT can precede any context check. It inverts the value returned by the context check.

Finally, you can use parentheses to group context checks and to control the sequence in which they are evaluated within a compound condition. As with all such syntax, the conditions are evaluated from the innermost parentheses out, with each parenthetical term being evaluated and then treated as a single entity.

In the following examples, assume that the context checks EvaluatesToTrue and EvalutesToFalse always return TRUE and FALSE respectively.

```
EvaluatesToTrue() #TRUE
NOT EvaluatesToTrue() #FALSE
EvaluatesToTrue() OR EvaluatesToFalse() #TRUE
EvaluatesToTrue() AND EvaluatesToFalse() #FALSE
EvalutesToTrue() OR NOT EvaluatesToFalse() #TRUE
NOT (EvalutesToTrue() AND EvaluatesToFalse() #TRUE
```

Guide Maker Context Checks

In addition to the external code modules provided in Standard Resources, Guide Maker itself includes two context checks that can be used as conditions:

```
radioButtonState(buttonTitle, panelName)
```

and

```
checkBoxState(checkBoxTitle, panelName)
```

Each returns TRUE if the named control on the specified panel is clicked.

Simple Condition Tests

Simple condition tests are used to modify the display of panels in a sequence. They normally take effect when the user clicks an arrow to go to the next or previous panel in a sequence. The condition is evaluated, and based on the result, one or another panel is shown.

Apple Guide looks ahead, attempting to perform the context checks required to move to the next panel, usually every 30 to 60 ticks (once or twice a second). As a result, a context check is often called repeatedly. Furthermore, it is almost always called before the user clicks the right arrow—often as soon as a new panel is displayed. If your context check does anything out of the ordinary (such as performing collateral actions), there may be significant consequences.

There are three sets of simple condition tests:

- If/Then/Else
- Skip If
- Make Sure

If/Then/Else

The If/Then/Else structure is familiar to all programmers. A condition is evaluated; if it is true, a section of code is executed. If it is false, another section is executed. The syntax is straightforward.

As in all cases, the condition is made up of one or more context checks and can be a compound condition, with context checks combined using parentheses, AND, and OR.

The <Else> clause is optional. You can simply test that the condition is true and execute one or more statements before the <End If> command.

Syntax: **<If>** *condition*

commands to execute if the condition is true—usually
panel(s) to be displayed

<Else>

commands to execute if the condition is true—usually
panel(s) to be displayed

<End If>

Example: This section from the "How do I change the colors in the Label menu?" sequence in Macintosh Guide first uses a context check to test whether the monitor is black and white. If it is, a panel is displayed telling the user that no colors are available. If it is a color monitor (the <Else> clause), a second context check is evaluated to see whether the Labels control panel can be found in the Control Panels folder. (This is one of the standard external code module context checks.) If the control panel is not found (note the NOT operator) a transition panel is shown and the user jumps to a new sequence explaining how to install the Labels control panel.

```
<IF> isMonoChrome()
<PANEL>"display: no colors"
<ELSE>
<IF>NOT InControlPanelFolder("Labels")
    <PANEL>"Labels: segue to install"
    <JUMP SEQUENCE>"Subsequence: Install Labels
  control panel"
<END IF>
<END IF>
```

Limitations:	**<If>** commands can be nested, but only to a depth of four levels.
When to Use:	As needed.

Skip If Command

The <Skip If> command provides a simple way to skip over a single panel if necessary. The command applies only to the first panel following it; if you want to skip several panels after testing for a single condition, use the <If> and <End If> commands. If the panel is preceded by one or more <Make Sure> commands (see next command), they are skipped as well.

Syntax:	**<Skip If>** *condition*
Example:	In another section of the sequence excerpted above, a panel prompting the user to set the colors on the monitor to 16 is skipped if the monitor is already set to a bid depth of four or more (i.e., 16 or more colors).

```
<SKIP IF> BitDepthAtLeast(4)
   <PANEL>"Label menu: set colors to 16"
```

Limitations:	Only applies to the next panel.
When to Use:	As needed.

Make Sure Command

The last simple condition test is the <Make Sure> command, which completes the functionality of the suite. The If/Then/Else syntax allows you to evaluate a condition, and then execute either of two series of commands. The <Skip If> command allows you to omit a single panel if the condition is true. The <Make Sure> command provides a somewhat more sophisticated mechanism.

The condition is evaluated, and if it is true, control passes to the next command in the guide file. If it is not true, an Oops sequence is launched. The Oops sequence consists of panels (preferably one) identifying the problem and instructing the user how to solve the problem. An **OK** button with the GoBack event attached to it closes the Oops sequence and returns the user to the primary sequence. The <Make Sure> command in the primary sequence is reevaluated at this time. If the condition is now true, the next panel in the primary sequence is displayed. If the condition remains false, Apple Guide searches backward in the primary sequence to find a panel that can be shown—either because it has no <Make Sure> command preceding it or because the <Make Sure> command evaluates to true.

An alternative design replaces the **OK** button with a **Continue** button, and is called a Continue sequence rather than an Oops sequence. With a Continue sequence, the problem is solved for the user—often by AppleScript commands. When the script has finished executing, the user clicks **Continue** and returns to the primary sequence as described.

The *condition* should not be a compound condition in the <Make Sure> command. Because you can attach up to three <Make Sure> commands to a single panel, use simple conditions, each with its own Oops sequence. The *oopsOrContinueSequenceName* is the name of the sequence to be shown if the condition is false.

When you have more than one <Make Sure> command preceding a panel, Apple Guide evaluates them in reverse order, starting with the <Make Sure> command immediately preceding the panel and continuing up.

Syntax:	**<Make Sure>** *condition, oopsOrContinueSequenceName*
Example:	The <Make Sure> command is often used in conjunction with the <Skip If> command, as shown in this further excerpt. If the active window is the Labels control panel, the subsequent panel with its two <Make Sure> commands is skipped.
	If the active window is not Control Panels, a Continue sequence "Auto open: Control Panels folder seq" is launched, which automatically opens the Control Panels window. (Remember that <Make Sure> commands are evaluated in reverse order up from the panel.)
	Then, if the monitor is not set for at least 16 colors, an Oops sequence is launched, prompting the user to set the colors to 16 or more.

When both conditions are true, the panel telling the user that the Labels control panel is being opened is displayed.

This type of structure is very common in Apple Guide files.

```
<SKIP IF>ActiveWindow('MACS',"Labels")
        <MAKE SURE> BitDepthAtLeast(4), "Oops:not 16
        colors"
        <MAKE SURE> ActiveWindow('MACS',"Control
        Panels"),"Auto open: Control Panels folder
        seq"
                <PANEL>          "Labels control panel:
                opening"
```

Limitations: A <Make Sure> command cannot precede the first panel of a jump sequence.

When to Use: As needed.

Persistent Condition Tests

Unlike the simple condition tests, which are evaluated at a single point in a guide file's execution, the <Start Making Sure> command is used to apply to a number of panels in the guide file.

Its syntax is the same as that of the <Make Sure> command, but it applies to all panels until the <End Making Sure> command is encountered. <Start Making Sure> commands can be nested. Like <Make Sure> commands, their conditions should be simple, not compound.

NOTE   The <If> command can be used to control a number of panels, but once its condition is evaluated, it is not referred to again. Thus, if you test whether File Sharing is turned on with an <If> command, you can then present a number of panels that are based on the assumption that File Sharing is on. Because the condition is not re-evaluated after the <If> command is processed, the user can turn File Sharing off part way through the sequence. The <Start Making Sure> and <End Making Sure> commands can be used to bracket all of the panels that share the assumption that File Sharing is on; the test will be performed over again for each panel in the sequence, preventing the user and the guide file from getting out of synch.

Start Making Sure and End Making Sure Commands

Syntax:	**<Start Making Sure>** *condition, oopsOrContinueSequenceName*
	<End Making Sure>
Example:	This example from Symposium Explorer checks that the graphics tool palette is torn off from the menu bar while panels that refer to it (and that make use of coach marks that will be drawn on it) are shown.

```
<Start Making Sure> ToolPaletteTorn(), "Oops, Tool
Palette not torn off"
  <Panel> "Resize"
  <Panel> "Multiple Select"
<End Making Sure>
```

Limitations:	A <Make Sure> command cannot precede the first panel of a jump sequence.
When to Use:	As needed.

SUMMARY

Far from just being a mechanism to determine what information to display on the screen, context checks provide a crucial part of the positive "hand-holding" experience of Apple Guide. If you have access to programming resources and have the need, you can add custom context checks to your application and to your guide files with external code modules. Even with no custom programming, you can add powerful context checks to your assistance, using the external code modules provided in Standard Resources.

By testing for various conditions in your guide file, you can keep track of where the user is and whether problems arise. When something untoward happens (or doesn't happen), an Oops sequence can guide the user through the steps necessary to return to the proper path. Even better, a Continue sequence that automatically performs the action for the user can keep the user's attention focused on the main goal.

To automatically perform actions for the user, you need to be able to specify events and lists of events for Apple Guide to execute. By a particularly fortunate coincidence, they are covered in the next chapter.

CHAPTER 13

Sequences III: Events

The last piece of the Apple Guide puzzle is its use of Apple events, either directly or through AppleScript. Apple events are a standard form of interapplication communication that can be used among processes running on the same or different machines. Together with coach marks and context checks, the use of Apple events takes Apple Guide truly into a dimension far beyond help.

Coach marks provide an immediately visible level of comfort: click here, type there. Users react positively because they can tell that they are in safe hands. Context checks provide an additional level of comfort, but it is one that is not necessarily visible to the user. Apple Guide just seems to "know" what panels to show and what instructions to give.

Events can lead the user beyond these levels of comfort into a realm of true service and assistance. A **Do It for Me** button is as visible as a coach mark, and its implications are very significant for the future of computing, work (and play), and computer interfaces.

You attach events to buttons that the user clicks; you also can cause events to be fired off when specific panels are created, destroyed, shown or hidden. Chapter 10, "Panels IIIControls," covered the commands to create buttons. In those commands, a *buttonEvent* parameter specified the event for that button.

In this chapter, you will see how to define events and groups of events (so that you can use them as *buttonEvent* parameters), and then how to attach events to panels.

Events can be fired in response to a user action (clicking a button). Events also can be fired by Guide Maker in anticipation (or lack) of a user action. When to use which event mechanism is covered in the section, "Putting It Together: Events and Context Checks in Apple Guide" later in this chapter.

Apple Guide provides 10 event functions. These are used frequently in guide files to execute AppleScript scripts, return from Oops sequences, and so on. The last section of this chapter describes the built-in events.

N O T E

Even if you don't define your own events, you almost always use some of the built-in event functions. The GoBack function in the guide file shells on the CD-ROM returns the user from an Oops sequence; the DoScript function runs an AppleScript; and the DoHuh and GoStart functions are usually attached to navigation bar buttons.

If you will not be defining your own events, you should feel free to skip over the Defining Events section in this chapter. If you are not going to use AppleScript or Apple events directly, you can also skip the section Attaching Events to Panels.

But remember that Apple events and AppleScript can add significant value to the service you provide your users through Apple Guide. They are the mechanism through which the Mac's graphical user interface can stop just lying there like a cute sunbather on the beach and get to work with and for the user.

DEFINING EVENTS AND EVENT LISTS

As with all Apple Guide objects that you reference from various places in a guide file, you define events before you use them. You also can define event lists that group up to six events together; you can then use the event list identifier any place where a single event identifier could be used. All of the events are then processed as a group.

Defining Events

Apple events are a powerful part of the Mac OS; Apple Guide itself relies extensively on them as it communicates with itself and the environment. Apple events are designed primarily for use by programmers, but Apple Guide provides a straightforward method for defining them.

A much more convenient interface for most people is AppleScript, which packages Apple events into a language that is fairly easy to read and to write, even for nonprogrammers. One of the built-in functions allows you to execute an AppleScript script as an event. You generally define an event (rather than invoking it through AppleScript) to improve performance; events that are fired off directly from Apple Guide are processed more quickly than those fired off from AppleScript, which in turn was fired off from Apple Guide.

N O T E   Apple events are conceptually very simple; in practice there are many nuances to their use. This section provides a brief overview, as well as enough information to use Apple events in your guide files. For the sake of clarity, a few simplifications have been made and are not noted as such. Thus, this section should be considered as an overview of Apple events only as they relate to Apple Guide.

Although Apple events provide a standard interface for communication among processes running under the Mac OS, that interface is very flexible. All Apple events are divided into classes, each identified by a four-character class identifier. Some classes, such as the core event class, are defined by Apple. (All applications that support any Apple events support the core event class.) Other classes are designed to handle Apple events specific to certain types of applications (spreadsheets, word processing, and so on). Within each class of events, individual events are given four-character event identifiers. The combination of class and event identifiers uniquely identifies a specific Apple event.

The syntax of each Apple event specifies the data that can be incorporated into the event. There may be a direct object that is what the event will affect—a document to print, for example. There also may be a number of optional parameters that may or may not be present: a number of copies parameter, a back-to-front printing option, and so on. Each optional parameter has a four-character identifying key. The Apple Event Manager provides routines for the sending and receiving applications to use to retrieve and set the data for each key in the Apple event.

The syntax for Apple events supported by a given application is provided either in the application's documentation or in the *Apple Event Registry*, which provides the standard events in the suites designed to support specific types of applications. (The Apple Events Registry is available from APDA as part of the Mac OS SDK or as part of E.T.O. For further information, see the References & Resources stack on the CD-ROM.)

With this very brief overview of Apple event terminology, the syntax for the Guide Script <Define Event> command should be clear.

Define Event Command

The *eventName* should be meaningful and must not contain spaces. When it is referred to later in your guide files, it is not enclosed in quotation marks and must be a single word.

Apple Guide will send the event to a specific application, whose four-character signature you provide in *targetApp*. You can use the constants FRONT and SELF to indicate that the event should be sent to the front-most process or to Apple Guide itself.

The next two parameters, *teventClass* and *teventID* are the two four-character identifiers for the class and event that you are interested in.

Although Apple events can have many optional parameters, Apple Guide allows only two to be passed to the Apple event. One parameter automatically has the keyword IOPT associated with it, and must be an integer. (You cannot use the IOPT parameter much; it is used internally by Apple Guide when it sends a 'scpt' event, which executes an AppleScript script. At that time it is the resource number of the 'scpt' resource in the guide file.)

The second parameter can have any keyword and any data that you supply, provided, of course, that they make sense to the Apple event. The four-character key is placed in the parameter *optKey*, and the data is placed in the parameter *optData*.

If you want to pass a direct object to the Apple event, you must do that when the event is used rather than in the <Define Event> command as, for example, in the <Standard Button> command:

```
<Standard Button> "OK", CENTER, myAppleEvent("my direct object")
```

Some events take no parameters of any kind. For example, the event 'quit' tells the application to which it is sent to quit. No parameters are needed.

Syntax:	**<Define Event>** *eventName, targetApp, teventClass, teventID [, IOPTData] [, optKey] [, optData]*
Example:	The PrintDocument event defined is designed to be invoked with a direct parameter, identifying the document to be printed:
	`<Define Event> "PrintDocument", FRONT, 'aevt', 'pdoc'`
Limitations:	The <Define Event> command is limited to two parameters, one of which is an integer with the key IOPT. You need not use either of the parameters, but you cannot add additional parameters.
When to Use:	As needed. Remember to consider using AppleScript scripts rather than events for ease of development and maintenance.

Defining Event Lists

Clicking on a button causes the event associated with that button to be processed. Sometimes, however, you want to combine several events together. Use the <Define Event List> command to consolidate up to six events into one identifier.

Define Event List Command

The parameters *event1* through *event6* can be treated as invocations of previously defined events. Thus, if an event requires a direct object, that direct object is specified in the parameter of the <Define Event List> command. An event list cannot itself contain a direct object. Guide Maker has no way of knowing which of the events to associate with the direct object.

If you have an event that is repeatedly used with the same direct object, you can define an event list that consists of only that one event, with the direct object specified in the <Define Event List> command. This can make for more readable code in your guide file. For example, consider the following <Define Event> command, which requires a direct object:

```
<Define Event> "PrintDocument", FRONT, 'aevt', 'pdoc'
```

If you find that you are using this event repeatedly with the same parameter, you might make an event list out of it. Thus, instead of writing:

```
<Standard Button> "Print Log", CENTER,
    PrintDocument("HD:Accounting:Transaction Log")
```

you could define an event list:

```
<Define Event List> "PrintLog"
    PrintDocument("HD:Accounting:Transaction Log")
```

and change the <Standard Button> command to:

```
<Standard Button> "Print Log", CENTER, PrintLog()
```

Syntax:	**<Define Event List>** eventListName, event1 [, event2] [, event3] [, event4] [, event5] [, event6]

Example:	Given these event definitions to print a document and then quit an application:
	
	```<Define Event> "PrintDocument", FRONT, 'aevt', 'pdoc'```
	```<Define Event> "QuitApplication", FRONT, 'aevt', 'quit'```
	
	you can create an event list as follows:
	
	```<Define Event List> "PrintLogAndQuit", PrintDocument("HD:Accounting:TransactionLog"), QuitApplication```

Limitations:	Up to six events can be combined in an event list; each may contain a direct object, but the event list itself cannot contain one.
When to Use:	As needed.

ATTACHING EVENTS TO PANELS

Events can be attached to buttons and hot objects in panels. When the user clicks them the event is processed. You can also attach events to panels, causing them to be processed in any of four cases:

- When the panel is created by Apple Guide, prior to its being shown.
- When the panel is destroyed by Apple Guide, after it has been closed.
- When the panel is shown, either after it is created or when the window's zoom box is clicked to expand a previously compressed window. A parameter lets you control whether the event is processed only the first time the panel is shown, or in all cases when it is shown.
- When the panel is hidden, either when it is being closed or when the window's zoom box is clicked and the panel is minimized. A parameter lets you control whether the event is processed only the first time the panel is hidden, or in all cases when it is hidden.

The commands are placed between the <Define Panel> and <End Panel> commands. The syntax for all four commands is similar.

On Panel Create and On Panel Destroy Commands

The *eventFunction* parameter is an event or event list that you have defined with the <Define Event> or <Define Event List> commands. Any direct object is enclosed in parentheses following the function name. If there is no direct object, the parentheses are required, but they enclose nothing. Although spaces normally do not matter in Guide Maker (except when enclosed in a quoted string), it does not like a space between the last character of the *eventFunction* parameter and the opening parenthesis.

You can have a number of <On Panel Create> or <On Panel Destroy> commands in any panel definition.

Syntax:	**\<On Panel Create\>** *eventFunction*
	\<On Panel Destroy\> *eventFunction*
Example:	`<On Panel Create>`
	`    DoScript("ScriptToBeProcessedOnCreate")`
	`<On Panel Destroy> PlaySound("Congratulations")`
When to Use:	As needed.

On Panel Show and On Panel Hide Commands

These commands cause the events to be processed not only when the panel is created or destroyed, but also when it is shown or hidden as a result of the user clicking the zoom box in the Apple Guide presentation window, which causes the panel to be compressed so that only the title and navigation bars are visible; the contents of the panel are hidden.

The *firstOrAlways* parameter is one of the constants FIRST and ALWAYS. If omitted, the default value is ALWAYS. Use FIRST if you want the event to be processed only the first time the panel is shown or hidden.

As with the preceding commands, you can attach multiple \<On Panel Show\> and \<On Panel Hide\> commands to a given panel.

Syntax:	**\<On Panel Show\>** *eventFunction [, firstOrAlways]*
Example:	The first command is executed whenever the panel is shown; the second command is executed only the first time the panel is destroyed:
	`<On Panel Show> DoScript`
	`   ("ScriptToBeProcessedWheneverPanelIsShown")`
	`<On Panel Destroy> DoScript`
	`   ("ScriptToBeProcessedWhenPanelIsHiddenFirstTime`
	`   "), FIRST`
When to Use:	As needed.

PUTTING IT TOGETHER: EVENTS AND CONTEXT CHECKS IN APPLE GUIDE

The context checks of the last chapter and the events of this chapter can be interwoven to provide a valuable service to the user.

Assisting the User in Setting the Mouse Control Panel

In coaching the user how to adjust the Mouse control panel (for track speed and double-click speed), it is necessary to first make certain that the Mouse control panel is open. In the following excerpt from Macintosh Guide, the authors guarantee that the Mouse control panel is open. First, a context check is used to check whether it is already open.

```
<SKIP IF>ActiveWindow('MACS',"Mouse")
    <PANEL> "Mouse control panel: opening"
```

If the context check fails (that is, if the Mouse control panel is not active), the user is prompted to open it in the "Mouse control panel: opening" panel, which looks like this:

```
<DEFINE PANEL>"Mouse control panel: opening"
<FORMAT> "Tag"
Do This
<FORMAT> "Body"
Open the Mouse control panel.
<COACH MARK>"Finder Coach Mouse"
<END PANEL>
```

All would be well and good except that the "Finder Coach Mouse" coach mark circles the Mouse control panel in the Control Panels window. What if that window is not open? The actual sequence of code in Macintosh Guide includes a third line, as follows:

```
SKIP IF>ActiveWindow('MACS',"Mouse")
    <MAKE SURE>ActiveWindow('MACS',"Control Panels"),"Auto open:
    Control Panels folder seq"
```

```
<PANEL> "Mouse control panel: opening"
```

Remember that if the context check is true (the Active window is the Mouse control panel), both the <Make Sure> and <Panel> commands will be skipped. If the context check fails, before the user is prompted to open the Mouse control panel, the <Make Sure> command guarantees that the Control Panels window is the active window. If it is not, the Oops sequence, "Auto open: Control Panels folder seq" is launched. And here is that sequence:

```
<DEFINE SEQUENCE>"Auto open: Control Panels folder seq"
<SEQ NAV BUTTON SET>NONE
<DEFINE PANEL>"Auto open: Control Panels folder"
<FORMAT> "Full"
Please wait a moment. Apple Guide is assisting you by opening the
Control Panels folder.
<3D BUTTON>1070,1072, Center, GoBack() # This is a Continue button
<On Panel Show>DoAppleScript(":Open AppleScripts:Open Control
   Panels folder")
<PANEL PROMPT>"AG Opened folder"
<END PANEL>
<END SEQUENCE>
```

When the panel is shown, an AppleScript is invoked (see the underlined code in the example above) that opens the Control Panels folder. Here is the AppleScript:

```
tell application "Finder"
    if application "Finder" is not frontmost then activate
    open control panels folder
end tell
```

Thus, if the <Make Sure> command detects that the Control Panels folder is not open, this Oops sequence, consisting of only one panel is shown. As soon as the panel is shown, the AppleScript is launched, and the user is told by the panel's text that Apple Guide is opening the Control Panels folder. Note that there are no navigation buttons in this sequence: the only way the user can continue is by clicking the **Continue** button (or closing the window).

The AG Opened Folder prompt set makes this clear:

```
<DEFINE PROMPT SET>        "AG Opened folder",
   "After the folder opens, click Continue.",
   "After the folder opens, click Continue.",
   "After the folder opens, click Continue.",
   " "
```

NOTE

The context checks and events in this excerpt are all built in to Apple Guide; a full description of these and the other built-in events is found at the end of this chapter.

Who Does What When

You might be tempted to think that two different approaches to the interface have been taken in the excerpt above: the Control Panels folder is opened automatically but the user is coached to open the Mouse control panel. In fact, the structures are parallel. In the section of code that precedes the lines shown here, the user is prompted to open the Control Panels folder in the same way in which the "Mouse control panel: opening" panel prompts the opening of the Mouse control panel. It is only if the user has not done this (or has clicked on another window so that the Control Panels folder is no longer the active window) that the Control Panels folder is automatically opened.

Such consistency is very important in guide files. People can learn very quickly how to respond to subtle cues in their environment, but this process is slowed and hindered when those cues are inconsistent. The Macintosh user interface goes a long way towards making the user interface consistent; each application—even when it conforms to the interface guidelines—develops its own environment in which the user quickly learns how to function. (An example of the unique environment of applications is the difference between the treatment of Preferences in Microsoft Word, where it's in the Tool menu, and in Microsoft Excel, where individual preferences, such as Toolbars, appear in the Options menu.)

Take the time to develop a design for your guide file's behavior that users will come to expect. A common design is as follows:

1. If no user action is needed, don't do anything. In other words, don't tell the user to open a window that is already open.

2. If an action is needed, tell the user to do it.

3. Assume that the user has done the action, but check to make sure. If it has not been done, launch an Oops sequence to automatically do it, telling the user that you are doing it, and prompting the user to click a **Continue** button when the action is complete.

There are other possibilities. For example, you could replace step 3 above with the following rule:

3a. Offer the user additional assistance (coaching, explanations, and so on) in performing the action.

Or,

3b. Offer the user a choice of additional assistance or a **Do It for Me** button.

In either case, make it clear how your guide file will behave in different circumstances. If you sometimes do the task for the user and sometimes don't, users will never know where they are.

Sometimes, you are constrained by other factors in the environment. If you are coaching an application that cannot perform a task, step 3a is the only possible solution. Then, for the sake of consistency, you can have to consider whether to automatically perform other tasks that are possible to carry out. One solution to this problem is to place a **Do It for Me** button on the Do This panel (rather than on the panel in the Oops sequence). This makes it clear that sometimes your guide file can carry out the action and sometimes (when the **Do It for Me** button isn't present) it cannot.

Remember that people react well to situations that they can understand and control, so make certain that there is a consistent, understandable logic to your guide files, and that users are always in control.

N O T E   An interesting consequence of this very human desire for understanding and control is the lengths to which people will go to find logic in a situation, even when it does not exist. Apple Guide provides you with enough tools to provide explicit and subliminal cues so that people need not construct their own (often bizarre) explanations for how guide files work. By combining panel text, the prompts at the bottom of the panel, buttons, and panel graphics, you should be able to make clear to the user whether the next panel will simply be more text, will check for and correct any errors, or will provide an option to carry out a task. The user is working with your guide file to get assistance in carrying out a task: don't make the assistance yet another obstacle to the user's objective.

BUILT-IN EVENT FUNCTIONS

There are 10 built-in event functions available to you: seven are provided by Guide Maker, and three others are defined in Standard Includes. Together with the built-in external code modules that perform basic context checks for you, you can create truly powerful guide files.

Using AppleScript Scripts as Events

AppleScript provides a common scripting language that can be used across many applications, from HyperCard, to QuarkXPress, to WordPerfect, to Excel, and even to the Finder. ScriptEditor, included with the Mac OS, lets you write, save, and execute AppleScript scripts. Some applications are recordable. You can have ScriptEditor (or another editing program) record your actions as you use an application. The resulting AppleScript commands can then be saved, edited, and executed. To complete its flexibility, AppleScript stores its commands in an internal format that is independent of the natural language of the user. Dialects exist so that you can write an AppleScript script in the English language dialect and convert it effortlessly to the French language dialect. Obviously, this makes for big savings in development, maintenance, and documentation of AppleScript scripts.

A single AppleScript script can send commands to several applications, combining them into custom solutions or hiding the intricacies of networks and file servers from users. Just as AppleScript can tie together several pieces of a complex operation, you can use Apple Guide to join together several AppleScript processes. Whereas AppleScript is particularly convenient for processing tasks and passing information back and forth, Apple Guide is particularly useful for providing a user interface that is very easy to use and understand. Together, they can be an unbeatable combination for custom solutions.

Preparing an AppleScript for Use As an Event

Write the script using ScriptEditor (or any other similar application). Test it thoroughly to make certain that it works, and make any changes that are necessary.

When you are finished, save it as a compiled script, which you will reference from your guide file.

Alternatively, you can use ResEdit to copy the 'scpt' resource from a compiled file or AppleScript application into the resource fork of a file. You can then use the <Resource> command to include that resource in your guide file.

DoAppleScript/DoScript

The DoScript or DoAppleScript event function can be used anywhere another event function would be used: attached to a button, in an event list, and so on.

DoScript/DoAppleScript Event Function

This is actually one function with two names. The *scriptResource* is either the name of a compiled AppleScript script (relative to the location of your source file), or the resource ID of a 'scpt' resource that you have extracted from an AppleScript file or application and inserted into a resource file as described previously. (Remember that if you are using the 'scpt' resource, you must have included the resource in your guide file with the <Resource> command.)

There is no difference between the DoScript and DoAppleScript functions.

Syntax:	**DoScript** (*scriptResource*)
	or
	DoAppleScript (*scriptResource*)
Example:	`DoAppleScript` `(":Compiled Apple Scripts:Repaginate Document")`
When to Use:	As needed.

Navigating With Built-In Events

Eight built-in functions allow you to attach navigation commands to buttons, panels, and event lists. The functions with parameters are built into Guide Maker, those without parameters are defined in Standard Definitions, which must be included in your guide file if you use them.

GoPanel Event Function

The <GoPanel> command displays the specified panel in the current sequence. The *panelNumber* parameter identifies the panel's sequence, with the first panel being 1, the second 2, and so on. As with all go to statements, this can easily cause problems. In the development of your guide file, panels are often inserted or removed, throwing panel numbers off. Just as in standard programming languages, if you notice <GoPanel> commands in your guide files, consider replacing the structure with If/Then/Else syntax.

Syntax:	**GoPanel**(panelNumber)
Example:	GoPanel(1)
When to Use:	Rarely. Try to restructure with If/Then/Else.

LaunchNewSequence Event Function

Sometimes you want to launch a new sequence as soon as the user clicks a button or other control. In other cases, you ask the user to click a check box or radio button and launch a new sequence depending on the control's value, but only when the user clicks the right arrow to continue. In the first case you use the LaunchNewSequence event function, attaching it to the control that you want to launch the new sequence. In the second case, you use the <Checkbox> or <Radio Button> commands described in Chapter 10, "Panels III Controls."

The parameter *sequenceName* is the name of a sequence that you have defined elsewhere in your guide file.

The LaunchNewSequence event closes the current window and launches the new sequence in its own window. The number of Apple Guide windows remains the same as before the LaunchNewSequence event was called.

For the sake of consistency, you should establish a standard in your guide file for how new sequences are launched. Avoid sometimes using the two-step process of a check box or radio button selection followed by the right arrow and other times using a button or hot object with the LaunchNewSequence event function attached.

Syntax:	**LaunchNewSequence**(*sequenceName*)
Example:	`LaunchNewSequence("HowTo:Remove The Background")`
When to Use:	As needed, but subject to the consistency constraint mentioned previously.

LaunchNewSequenceNewWindow Event Function

The LaunchNewSequenceNewWindow event function is identical to the LaunchNewSequence event, except that the new sequence is launched in its own window that is opened in addition to the previously opened Apple Guide windows. After the LaunchNewSequenceNewWindow event is processed, there is one more Apple Guide window open than before it was processed.

Syntax:	**LaunchNewSequenceNewWindow**(*sequenceName*)
Example:	`LaunchNewSequenceNewWindow("HowTo:Remove The Background")`
When to Use:	As needed, but subject to the consistency constraint mentioned for the LaunchNewSequence event function.

StartTopicOops Function

Oops sequences (and their syntactically identical companions, Continue sequences) are normally launched from <Make Sure> commands that fail. Apple Guide manages the opening and returning from the sequence with no additional help from you. Sometimes, you want to explicitly start and return from an Oops sequence. You can use the StartTopicOops event function for that purpose. The *sequenceName* parameter is the name of any Oops sequence that you have defined elsewhere in your guide file.

Syntax:	**StartTopicOops**(*sequenceName*)
Example:	`StartTopicOops("Doing:Remove The Background")`
When to Use:	Rarely. Use the <Make Sure> or <Start Making Sure> commands, which automatically manage the Oops sequence.

QuitTopicOops Function

Like the StartTopicOops event function, QuitTopicOops is rarely used, but is presented here for completeness. The optional parameter *panelNumber* is the number of the panel in the original sequence to which to return. If it is omitted, QuitTopicOops returns to the panel from which it came.

Syntax:	**QuitTopicOops**(*[panelNumber]*)
Example:	QuitTopicOops(3)
When to Use:	Rarely. Use the GoBack event function described later. QuitTopicOops with its explicit panel number poses all the potential problems of the GoPanel event function.

DoHuh Event

The DoHuh event has the same effect as if the user had clicked the **Huh?** button. If the **Huh?** button does not exist or is dimmed, nothing will happen. DoHuh is defined in Standard Definitions; you must either include this file in your guide file or include the definition:

```
<Define Event> "DoHuh", 's***', 'help', 'dhuh'
```

You might attach a DoHuh event to a hot object that you want to function in the same way as the **Huh?** button.

Syntax:	**DoHuh**()
Example:	<Hot Text> "Explanation", FIRST, DoHuh()
When to Use:	Rarely. Let the user use the **Huh?** button; you can be adding inconsistent behavior to your guide file.

GoBack Event Function

The GoBack event function is most often attached to the **OK** or **Continue** button at the end of an Oops or Continue sequence. It returns the user to the last successful panel in the main sequence. (Remember that <Make Sure> conditions are reevaluated as the GoBack event is processed; the user might be returned to an even earlier position in the guide file if intervening events have caused other <Make Sure> conditions to fail.)

DoHuh is defined in Standard Definitions; you must either include this file in your guide file or include the definition:

```
<Define Event> "GoBack", 's***', 'help', 'gobk'
```

Syntax:	**GoBack()**
Example:	`<Standard Button> "OK", CENTER, GoBack()`
When to Use:	Always for the OK or Continue button in an Oops or Continue sequence.

GoStart Event Function

The GoStart event function returns the user to the access window. It is usually attached to the **GoStart** button at the left of the navigation bar.

GoStart is defined in Standard Definitions. You must either include this file in your guide file or include the definition:

```
<Define Event> "GoStart", 's***', 'help', 'stac'
```

Syntax:	**GoStart()**
Example:	`<Define Nav Button>"GoStart",103,113,123,GoStart()`
When to Use:	Almost always for your standard navigation bar buttons.

Sound as an Event

The last function provided with Apple Guide allows you to play a sound resource. Be careful with sounds! As with color, sound should never be the sole means of communicating information. Speakers can be turned off or unplugged, users may be hearing-impaired, the room may be noisy, or many other circumstances could cause the sound to be lost or misinterpreted.

You may be tempted to associate a sound with an Oops panel, using the <On Panel Create> command. Consider the temptation before you act on it. Apple Guide windows are always front-most on the computer screen: the user is not likely to miss seeing them. Furthermore, you are supposed to be providing a service that is supportive and helpful; calling undue attention to an errorpossibly attracting attention to the user in a crowded room of other peopleis hardly helpful. Sound can be valuable as an additional means of communicating when the information is of more importance than usual. An Oops sequence invoked because the application that you are coaching is no longer running might legitimately earn such a higher degree of importance, as would the loss of a network file server, the unexplained change in configuration of the computer (for example, a change in monitor depth in the midst of a color-intensive process), and so on.

PlaySound Event Function

The *soundResource* parameter can be either the ID of a resource that you have included in your guide file using the <Resource> command or the name of a file (relative to your source code) that contains a sound resource.

Syntax:	**PlaySound** (*soundResource*)
Example:	<On Panel Destroy> PlaySound(":Sounds:End of Chapter Sigh")
When to Use:	For important notification only. Sounds are not always heard and may be annoying to people nearby.

SUMMARY

This chapter concludes the Guide Script commands. You should feel relatively comfortable with the basic concepts of Apple Guide:

- Access windowsthe way users navigate to the information of a guide file
- Panelsthe information shown to users, together with coach marks and controls, such as buttons and hot objects
- Sequencesthe panels that are shown as the user navigates with navigation bar buttons and panel controls; the conditions and context checks that can alter that sequence; and the events that can be invoked by conditions and panel controls

CHAPTER 14

Mixins

You can modify a guide file at the time it is opened by using *mixins*. When a guide file is opened, mixin files that are coresident with it are examined to see whether they should be combined with the main guide file. If they pass the tests, their contents are added to (or removed from) the main guide file. This allows you to customize guide files on the fly.

There are several reasons for using mixins, but the most frequent one is when major sections of your assistance are only applicable to a certain configuration of hardware, application software (such as a specific version), or the system software environment. In the Macintosh interface, menu items are typically disabled and grayed-out when a certain command is unavailable. Because topic areas and index headers (not to mention topics themselves) cannot be grayed-out in the Apple Guide Access windows, users click on items only to find out that it is inappropriate to provide assistance on that topic (typically when you use a context check to make sure that there is a printer attached, and so forth).

Although this paradigm is appropriate in many cases, if you have a topic area that is large, such as an area relating to speech synthesis, it can be annoying to the user to see all of this information if PlainTalk text-to-speech is not installed. In such a case, you might only want to add that topic area if you have ascertained that PlainTalk is available. If it is not, you might want to do nothing, or to install a much smaller topic area with one sequence that explains what PlainTalk is and how to get it. This is a perfect job for a mixin.

Another case where a mixin is appropriate is where you have a temporary modification to a main guide file, often because a bug requires a different set of instructions or because a minor revision has added or modified functionality of the application.

Remember that other ways of customizing guide files are at compilation time, using the <Include> command to compile certain sequences or not, and during execution, using context checks.

N O T E

MANAGING MIXIN FILES

The <Mixin> command allows you to create a mixin file. The <Mixin Match> command determines whether a specific guide file should be merged with a main guide file when the main guide file is opened. If <Gestalt> commands are present in the mixin file, these are executed as well when the main guide file is opened and Apple Guide is determining whether to mix in a mixin file. If <App Creator> was specified, that test is also performed before considering a mixin file for inclusion in a main guide file. All Gestalt and <App Creator> tests must pass and the mixin match (if present) must also pass before the mixin file is in fact added to the main file.

<Mixin> Command

The <Mixin> command specifies that a guide file is to be compiled as a mixin file (type 'mixn'). The *symNameOrStartResNum* parameter identifies either the guide file to which it will be mixed in (specifically the .SYM file for that guide file that Guide Maker produced during compilation) or it identifies the resource number that Guide Maker should use to start assigning the resources that it creates from the mixin guide file source.

If you are defining topics, topic areas, and so forth, you can use either the .SYM file or the resource number in *symNameOrStartResNum*. If you will be deleting, inserting, or replacing items, you must use the .SYM file.

Syntax:	**<Mixin>** *symNameOrStartResNum*
Example:	`<Mixin> "Virgil Help.SYM"`
	or
	`<Mixin> "5000"`
Limitations:	The <Mixin> command must be the first line of the source code file.
When to Use:	Whenever you create a mixin file.

<Mixin Match> Command

The <Mixin Match> command provides a further link between a main guide file and a mixin file. The *matchingCreator* parameter is a four-character value in the mixin file that must match a corresponding value in the main guide file for Apple Guide to actually mix in the mixin file. Use the <Mixin Match> command with identical values for *matchingCreator* in both the main and mixin files.

The mixin match value can be used to link versions of files, with a mixin file used to temporarily modify the main guide file to reflect an anomaly ("bug" or "workaround"). Thus if you are using a mixin guide file as a temporary addition to the main guide file to cover such a situation, the mixin match value might be '1.0'. When a revision of the software—and its main guide file—is done, the mixin match value for the main guide file might be '2.0'. The 1.0 mixin match value for the mixin file would not match and it would no longer be mixed into the (new) main guide file, which presumably incorporates the modification that was previously done on the fly with the mixin file.

N O T E The absence of a <Mixin Match> command is taken as a value. Thus, a guide file with no <Mixin Match> command matches only with a mixin file that also contains no <Mixin Match> command. The value '****' matches any guide file, but must be specified explicitly with a <Mixin Match> command.

Syntax:	**\<Mixin Match\>** *matchingCreator*
Example:	`<Mixin Match> "PSM3"`
Limitations:	The \<Mixin Match\> command should appear only once in each guide file (the mixin and the main guide file).
When to Use:	Whenever you create a mixin file.

USING GUIDE SCRIPT COMMANDS IN MIXIN FILES

You can use any of the Guide Script commands that you would use in a main guide file in a mixin guide file. That is, you can create topics, sequences, panels, and so forth. If you are using a .SYM file in the *symNameOrStartResNum* parameter of the \<Mixin\> command, Guide Maker is able to access information from the main guide file at compilation time. This information consists of the topics, topic areas, sequences, and so forth of the main guide file. Prompts, formats, and other objects that are defined in the main guide file are not available to the mixin guide file: you must specify (or respecify) them. (This is a case where the judicious use of \<Include\> files can save time and typing.)

MIXIN-SPECIFIC COMMANDS

To use mixin-specific commands, you must specify a .SYM file in the *symNameOrStartResNum* parameter of the \<Mixin\> command. Without it, Guide Maker has no way of locating the referenced objects and cannot generate code for the mixin file.

The mixin-specific commands are of three types:

- Insert commands let you replace headers and topics.
- Delete commands let you remove items from a main guide file.
- The Replace command lets you replace a sequence.

Insert Commands

In deciding how to structure your main and mixin files, you can choose from two strategies. You can use the insert commands to add items to your main guide file that are appropriate for a specific configuration (for example, when two monitors are present) or you can use the delete commands to delete items from the main file that are inappropriate for that configuration. The choice is most often made so that the most frequent case will not require modification. Thus, if your users generally do not have two monitors, you would insert items in the case where they did have two monitors. If your users generally do have access to a network, you would delete items with a mixin file for the few users who do not have that access. Your goal should be to do the minimum with your mixin files. This makes it easier to maintain your guide files and provides some efficiencies when Apple Guide opens the guide file and performs the mixin process.

Of course, if you are using mixin files to modify the main guide file to reflect modifications to (or bugs in) your application, you have no choice; you do whatever is appropriate.

Insert Commands

You can insert topics and headers within topic areas and index terms using a mixin file. To insert a new topic area or a new index term, use the <Topic Area> or <Index> commands, which are discussed in Chapter 11, "Sequences IDefinitions and Controls." (The <Topic Area> command has an option *mixinOrder* parameter that allows you to specify where the new topic area should be inserted.)

Because you use the standard commands to create topic areas or index items, it is only necessary for Guide Maker to provide you with special mixin commands to insert headers and topics under existing topic areas or index items.

Inserting Headers and Topics to Topic Areas

Two commands let you modify an existing topic area.

<Insert Topic Area Header> Command

If you want to add a header to an existing topic area, use the <Insert Topic Area Header> command. This header will have no topics, unless you explicitly add them with the <Insert Topic Area Topic> command (discussed next). The parameter *sortOrder* consists of either the constants FIRST or LAST, or a string containing the name of the already-defined header, which should immediately precede the new inserted header.

Syntax:	**<Insert Topic Area Header>** header, topicArea [, sortOrder]
Example:	`<Insert Topic Area Header> "New features in version 2.0", "File"`
When to Use:	As needed.

Insert Topic Area Topic> Command

You use this command to add a new topic to a header, either one that exists in the main file or one that you have created in your mixin file with the <Insert Topic Area Header> command.

The *seqName* sequence is associated with the new topic.

Syntax:	**<Insert Topic Area Topic>** topic, seqName, topicArea [, sortOrder]
Example:	`<Insert Topic Area Topic> "Disk-mirroring", "About Disk-mirroring", "Files"`
When to Use:	As needed.

Inserting Topics and Headers to Index Items

A pair of comparable commands let you add topics and headers to index terms.

<Insert Index Header> Command

If you want to add a header, to an existing index term , use the <Insert Index Header> command. This header will have no topics, unless you explicitly add them with the <Insert Index Topic> command (discussed next).

Syntax:	**<Insert Index Header>** *header, indexTerm [, sortOrder]*
Example:	`<Insert Index Header> "New features in version 2.0", "files"`
When to Use:	As needed.

Insert Index Topic Command

You use this command to add a new topic to an index term, either one that exists in the main file or one you have created in your mixin file with the <Insert Index Header> command.

The *seqName* sequence is associated with the new topic.

Syntax:	**<Insert Index Topic>** *topic, seqName, indexTerm [, sortOrder]*
Example:	`<Insert Index Topic> "Disk-mirroring", "About Disk-mirroring", "files"`
When to Use:	As needed.

Delete Commands

In a Full Access window, you can create topics and headers that are presented within topic areas or index items. These are shown when the **Topics** or **Index** button is clicked in the Full Access window. Commands for deleting them are divided into those that apply to topic areas and those that apply to the index view.

Deleting Topics Areas and Their Components

In the Full Access window, you can define topic areas that contain topics. You can optionally place a header below the topic area to group topics. Thus, you may have the following group of phrases (taken from Macintosh Guide):

Files—topic area

How do I—header

open an Item?—topic

The commands discussed in this section let you delete any such items from a main guide file with commands in the mixin file.

<Delete Topic Area> Command

This command deletes the highest level of object shown in the Topics view of a Full Access window. Topic areas are shown in the left pane of the Full Access window. An example is "Files" in the phrases shown previously.

Syntax:	**<Delete Topic Area>** *topicArea*
Example:	`<Delete Topic Area> "Files"`
When to Use:	As needed.

<Delete Topic Area Header> Command

This commands deletes the header that you may have specified beneath a topic area, "How do I" in the previous example. You specify the topic area in which the header is found in the *topicArea* command.

Syntax:	**<Delete Topic Area Header>** *topicArea, topicAreaHeader*
Example:	`<Delete Topic Area Header> "Files", "How do I"`
When to Use:	As needed.

<Delete Topic Area Topic> Command

If you want to delete a topic from a topic area, such as "open an item?" in the previous example, use this command.

Syntax:	**<Delete Topic Area Topic>** *topicArea, topicAreaTopic*
Example:	`<Delete Topic Area Topic> "Files", "open an Item?"`
When to Use:	As needed.

Deleting Index Items and Their Components

Similarly, you can have headers and topics within index terms. An example from the Macintosh Guide file is

files—index item

How do I—header

create a folder?—topic

<Delete Index> Command

This command deletes an index item, "files," in the previous example.

Syntax:	**<Delete Index>** *indexTerm*
Example:	<Delete Index> "files"
When to Use:	As needed.

<Delete Index Header> Command

To delete a header that was placed beneath an index ("How do I" in the example), use this command.

Syntax:	**<Delete Index Header>** *indexTerm, indexHeader*
Example:	<Delete Index Header> "files", "How do I"
When to Use:	As needed.

<Delete Index Topic> Command

Finally, to delete a topic from an index term, use the <Delete Index Topic> command.

Syntax:	**<Delete Index Topic>** *indexTerm, indexTopic*
Example:	<Delete Index Topic> "files", "create a folder?"
When to Use:	As needed.

Replace Command

The final mixin command is the simplest. It allows you to replace a sequence from a main guide file with one from the mixin guide file.

<Replace Sequence> Command

This is a very simple way to correct misspellings or other errors in the main guide file. By replacing the sequence with a mixin file, you can minimize the potential side effects that could occur if you recompiled the main guide file incorporating a trivial change.

Syntax:	**<Replace Sequence>** *oldSequenceName, newSequenceName*
Example:	`<Replace Sequence> "sequence with misspellings",` `   "corrected sequence"`
When to Use:	As needed.

SUMMARY

Using mixin guide files, you can easily modify your main guide file to accommodate itself to specific environmental considerations, as well as to easily make minor modifications reflecting errors in either the main guide file or the application.

Using Guide Maker and Organizing Source Files

Now that you've seen the concepts of Apple Guide and the syntax of Guide Script, all that remains is to write and compile your own guide files. In this chapter, you will see how to use Guide Maker, Apple's tool for compiling and debugging guide files.

An important point to remember is that the tools you have available to you are the same tools that were available to the authors and designers of Macintosh Guide. Guide Maker and the external code modules from Standard Resources—together with a lot of thought, design, and experimentation—are all that were used to develop the basic assistance that ships with System 7.5. Anything you see in Macintosh Guide can be achieved with the tools provided here.

All of the files and resources mentioned in this chapter—Guide Maker, Standard Resources, the basic XTND system, guide file template documents—are located on the CD-ROM that accompanies this book.

NOTE

One often-overlooked feature of Guide Maker is its testing and diagnostic features. All panels should be reviewed for spelling, syntax, adherence to standards (your own and those of the Mac OS). When you use context checks to conditionally show or hide panels, it is easy to miss a few. Using Guide Maker's utilities which ignore the context checks makes it easy to test your guide file.

In this chapter, the main points of Guide Maker use are covered:

- Creating and Building Guide Files with Guide Maker
- Testing Look For Phrases with Guide Maker
- Converting and Localizing Guide Files
- Guide Maker Utilities and Reports

CREATING AND BUILDING GUIDE FILES WITH GUIDE MAKER

Guide Maker is designed to be used in conjunction with a word processing application which you use to actually create the source file for your Apple Guide assistance. Styled text (colors, fonts, underlining, etc.) is used for clarity of the guide files that the user sees and of the source files which you develop. (Windows Help implements the equivalent of Guide Script commands with some of these text styles. In Apple Guide, text styles are used in whatever way the author feels is appropriate to convey information to users; Guide Script commands are commands and text styles are text styles in Apple Guide.)

The <Format> commands which you use in your guide file may override the styling that you have applied to the Guide Script commands in your source file. For example, the font, size, and style of text in most Apple Guide windows is standard — 10 point Espy Serif black. The styling that you apply to Guide Script commands themselves (<Define Panel>, <If>, etc.) makes no difference in the guide file produced by Guide Maker. Many Apple Guide authors use these facts to take advantage of the styles in their word processing applications to make the source code of their guide files more legible.

The shell guide files on the CD-ROM include several variations of guide file layout, and include WordPerfect and Microsoft Word samples which use document styles to make the source code more legible. These should be taken as examples, not hard and fast rules.

Using XTND translators

Guide Maker uses the XTND translation system to read your source files. This system allows files created by one application to be read by another. An excellent way of easily moving among applications from different vendors, XTND suffers from one significant problem: not all vendors fully support it. Many vendors feel that it is in their best interests to be able to read files created in other applications but not to export them. (The logic apparently is that their product is the ultimate achievement in its category, and there is no reason why you would ever want to take a document and work on it in another environment.) Anyone who has used a desktop publishing program to import text from word processing applications has run up against this problem. Having created your newsletter or brochure, there is no Export command to reverse the process, creating a plain-text version suitable for posting to an on-line service.

Fortunately, XTND translators are fairly easy to obtain—the basic XTND system and basic translators are included on the CD-ROM. If you are uncertain as to whether or not you have an XTND translator, take any word processing document (not necessarily Guide Maker input) and attempt to use it as a source file for a Guide Maker build. If you get a clean compilation or syntax errors, you have the translator. If you don't have the translator, Guide Maker will give you the error message, "Could not find an appropriate XTND translator for this text file."

XTND translators should bring all of your styled text into Guide Maker. On occasion—particularly in documents with many styles—XTND may get a little confused. If you find styling information in the wrong places in your guide files (wrong color text, for example), save the source file to a new file with the Save As... command. This should eliminate the problem.

Creating Source Files Without XTND Translators

If you do not have an XTND translator that Guide Maker can use to read your source file, you can create your source file as a plain text file using TeachText or SimpleText. With the Guide Script <Define Format> command, you can style the text for presentation to the user in whatever font, size, color, etc. you want. You can also save a word processing document as a plain text file.

Organizing Source Files for Guide Maker

The easiest way to manage the source files for your guide files is to create a folder for each guide file, and to use a make file with <Include> commands to combine the necessary files. A sub-folder can be created to contain AppleScript files referenced by the guide file, and you may want to create another sub-folder for PICT graphics and other resources that will be included.

The sample files in The Cookbook folder on the CD-ROM will give you a number of suggestions as to how to organize your source code.

Standard Resources is included in most guide files—it contains that basic external code modules and a number of 3D buttons. A common modification to it is to remove PICT graphics 501 and 502 from Standard Resources: these are the default images that Apple Guide places at the top of an access window. You generally want your own graphic or at least your application name using the <App Text> command. Versions both with and without these graphics are on the CD-ROM.

If you are writing several guide files for a single application or project, you may place all the files in a single folder, with separate make files for each guide file. This facilitates re-use of source code.

TESTING LOOK FOR PHRASES WITH GUIDE MAKER

Rather than just providing the user with a list of keywords, Apple Guide also provides the user with the possibility of typing in a word or phrase to locate information. (See Chapter 7, "Access Windows.") It is safe to say that no one can create a useful set of look for keywords without extensive testing. The Test Look For window is invaluable for this purpose, particularly if you have used the <Exception>, <Ignore>, and <Synonym> commands (as you should have).

Figure 15.1 shows the Test Look For window with the result of several searches.

The current phrase being searched is "mouse pads." As you can see from the top window, "pads" is stemmed to "pad" and "mouse" is left alone. Although there are hits on "mouse," there are none on "pad". It is important that people other than the Apple Guide designers test the look for feature. Just as an office secretary—and no one else—knows that sugar packets are stored in a file drawer marked "C" (for coffee), your idiosyncratic usages, spellings, and synaptic leaps need to be checked in the prism of other people's searches.

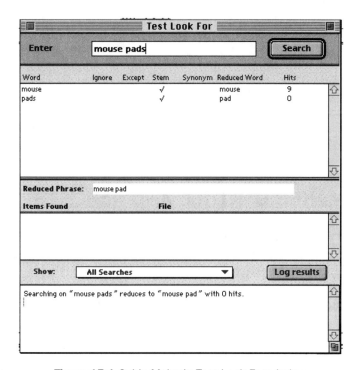

Figure 15.1 Guide Maker's Test Look For window.

CONVERTING AND LOCALIZING GUIDE FILES

Guide Maker is able to read Windows Help source files and convert them to Apple Guide source files. Because Windows Help and Apple Guide have distinct and different points of view, the conversion cannot be total or automatic, but it often comes close. Chapter 26, "Apple Guide and Windows Help," explores this issue in detail.

Guide Maker can also assist in the localization of your guide files. The Localize menu contains commands that extract strings from panel definitions and other Guide Script commands, storing them in a file, which you can then translate to another language or dialect. The strings are identified as to their source, and Guide Maker saves a file with references to where in your source files the strings came from. After translation, you can then merge the translated strings back in, recompile, and have a translated guide file ready to go. Chapter 27, "Localizing Apple Guide," discusses this process more fully.

NOTE

The extracted strings can be used for purposes other than translation. Because all visible text is extracted during this process, a copy editor may find it easier to edit the extracted text rather than the source files with Guide Script commands interspersed. Of course, the final edit and quality control check must be done using Apple Guide itself, reviewing the panels as they are actually shown.

GUIDE MAKER UTILITIES AND REPORTS

Guide Maker has a number of utilities and reports that can provide diagnostics helpful in managing Apple Guide projects. The .SYM file that is automatically created during guide file compilation contains information that is displayed in many of these reports. Particularly if you are managing large Apple Guide projects with several people working on guide files, you may find the reports useful in making certain that the project is under control.

In addition to the static reports, Guide Maker allows you to display sequences and panels directly, without having the target application open. This can provide an easy way of doing a final check of a guide file. The alternate extension, Apple Guide.Debug, can be installed instead of Apple Guide itself. If the debug version is installed, even more extensive diagnostics are provided by Guide Maker.

SUMMARY

Guide Maker provides an array of services to the Apple Guide author that should make the creation of useful assistance fairly easy. Although some of the support tools may seem like overkill for a small Apple Guide project, nowhere is it written that you must use them all. It is hard to think of an authoring problem that can't be solved by recourse to the Guide Maker utilitiesand by careful observation of the user.

In this part of the book, you have seen how to create guide files using the Guide Script commands and how to compile your guide files using Guide Maker. By now, you should feel fairly comfortable with Apple Guide and with what it can do. The next step, of course, is to see what applications can do with Apple Guidehow tightly integrated assistance can magnify the power of Apple Guide by itself.

CHAPTER 16

When to Create and Modify Applications to Use Apple Guide

N O T E   This part of the book is primarily addressed to developers who create and modify applications that use Apple Guide extensively and that have sophisticated links to the Apple Guide software. If you are not in that category, feel free to skip this part, or to skim through it to get an idea of the types of things that you can do with applications that support Apple Guide in this way.

You can add Apple Guide assistance to applications without making any modifications to them at all. This assistance can be quite extensive and can go far beyond the help of many applications that have been heavily modified to support on-line help. If you incorporate the context checks of the external code modules that are provided in Standard Resources, and if you add the context checks that you can create based on menus, windows, and dialog items, you can provide a remarkably robust and supportive system of assistance. All of this can be done without touching the application.

If the application you are coaching supports Apple Events and AppleScript, you are several steps ahead. You can add events to buttons and other panel controls and hot objects.

REASONS TO ADD CUSTOMIZED APPLE GUIDE SUPPORT TO AN APPLICATION

When you are creating or revising an application, it is worth considering adding more extensive Apple Guide support. The reasons are varied:

- It is very simple to add Apple Guide support to an application.

- The code that is added to support Apple Guide is isolated. None of it is executed unless Apple Guide is installed, and the major routines (context check and coach mark callbacks) are executed only in response to Apple Guide requests. It is unlikely to have adverse effects on the rest of your application.

- You can make more sophisticated use of Apple Guide, including control over where guide files are located, invocation of Apple Guide other than from the Guide menu (such as from a **Help** button in a dialog, next to the **OK** and **Cancel** buttons), and the ability to fine-tune assistance by opening guide files directly to the topic that is needed.

- If you publish the Apple Guide hooks (context checks, coach marks, and events) that you provide, third-party solution providers can more easily incorporate your application into custom solutions, as well as providing their own guide files to supplement your own. (It's awfully nice to have other people support your application: it relieves you from some of the burden and suggests to customers that your application is more competitive than others, which are supported by only their developer.)

- With fully integrated Apple Guide assistance, you may be able to reduce other forms of support materials, reducing the costs of printed documentation as well as the demands on technical support staff.

Above all, remember that you can add Apple Guide support to an application without making any modifications whatsoever. The modifications merely provide more extensive use of Apple Guide.

JUSTIFYING MODIFYING AN APPLICATION FOR CUSTOMIZED APPLE GUIDE SUPPORT

The decision to make modifications to support more extensive Apple Guide support should be based on an evaluation of the points just presented, as well as the specific issues relevant to your application. This is often not a straightforward decision. The main point to remember is that, although many of the benefits are intangible (and thus unquanitifiable), the costs can be minimal (little code disruption and relatively little effort). Such an equation, particularly in a competitive world, quickly tips in favor of adding the feature.

Even then, two questions quickly arise:

- what about pre-System 7.5 users who can't use Apple Guide, and
- what about cross-platform compatibility with other versions of the application?

Sometimes you are very lucky, as in the case of designing a new application that is specified only to run on System 7.5 or later. In that case, the choice of Apple Guide support is trivial.

In the case of an application that must run on systems that don't support Apple Guide, the choice is more difficult, but not impossible. Experience has shown that users eventually do upgrade to new versions of their operating systems. It may take a while, but the accountant in a home office eventually comes to the conclusion that it is cost-effective to add a hard drive to that old Macintosh Plus and run System 7 as well as the latest version of Excel. The more extensive your Apple Guide support, the more likely users are to upgrade to a new version of your application, or to purchase it in the first place.

There is even an answer to the argument that adding Apple Guide support in the short term increases rather than decreases support costs: by supporting two types of assistance, you have to continue to produce paper documentation as well as incurring the costs of developing Apple Guide assistance. If this is a concern, consider the minimal investment of adding Apple Guide support only in the form of the call-back routines for custom context checks, object-based coach marks, and Apple Events that will fit well with **Do It for Me** buttons. This will allow third parties to provide Apple Guide assistance for your product and to incorporate it into multi-application custom solutions that are tied together with Apple Guide.

As to the problem of keeping cross-platform applications consistent, this is an old issue and one that certainly cannot be resolved here. Suffice it to repeat the basic issue: is it to be a cross-platform application that is consistent by being the lowest common denominator of all platform features, or is it to be a cross-platform application that takes advantage of each platform's capabilities to the fullest. From the point of view of the developer and support staff, it is most important that the application be as similar as possible across all platforms that are supported. From the user's point of view (remember the user?), it is most important that all applications on a single platform be as similar and consistent as possible, taking advantage of each platform's features and idiosyncrasies.

Finally, there is one more benefit, albeit another intangible one, to just considering the possibility of modifying an application to use Apple Guide. In a one-hour session, involving product managers, designers, developers, and support staff (be they one person or a dozen), you will most likely reap a number of new ideas simply from examining your application and its interface in the light of possible Apple Guide modifications. Every time you look at an application's interface from a new perspective you gain such insights.

SUMMARY

What it all boils down to is this:

- New applications should be designed with the possibility of providing custom Apple Guide support. In many cases, no such support is necessary, but it should be on the design checklist.
- When existing applications are revised, if custom Apple Guide support is require—deither now or in the future—it should be added due to its relatively low cost and isolation from the rest of the code.

How easy is it to provide custom Apple Guide support? In this Part you will see the basic API calls, which are covered in Chapter 17. The two chapters that follow demonstrate the addition of custom Apple Guide support to OpenDoc parts and containers as well as to applications written with MacApp. (Chapter 19, "MacApp and Apple Guide," covers the most basic procedures for adding custom Apple Guide to any solution, even if it is not based on MacApp and is not even object-oriented.)

CHAPTER 17

The Apple Guide API

It is not necessary to modify any application or write any code to use Apple Guide. You can create very powerful and effective guide files without touching a compiler. By the same token, there are some things that you can do and often want to do that require modifications to applications. In this chapter, the Apple Guide API is discussed, showing you the range of features that are available to you.

There are two cases when you may write code that interacts with Apple Guide without modifying an application. If you write external modules to perform context checks, you will write code and compile it, following the syntax described in Chapter 12, "Sequences II Context Checks." In the other case, you may use AppleScript to write scripts that are executed to identify coach marks or to perform tasks in which the AppleScript script is associated with an Apple Guide event. Apple Guide itself provides a suite of events that are accessible to AppleScript authors; these are most often used in custom solutions, and are described in Chapter 21, "The Apple Guide Core Suite of Events," which is in Part 4, "Adding Apple Guide to Custom Solutions and Content."

Many of the modifications that you make to applications to integrate them more fully with Apple Guide are not covered in this chapter, because they do not involve Apple Guide *per se.* Because Apple Guide uses Apple events so extensively, and because they are so easy to generate from your guide files, you may decide that this is the time to make your application scriptable, supporting at least the core suite (open document, open application, print document, and quit). Depending on your application and the types of Apple Guide assistance that you want to support, you may decide to implement other Apple Events specifically to be called from Apple Guide for example Apple Events to be linked to **Do It for Me** buttons in guide files.

The Apple Guide API consists of routines that allow you to do the following:

- create Gestalt selectors that let you test for the presence of Apple Guide
- create custom context checks and coach marks
- open and close guide files from your application
- interrogate attributes of guide files
- manage housekeeping functions for Apple Guide

N O T E

The rest of this chapter is unabashedly directed to developers and programmers. It assumes a basic knowledge of programming for the Mac OS as well as a familiarity with Apple Guide (such as should be developed by reading the previous chapters).

For historical reasons, "guide file" and "database" are used to describe guide files. Except where "database" appears in a command's syntax, the preference is to use "guide file."

USING THE APPLE GUIDE API

The basic Apple Guide interface file is AppleGuide.h, which is provided on the Real World Apple Guide CD-ROM, along with all the other interface and library files mentioned in this chapter. Some of the routines in the API are implemented in the AGFileLib library, whose interface is AGFile.h. Routines in the AGFileLib are identifiable by their names. They all start with "AGFile," such as "AGFileCountType," for example. AGFileLib does not require Apple Guide to be present on a computer, so you need not check Gestalt before using these routines.

Normally, you include the AppleGuide.h header in your source code in order to use Apple Guide routines. If you also use AGFile routines, include the AGFile.h header and link in AGFileLib. (Examples are given in Chapter 19, "MacApp and Apple Guide.")

CHECKING FOR APPLE GUIDE

Before using any feature of the operating system or hardware, you should always check that it exists using Gestalt. The Gestalt selector for Apple Guide is *gestaltHelpMgrAttr*, which was first defined for the Help Manager (Balloon Help) in System 7. Two bits in the long integer that is returned tell you whether Apple Guide is present and whether the debug version of Apple Guide is present:

```
long result = 0;
OSErr err = Gestalt (gestaltHelpMgrAttr, &result);
if (err == noErr && (result & 1 <<gestaltAppleGuidePresent)))
    //Apple Guide is present
if (err == noErr && (result & 1 <<gestaltAppleGuideIsDebug)))
    //debug version is present
```

Always check whether Apple Guide is present before using any of its features. Test whether the debug version is available as necessary.

CUSTOM CONTEXT CHECKS AND COACH MARKS

By far the most frequent use of the Apple Guide API is to install custom coach marks and context checks. The process is similar for both cases. You write a call-back routine that will actually handle the coach mark or context check request. You then install the routine, usually when your application starts up, and deinstall it, usually when your application quits. As with all call-back routines, your custom coach mark and context check routines should be in locked, unpurgeable segments (such as the main segment of your application).

The examples shown in this section are drawn from Symposium Explorer's Apple Guide support. Symposium Explorer, part of Philmont Symposium System, is a multimedia presentation tool. It has support for Apple Guide not only for itself, but it also has custom coach marks and context checks that can be used by authors to provide Apple Guide assistance for the multimedia content of Symposia.

Custom Context Checks

In Symposium Explorer, the Controller contains a list of parts that can be seen by clicking on their names in the list. The parts list can be toggled among several displays:

- Topics, similar to chapter headings
- Subparts, parts contained within the current part
- Path, a sequential list of the parts that the user has opened
- Next/Previous, parts adjacent to the current part

Four buttons above the parts list are used to choose which items are displayed in the parts list (see Figure 17.1).

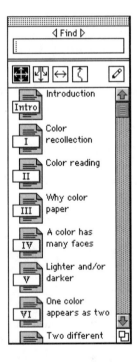

Figure 17.1 Symposium Explorer's controller.

Four context checks are defined, which allow the Apple Guide author to test which of the four buttons is clicked:

```
<Define Context Check> "TopicButton", 'cntT', 'PSM3',
  OSTYPE:'Btop'
<Define Context Check> "SubPartsButton", 'cntT', 'PSM3',
  OSTYPE:'Bsub'
<Define Context Check> "PathButton", 'cntT', 'PSM3', OSTYPE:'Bpth'
<Define Context Check> "NextPrevButton", 'cntT', 'PSM3',
  OSTYPE:'Bnxt'
```

All four context checks have the same *codeResSpec* parameter (cntT), which means that they will all be processed by the same context check in Symposium Explorer (whose application signature is PSM3). Each context check has a different parameter, identifying which button is in question.

Given these Guide Script commands, now consider what you must do on the application side to implement the context check.

Defining a Context Check

A context check function's header looks like this:

```
pascal OSErr ContextCheckReply (Ptr pInput, Size inputDataSize,
  Ptr *ppOutput, Size *pOutputDataSize, AGAppInfoHdl hAppInfo)
```

The parameter *pInput* contains the parameters defined in the <Define Context Check> command; *inputDataSize* is the length of the *pInput* data structure. You return the result of your context check as a 0 (FALSE) or 1 (TRUE) Boolean in *ppOutput*, and its size in *pOutputDataSize*.

The *hAppInfo* parameter is a struct that is defined as follows:

```
typedef struct AGAppInfo
    {
    AEEventID  eventId;
    long       refCon;
```

```
void*        contextObj;// private system field
}
AGAppInfo, *AGAppInfoPtr, **AGAppInfoHdl;
```

As you will see, the *eventID* in the AGAppInfo structure is the key to the link between Apple Guide, the <Define Context Check> command in your guide file, and your application.

 You may want to review the discussion of a context check's processing as discussed in Chapter 12, "Sequences II Conditions and Context Checks", or the more detailed discussion of this context check in Chapter 19, "MacApp and Apple Guide".

N O T E

AGInstallContextHandler Function

Having defined a context check, you must install it so that it will be called by Apple Guide when the context check that you defined in your guide file is evaluated. To install a context check, you call AGInstallContextHandler.

contextReplyProc is the function that you defined to perform your context check. The *eventID* parameter is the four-character *codeResSpec* in your <Define Context Check> command; in the example above, 'cntT'. This is the link between your guide file and your application's context check.

The *refCon* parameter is anything that you want it to be: it will be passed to your context check function in the structure *hAppInfo*, which also will contain the *eventID* parameter you specified in AGInstallContextHandler. Normally, the *refCon* parameter contains a pointer to some data structure that is of interest to the context check (in the case of object-oriented programs, this data structure is likely to be the application object itself). Because the *refCon* parameter's value will be used when the call-back routine is processed, you should make certain that it points to a structure that will exist and be in the same place when that occurs.

The *eventID* parameter forms the link between the guide file's context check and the context check function in your application. This link is a unique, one-to-one link. However, a single context check function can be installed to respond to several different context checks in a guide file. Thus, you may need to check the value of *hAppInfo.eventID* in your context check to know which context check you are supposed to be evaluating.

Finally, the *resultRefNum* parameter is provided to uniquely identify this context handler. Save it, and use it to deinstall the context check.

Syntax: **OSErr AGInstallContextHandler (ContextReplyProcPtr, contextReplyProc,**

```
AEEventID eventID,
long refCon,
AGContextRefNum *resultRefNum);
```

Result Codes:
```
noErr   0
kAGErrCannotInitContext      -2953
kAGErrMissingAppInfoHdl      -2958
kAGErrMissingContextObject   -2959
```

Example: This is the code that installs a context check to handle the context checks defined above. The constant kControllerTool is defined as 'cntT' the value used in the <Define Context Check> command. This code is part of a MacApp application; the FailOSErr routine checks for a value other than *noErr* from the installation routine and takes appropriate action. It is called from a method of the application object, so *this* is a pointer to the application object itself. Note that the *resultRefNum* is stored in an array with other context check handlers for use later on.

```
FailOSErr (AGInstallContextHandler(
(ContextReplyProcPtr)ContextCheckReply,
 kControllerTool,
 (long)this, // the application object
 &(this->fContextRefNum[5])));
```

When to Use: Whenever you have a context check in your application.

What Happens When You Call a Context Check

The context check function that processes the context checks shown contains two sections of code that are of interest. In the first, the application object associated with the context check handler during the installation process in the *refCon* parameter is dereferenced. Using that object and its methods, a document is found, and the Controller for that document is located.

```
TVirgil* ourApp = (TVirgil*)(**hAppInfo).refCon;
if(ourApp)
   {
   TDocument* aDocument = ourApp->GetKioskDocument();
   if (aDocument)
      {
      hasKioskDocument = TRUE;
      aKioskDocument = (TKioskDocument*) aDocument;
      theController = aKioskDocument->GetController();
      };
   };
```

This particular context check handler is used to process several context checks. Thus, the other element of *hAppInfo*, the *eventID*, is also used during the callback routine. It is used to control a switch statement, each case of which handles a different context check. The beginning of that switch statement follows:

```
switch ((**hAppInfo).eventId)
   {
   case kControllerTool:
      {
      if (theController)
         {
         if(pInput && inputDataSize>0)
```

```
        inputType = *((OSType*)pInput);
     result = theController->IsToolSelected (inputType);
        };
     };
```

The use of the constant kControllerTool (defined as 'cntT') makes the code easier to read and helps ensure the consistency between the installation routine and the context check handler.

The data from the <Define Context Check> command (in this case an OSType) is passed in the *pInput* parameter. This pointer is dereferenced and coerced back to an OSType. It is then passed to the Controller's IsToolSelected method, which checks to see whether the button in question is clicked.

This context check handler shows two types of code efficiency:

- By using the OSType parameter, a single context check can be implemented to handle four different <Define Context Check> commands.

- By using the *hAppInfo.eventID* parameter within the context check handler, a switch statement can process several context checks within one function. This is particularly useful when the different context checks share certain characteristics (in this case, they are all context checks that relate to the Controller).

Using techniques like these, you can get the most mileage out of your context check handlers; having implemented one context check, adding additional checks-particularly when they are parameterized variants of the first-is quite simple.

AGRemoveContextHandler Function

When your application quits, you should deinstall all the context check handlers you installed. Use the refNum that was returned from each context check's installation.

Syntax:	**OSERR AGRemoveContextHandler (AGCoachRefNum *theRefNum);**
Result Codes:	noErr 0
Example:	This code removes all of the context check handlers that are installed in Symposium Explorer:

```
for (short i = 0; i <= fContextRefNumCount; i++)
    FailOSErr (AGRemoveContextHandler
        (&this->fContextRefNum[i]));
```

When to Use:	Whenever you have a context check in your application.

Custom Coach Marks

Coach marks are handled very similarly to context checks. You define a handler and install it; Apple Guide calls it when necessary; and then you deinstall it when your application is finished.

In this section, four coach marks on Symposium Explorer's Controller are shown. They refer to the same four buttons at the top of the parts list, and their definitions are as follows:

```
<Define Object Coach> "Controller Topics", 'PSM3', REDCIRCLE,
  "Controller-Btop"
<Define Object Coach> "Sub-parts Button", 'PSM3', REDCIRCLE,
  "Controller-Bsub"
<Define Object Coach> "Next/previous Button", 'PSM3', REDCIRCLE,
  "Controller-Bnxt"
<Define Object Coach> "Path Button", 'PSM3', REDCIRCLE,
  "Controller-Bpth"
```

N O T E   In this particular case, it would be possible to coach these buttons using the <Define Window Coach> command, because the buttons remain in the same location on the Controller at all times. In Symposium Explorer, all interface objects are coached using coach mark handler call-backs because the majority of them, in fact, do move around. For example, a coach mark is defined for the parts list section of the Controller. As you can see from Figure 17.1, the Controller is resizable, and so the parts list—although its top is always in the same place—may be of varying lengths. In such a case, no static coach mark definition can properly identify the object to be coached.

Defining a Coach Mark Handler

A coach mark handler's header looks like this:

```
pascal OSErr CoachMarkReply (Rect* pItemRect, Ptr pNameIn,
   long refCon)
```

Like a context check function, this function returns an OSErr that lets Apple Guide know whether it was able to process the request. The constant

```
kAGErrItemNotFound = -2925
```

should be returned if you cannot identify the object requested.

The *pItemRect* rectangle that you return is the rectangle on which the coach mark is based. In the case of a circle, it is drawn around the outside of the rectangle. Other coach marks (such as arrows) use the rectangle in different ways (see Chapter 9, "Panels IICoach Marks").

The *pNameIn* parameter is a pointer that contains the name of the item requested—the *objectName* parameter from the <Define Object Coach> command. This is a zero-terminated string.

The *refCon* parameter is comparable to the *hAppInfo.refCon* value in context check handlers. It is set when you install the coach mark handler and is usually used to store a pointer to a relevant data structure.

AGInstallCoachHandler Function

Use the AGInstallCoachHandler routine to install your coach mark handler. The *coachReplyProc* is your coach mark handler routine; the *refCon* is whatever value you want to pass so that your handler will have it handy, and the *resultRefNum* is returned for you to save and use when you deinstall the routine.

If you compare the coach mark and context check handlers and installers, you will notice that context checks have an additional parameter: the four-character *eventID* used to associate a context check handler with a specific context check in a guide file. Coach mark handlers do not have a comparable parameter, and thus all object coach mark requests to a given application are processed by a single handler. You should install only one handler.

Syntax:	**OSErrAGInstallCoachHandler (CoachReplyProcPtr CoachReplyProc, long refCon, AGCoachRefNum* resultRefNum);**
Result Codes:	`noErr    0` `kAGErrCannotInitCoach  -2952`

Example:	This is the code that installs the custom coach mark handler for Symposium Explorer. It is called from a method of the application object, so *this* is a pointer to the application object itself. Because only one coach mark handler is installed, there is a simple variable rather than an array to store the *resultRefNum*.
	
	`FailOSErr( AGInstallCoachHandler(`
	`  (CoachReplyProcPtr)CoachMarkReply,`
	`(long)this, &(this->fCoachRefNum)));`

Limitations:	Install only one coach mark handler in your application.
When to Use:	Whenever you have a coach mark handler in your application.

What Happens When You Call a Coach Mark Handler

Whenever Apple Guide needs to evaluate a <Define Object Coach> command, it calls the handler in the appropriate application, passing it the object name as specified in the <Define Object Coach>. As you can infer from the four object coaches defined above, this coach mark handler splits the name into two parts so that the coach mark handler can process a number of requests easily.

The bulk of the coach mark handler is comparable to the context check handler above; the application object is found in the *refCon*, and the Controller itself is located by the application object. The name from the <Define Object Coach> command is parsed into two parts: the first ("Controller") identifies the application object containing the item to be coached; the second contains the four-character identifier of a subview that is the target of the inquiry.

Remember that this is only an example of the sort of thing that you can do. You can establish any naming conventions that you want to interpret object coach requests.

N O T E

The first half of each name happens to have a unique first letter in this application's design. As a result, a switch statement contains a case for 'C' (Controller) as follows:

```
case 'C': //controller
{
  if (aKioskDocument)
      result = (aKioskDocument->GetController())->
      GetControllerRects (*((OSType*)inName2), pItemRect);
  break;
};
```

Several points are worth noting here. The two-part identification scheme for object names (Controller-Bpth, for example) actually is implemented with only the first character of the first name being used. For ease of readability and maintainability, authors of Apple Guide files for Symposium Explorer did not know (until now) that they could write "C-Bpth."

Why, therefore, is the second part of the identification scheme not equally clear? In this case, the balance comes down on the side of efficiency at the (slight) cost of readability. This excerpt is from a MacApp application; every part of a window in a MacApp is a subview, and each subview has a four-character identifier. By using this four-character identifier as part of the object name in the <Define Object Coach> command, the coach mark rectangle can ultimately be found with these lines of code in the Controller method GetControllerRects:

```
TView* theView = this->FindSubView (whichOne);
//whichOne is the four-character subview identifier
if (theView)
    theView->GetExtent (theVRect);
//returns the subview's rectangle
```

Once again, it is important to realize how easy it is to install custom coach marks, particularly when you can take advantage of already-existing application identifiers for the objects to be coached. Nowhere in the *coachMarkReply* procedure is the identifier of each object specified. The procedure is written only to discriminate among the different types of windows and send the second half of the object's name to the appropriate method of the appropriate window, where it is processed.

One final point must be made in relation to the processing of coach marks. The rectangle that is returned must be in global coordinates. Use the Toolbox LocalToGlobal routine to do this.

AGRemoveCoachHandler Function

Finally, just as you deinstalled a context check handler, you deinstall a coach mark handler.

Syntax:	**OSErr AGRemoveCoachHandler (AGCoachRefNum *theRefNum);**
Result Codes:	noErr 0
Example:	This code removes the coach mark handler that is installed in Symposium Explorer:
	`FailOSErr (AGRemoveContextHandler (&this->fCoachRefNum));`
When to Use:	Whenever you have a coach mark handler in your application.

OPENING AND CLOSING GUIDE FILES FROM AN APPLICATION

Normally, Apple Guide builds the Guide menu from the appropriate guide files that are coresident with the application and that pass the tests necessary for inclusion in the menu (<Gestalt>, <App Creator>). When the user selects a file from that menu, Apple Guide opens it automatically to the startup window.

Sometimes you want to open guide files yourself in an application. This usually happens in one of two ways:

- You want to open guide files in response to other menu commands, button events (a **Help** button in a dialog, for example), or situations to which your program is sensitive (repeated unsuccessful attempts to do something).
- You build the Guide menu yourself, incorporating guide files from locations other than coresident with the application. If you build it yourself, you have to manipulate it yourself. The most common reason for doing this is when you have guide files that need to be coresident with documents rather than with an application, such as when you use Apple Guide with multimedia content.

Opening Guide Files

Four routines let you open guide files. You may choose to open them:

- normally, displaying the Access window, AGOpen,
- displaying the Full Access window with the **Look For** button clicked and with a specified phrase already searched for, AGOpenWithSearch,
- at the start of a specific sequence, AGOpenWithSequence, or
- a specific view of the Access window, Look For, Topics, Index, Howdy.

All of the routines have similar syntax, and because they all have parameters that are reserved for future expansion but are not used now, they may appear more challenging than they are. In all the following cases, the parameter *mixinControl* should be set to NIL and *flags* should be set to 0.

AGOpen Function

The *fileSpec* parameter is the standard file system specification record. It can be replaced by the constant kAGDefault; Apple Guide will then open the default help guide file.

The *resultRefNum* is returned and provides your application with a unique reference to this guide file. (You can use the AGGetFSSpec routine to convert a *resultRefNum* back to a FSSpec.

The result codes and limitations are the same for all four commands, as is the advice on when to use them.

Syntax:	**AGErr AGOpen (FSSpec *fileSpec,**
	UInt32 flags, //always 0
	Handle mixinControl, //always NIL
	AGRefNum *resultRefNum);
Result Codes:	noErr 0
	kAGErrCannotOpenAliasFile -2954
	kAGErrNoAliasResource -2955
	kAGErrDatabaseNotAvailable -2956
	kAGErrInsufficientMemory -2962
Limitation:	Apple Guide must be installed to use these routines. Use the Gestalt selector described previously before using any of these routines.
When to Use:	Whenever you open a guide file from your program, that is, whenever you want to open a guide file from your own menu command, from a button in a dialog box, or when you have built the Guide menu yourself. If you use Apple Guide's default Guide menu, you never open or close guide files yourself

AGOpenWithSearch Function

To open a guide file to the Look For view and perform a specified search, use AGOpenWithSearch. Specify the string to search for in *searchString*.

> *Syntax:* **AGErr AGOpenWithSearch (FSSpec *fileSpec,**
> **UInt32 flags, //always 0**
> **Handle mixinControl, //always NIL**
> **ConstStr255Param searchString,**
> **AGRefNum *resultRefNum);**

AGOpenWithSequence Function

To open a guide file to a specific sequence, use AGOpenWithSequence.

The *sequenceID* parameter refers to the identifying number that Guide Maker assigns to each sequence. Use the Text to IDs report from Guide Maker to find this number. Remember that Guide Maker can assign different numbers to the same sequence in a guide file on different occasions (as other sequences are added or removed). When you use this routine, you must make certain that the application-defined sequence identifier matches that of the most recent Guide Maker run.

> *Syntax:* **AGErr AGOpenWithSequence (FSSpec *fileSpec,**
> **UInt32 flags, //always 0**
> **Handle mixinControl, //always NIL**
> **short sequenceID,**
> **AGRefNum *resultRefNum);**

AGOpenWithView Function

To open a guide file to a specified view of the Access window, use AGOpenWithView.

You can use the following constants for the *viewNum* parameter (the names are self-explanatory):

kAGViewFullHowdy = 1

kAGViewTopicAreas = 2

kAGViewIndex = 3

kAGViewLookFor = 4

kAGViewSingleHowdy = 5

kAGViewSingleTopics = 6

Syntax:	**AGErr AGOpenWith View (FSSpec* fileSpec,**
	UInt32 flags, //always 0
	Handle mixinControl, //always NIL
	short viewNum,
	AGRefNum *resultRefNum);

Closing Guide Files

If you opened it, you close it.

AGClose Function

The *resultRefNum* is the same parameter that was returned from any of the previous example opening routines. Because you can close a guide file using only this value (in other words, you cannot close a guide file by name), you can close only those files that you have opened. Apple Guide remains running in the background even after the last guide file has been closed. You must call AGQuit to terminate it.

Syntax:	**AGErr AGClose (AGRefNum *resultRefNum);**	
Result Codes:	noErr 0	
	kAGErrDatabaseNotOpen	-2957
	kAGErrInvalidRefNum	-2960
Limitation:	Apple Guide must be installed to use these routines. Use the Gestalt selector described previously before using any of these routines.	
When to Use:	Whenever you have opened a guide file from your program.	

Getting Information about Open Guide Files

The routines in this section are used to get information about specific open Apple Guide files; they all take as a parameter an AGRefNum, which is the value returned in the *resultRefNum* when the guide files are opened. Apple Guide must be installed to use these routines. Use the Gestalt selector described previously before using any of these routines.

AGGetFSSpec Function

Sometimes, you need to convert the *resultRefNum* back to a FSSpec record. You can use the constant kAGFrontDatabase in the *refNum* parameter to get the FSSpec for the front-most database.

Syntax:	**AGErr AGGetFSSpec (AGRefNum refNum,** **FSSpec* fileSpec);**
Result Codes:	noErr 0
	kAGErrDatabaseNotOpen -2957
When to Use:	As needed.

AGIsDatabaseOpen Function

You may want to know whether a guide file is still open. Use AGIsDatabaseOpen for that purpose.

Syntax:	**Boolean AGIsDatabaseOpen (AGRefNum refNum);**
When to Use:	As needed.

AGGetFrontWindowKind Function

If a database is open, you can find out what kind of window is front-most with AGGetFrontWindowKind. You can use the constant kAGFrontDatabase in the *refNum* parameter to get the FSSpec for the front-most database.

Syntax:	**AGWindowKind AGGetFrontWindowKind (AGRefNum refNum)**
Result Codes:	kAGNoWindow 0
	kAGAccessWindow 1
	kAGPresentationWindow 2
	Any other value means either that the database in question is not the front database or that Apple Guide is not running.
When to Use:	As needed.

INTERROGATING APPLE GUIDE FILES

If you are going to build your own Guide menu or want to associate guide files with buttons or other interface elements of your application, you may need to find out about the guide files that are available. The routines in the AGFile library, which are described in this section, perform those functions.

To use these routines, you must include the AGFile.h header in your application, and you must link in the AGFileLib. Apple Guide need not be installed or running to use these routines.

AGFileGetDBCount Function

To count the guide files within a folder, use AGFileGetDBCount. The *vRefNum* and *dirID* are standard File System parameters that identify the folder in question. The *databaseType* parameter should be set to one of these constants:

kAGFileDBTypeAny	0
kAGFileDBTypeHelp	I
kAGFileDBTypeTutorial	2
kAGFileDBTypeShortcuts	3
kAGFileDBTypeAbout	4
kAGFileDBTypeOther	5

If *wantMixin* is TRUE, all guide files in the folder will be counted; if it is FALSE, only main guide files will be counted.

The result is returned as a type AGFileCountType, which is a short.

Syntax:	**AGFileCountType AGFileGetDBCount (short vRefNum, long dirID, AGFileDBType databaseType, Boolean wantMixin);**
Result Codes:	noErr 0
	nsvErr -35
	ioErr -36
	fnOpnErr -38
	eofErr -39
	posErr -40
	tmfoErr -42
	fnfErr -43
	fLckdErr -45
	rfNumErr -51
	dirNFErr -120
	afpAccessDenied -5000
When to Use:	As needed.

AGFileGetIndDB Function

After you have counted the guide files in a folder, you often want to deal with individual files. To get the File System FSSpec record for a single guide file in a folder, use AGFileGetIndDB.

The first four parameters are the same as for AGFileGetDBCount. The *dbIndex* simply identifies each of the guide files in the folder, starting with an index number of 1. Typically, you write a loop to iterate from 1 to the value returned by AGFileGetDBCount to get the file specification record for each guide file in turn. The file specification record is returned in *fileSpec*.

Syntax:	**OSErr AGFileGetIndDB (short vRefNum,**
	long dirID,
	AGFileDBType databaseType,
	Boolean wantMixin,
	short dbIndex,
	FSSpecType *fileSpec);
Result Codes:	As above.
When to Use:	As needed.

The following set of functions lets you get various information about a guide file after you have found its FSSpec record using AGFileGetIndDB. Almost all of the values that you set with the Guide Maker commands discussed in Chapter 6, "Setting Up Guide Files," can be accessed here. The example at the end of this section shows a common use of some of these functions.

AGFileGetMenuName Function

To get the name under which a file will be shown in the Guide menu (which you set using the <Help Menu> command), use AGFileGetMenuName.

Syntax:	**OSErr AGFileGetMenuName (AGFileFSSpecType *fileSpec,**
	AGFileDBMenuNamePtr menuItemNameStr);
Result Codes:	As above.
When to Use:	As needed.

You need this information if you are building your own Guide menu.

AGFileGetHelpMenuBalloonText Function

If you are associating a guide file with a button in a dialog box, you might want to use the Balloon Help text for that button. To get the Balloon Help text associated with a guide file (which you set using the <Balloon Menu Text> command), use AGFileGetHelpMenuBalloonText.

Syntax: **OSErr AGFileGetHelpMenuBalloonText (AGFileFSSpecType**
            *fileSpec, AStr255 helpMenuBalloonString);

Result Codes: As above.

When to Use: As needed.

AGFileGetDBCountry Function

To get the WorldScript information that you specified with the <World Script>
command, use AGFileGetDBCountry.

Syntax: **OSErr AGFileGetDBCountry (AGFileFSSpecType *fileSpec,**
            AGFileDBRegionType *script,
            AGFileDBRegionType *region);

Result Codes: As above.

When to Use: As needed.

AGFileGetDBType Function

If you used the value kAGFileDBTypeAny in the call to AGFileGetDBCount, you
may need to check which type of guide file you have found.

Syntax: **OSErr AGFileGetDBType (AGFileFSSpecType *fileSpec,**
            AGFileDBType *dataBaseType);

Result Codes: As above.

When to Use: As needed.

AGFileGetDBVersion Function

The guide file version information that you set with the <Version> command is
interrogated with AGFileGetDBVersion.

Syntax: **OSErr AGFileGetDBVersion (AGFileFSSpecType *fileSpec,**

                    AGFileMajorRevType *majorRev,

                    AGFileMinorRevType *minorRev);

Result Codes: As above.

When to Use: As needed.

AGFileGetHelpMenuAppCreator Function

To find out the creator type set with the <App Creator> command, use AGFileGetHelpMenuAppCreator.

Syntax: **OSErr AGFileGetHelpMenuAppCreator**

                    (AGFileFSSpecType *fileSpec,

                    OSType *helpMenuAppCreator);

Result Codes: As above.

When to Use: As needed.

AGFileIsMixin Function

If you used the value TRUE for the *mixin* parameter in AGFileGetDBCount, you may need to determine whether an individual guide file is a mixin or a main file.

Syntax: **Boolean AGFileIsMixin (AGFileFSSpecType *fileSpec);**

Result Codes: As above.

When to Use: As needed.

AGFileGetMixinMatchSelector Function

For mixin files, you specify a matching creator type using the <Mixin Match> command. If you have a mixin file, you can find out what that value is by using AGFileGetMixinMatchSelector.

Syntax: **OSErr AGFileGetMixinMatchSelector**
           (AGFileFSSpecType *fileSpec,
              OSType *mixinMatchSelector);

Result Codes: As above.
When to Use: As needed.

AGFileGetSelectorCount Function

You can specify up to three <Gestalt> tests that determine whether an individual guide file should be added to the Guide menu. To find out how many Gestalt tests are actually specified in a guide file, use AGFileGetSelectorCount.

Syntax: **AGFileSeletorCountType**
           AGFileGetSelectorCount(AGFileFSSpecType *fileSpec);
Result Codes: As above.
When to Use: As needed.

AGFileGetSelector Function

To get the values for a specific Gestalt selector in a guide file, use AGFileGetSelector. The parameter *selectorNumber* is an index that runs from 1 to the value returned by the AGFileGetSelectorCount function.

Syntax: **OSErr AGFileGetSelector(AGFileFSSpecType *fileSpec,**
           AGFileSelectorIndexType selectorNumber,
           AGFileSelectorType *selector,
           AGFileSelectorValueType *value);

Result Codes: As above.
When to Use: As needed.

Putting It Together

This section of code is used to find guide files with the application's signature that are located in the Preferences folder, a nonstandard alternative to the coresidency that Apple Guide normally uses.

```
//get the Preferences folder volume and director
myOSErr = FindFolder(kOnSystemDisk,kPreferencesFolderType,
  kCreateFolder, myVolID, myDirID);


//how many guide files are in the folder?
newFileCount = AGFileGetDBCount (myVolID, myDirID,
  kAGFileDBTypeAny, FALSE);


//if there are any,
if (newFileCount >0)
    //for each guide file in the folder,
    for (short i = 1; i <= newFileCount; i++)
        //if we can get the FSSpec for this guide file,
        if (AGFileGetIndDB (myVolID, myDirID, kAGFileDBTypeAny,
          wantMixin, i, &fileSpec) == noErr)
        {
            //is the <App Creator> in this guide file the same
            //as this application's?
            myOSErr = AGFileGetHelpMenuAppCreator
              (&fileSpec, &theType);
            if (theType == kSignature)
                //if we can get the name for the Guide menu,
                if (AGFileGetDBMenuName
            (&fileSpec, menuName)==noErr)
                    //..add this file to our Guide menu
```

APPLE GUIDE HOUSEKEEPING FUNCTIONS

The final set of Apple Guide routines lets you control the environment, send Apple Events to Apple Guide itself, and check the Guide menu's contents.

AGGetStatus Function

To find out the current status of Apple Guide, use the AGGetStatus routine. Before the first guide file is opened, the status is kAGIsNotRunning.

Syntax:	**AGStatus AGGetStatus (void);**	
Result codes:	kAGIsActive 0	Apple Guide is active and a guide file is open
	kAGIsNotRunning 1	Apple Guide is not loaded
	kAGIsSleeping 2	Apple Guide is loaded, but no guide file is open
Limitation:	Apple Guide must be installed to use this routine.	
When to Use:	As needed.	

AGStart Function

You can start Apple Guide explicitly with the AGStart routine.

Syntax:	**AGErr AGStart (void);**
Limitation:	Apple Guide must be installed to use this routine.
When to Use:	Rarely. AGStart is called automatically when you open a guide file.

AGQuit Function

You quit Apple Guide with the AGQuit function. It leaves Apple Guide with the status kAGIsNotRunning, and it frees memory.

Syntax:	**AGErr AGQuit (void);**
Result Codes:	noErr 0
	kAGErrDatabaseOpen -2961
Limitation:	Apple Guide must be installed to use this routine. You cannot quit Apple Guide if any guide files are open.
When to Use:	As needed.

AGGeneral Function

When you have opened a guide file from your application, you can use the AGGeneral function to send Apple Events to it. This can be useful in debugging and could be used in special cases where you want to programmatically navigate through a guide file, rather than having the user click the left and right arrows. Before using this function to change the behavior of a guide file, consider whether such a drastic step is worthwhile.

The following constants can be used for *theEvent*:

Constant	event ID	meaning
kAGEventDoCoach	'doco'	draws the coach mark defined on the current panel
kAGEventGoNext	'gonp'	same action as clicking the right arrow in the navigation bar
kAGEventGoPrev	'gopp'	same action as clicking the left arrow in the navigation bar
kAGEventHidePanel	'pahl'	collapse the current panel (same action as clicking the zoom box on an uncollapsed panel)
kAGEventReturnBack	'gobk'	return from an Oops sequence
kAGEventShowPanel	'pash'	expand a collapsed panel (same action as clicking the zoom box on a collapsed panel)
kAGEventTogglePanel	'patg'	same action as clicking the zoom box on a panel whether it is collapsed or not

N O T E

A complete list of all Apple events in Apple Guide's suite is provided in Chapter 21, "The Apple Guide Core Suite of Events."

Syntax:	**AGErr AGGeneral (AGRefNum refNum, AGEvent theEvent);**
Result Codes:	noErr 0
	kAGErrDatabaseNotOpen -2956
	kAGErrInvalidRefNum -2960
Limitation:	Apple Guide must be installed to use this routine.
When to Use:	Primarily for testing.

AGGetAvailableDBTypes Function

If you have built the Guide menu yourself, you know what files are in it and what their names and types are. If Apple Guide has constructed the menu (the most common situation), you do not know what it contains. The AGGetAvailableDBTypes function returns bit flags in a word that indicate the types of files in the Guide menu.

Syntax:	**UInt32 AGGetAvailableDBTypes (void);**
Result codes:	The bit values are
	kAGDBBitAny $0001
	kAGDBBitHelp $0002
	kAGDBBitTutorial $0004
	kAGDBBitShortcuts $0008
	kAGDBBitAbout $0010
	kAGDBBitOther $0080
Example:	If you wanted to customize your About guide file, you could include a context check that calls back to your application where AGGetAvailableDBTypes would be called. Based on the results of the context check, your About guide file might display panels explaining what Tutorial guide files are, what Shortcuts guide files are, and so forth, but only if the particular type of guide file exists in the Guide menu.
Limitation:	Apple Guide must be installed to use this routine.
When to Use:	As needed.

SUMMARY

For many developers, their only use of the Apple Guide API is to write custom context checks and coach marks, a simple and straightforward process. For others, application designs that use nonstandard locations for guide files, that open guide files from the application directly, or that build the Guide menu, require use of various parts of the API.

In the following chapters, you will see how you can add integrated Apple Guide support to MacApp and OpenDoc applications.

OpenDoc and Apple Guide

OpenDoc is a revolutionary technology that brings a new class of applications and documents to the Windows, Macintosh, OS/2, UNIX, and other personal computer platforms. With OpenDoc, hardware and software developers can deliver new software technologies to individual users, better server integration to corporate users, and enhanced multimedia content to all users.

OpenDoc enables the creation of cooperative component software that supports compound documents, that can be customized, that can be used collaboratively, and that is available across multiple platforms. In doing so, OpenDoc fundamentally changes the nature of software development for personal computers.

OpenDoc Programmer's Guide, preliminary edition

Although volumes are being written about OpenDoc itself, it is useful to note that on the Mac OS, OpenDoc and Apple Guide complement each other very well. OpenDoc allows users and solution providers to assemble compound documents from various parts. OpenDoc itself guarantees that the parts work together properly. Apple Guide excels at guiding the user through a sequence of steps in order to accomplish a task. To successfully carry out a task in the OpenDoc world, you need both the step-by-step assistance that Apple Guide provides as well as the functional integration that OpenDoc provides. Together they answer the question of how parts from different vendors can possibly work together more easily than a monolithic program from one vendor.

In the world of monolithic applications, users often find themselves using applications that aren't quite right for the tasks that they want to perform—they're too complicated, don't exactly handle certain aspects of the work, and so on. Despite the drawbacks of monolithic applications in general and specific applications that users may have, there is a level of comfort and assurance (whether it is justified or not) that someone somewhere is responsible for everything working together. With the OpenDoc's functional integration and Apple Guide's behavioral integration, parts can be assembled by users without worrying that they are going out on a limb. In fact, they may for the first time be able to get exactly what they want from their computer.

 This chapter assumes some basic familiarity with OpenDoc and component architecture.

N O T E

THE GUIDE MENU IN OPENDOC

The Guide Menu in traditional applications always reflects the guide files for the current application. In OpenDoc, where applications as such do not exist, the Guide Menu reflects the guide files appropriate to the active part of the document.

In OpenDoc, a guide file is automatically provided that describes the basic functionality of an OpenDoc document: saving, opening, and most important of all, manipulating parts. If a guide file is provided for individual parts of the document, the relevant guide file is shown in the guide menu whenever a part is active. In this way, the user has access to assistance for the part as well as for the basic OpenDoc concepts.

Just as you can open a guide file other than from the Guide menu, and just as an opened guide file can coach the user through actions involving several applications, you can do the same things with OpenDoc applications.

SCRIPTABILITY

OpenDoc parts can provide scriptability, with content-centered scripting allowing access to a part's data. Apple Guide, with its extensive use of Apple events, already has many hooks that allow AppleScript to be used by it—and to let it be used by scripts.

OPPORTUNITIES

In a world of composite documents, more and more applications will look like the custom solutions discussed in Part 4 of this book. OpenDoc will provide the functional integration. Tremendous opportunities exist for Apple Guide authors to add assistance to these solutions, as well as to use Apple Guide itself as an integrating force.

CHAPTER 19

MacApp and Apple Guide

MacApp is Apple's object-oriented application framework, the granddaddy of most of the application frameworks available today. Integrating Apple Guide with MacApp is as straightforward as with any application. Because so many applications are written using MacApp (including many in-house custom solutions), this chapter goes right to the specific code that you need to adjust.

If you are not using MacApp, the code samples in this chapter will still give you an overview of the basics of integrating Apple Guide assistance. Few people will need to use all of the features demonstrated in this chapter, so don't feel that you have to go overboard in your implementation of Apple Guide.

NOTE

The examples in this chapter are relative to MacApp version 3.0. Version 3.5 is a pointer-based version of MacApp and incorporates more explicit support for scripting. Most of the code given here is also applicable to version 3.5.

SUPPORT FOR APPLE EVENTS AND SCRIPTING

As noted in Chapter 17, "The Apple Guide API," many of the changes that you may want to make to integrate Apple Guide into your application do not involve

Apple Guide directly. One of those changes is a reconsideration of your application's support for Apple events.

Apple events expose your application's functionality to the wide world of AppleScript writers, as well as making your application easier to integrate into custom solutions. When first considering Apple event support, you most likely looked at it solely from this point of view. When you are looking at Apple event support from the point of view of Apple Guide, it often looks different.

For example, if your application has a set of preferences, you may define an Apple event such as 'pref' (preferences), which takes parameters that specify an individual preference and the value to which it should be set. When you consider using Apple Guide, you might want a different type of Apple event, perhaps a 'shpf' (show preferences) event that opens the Preferences window for the user. A show preferences event is easily attached to a Do It for Me button or an <On Panel Create> event. The events that are most useful for Apple Guide authors are often interface-based events rather than data manipulation events. They correspond to the instructions on a Do This Apple Guide panel, often choosing a menu command.

Fortunately, these events are trivial to add to MacApp applications. Even if you already have extensive Apple Guide support in your application, you may find that you want to add some of these interface events to make Apple Guide scripting easier.

To add interface-based events to your application, you do the following:

1. Add an 'aedt' resource to your application to map the Apple event to an existing menu command.
2. Add a DoAppleCommand method to your application.
3. Add an 'aete' resource to your application describing the events you have added.

Before adding one of these events to your application, you should plan for its use. Specifically, if you are going to use the event to automatically do something that the user doesn't do, you should plan to implement a context check to determine first that the user has actually not done the action. By checking the window title with the external code module provided, you may be able to do this easily (is a window open called Preferences?). In the case of some of your menu commands, you may need to implement custom context checks within your application.

Adding an 'aedt' Resource to Your Application

MacApp itself properly handles Apple Events that are directed to it, as long as it knows what they are. The 'aedt' resource identifies the events it should expect and associates each one with a command.

Here is the definition of the resource:

```
type 'aedt' {
    wide array {
        unsigned longint; // Event Class
        unsigned longint; // Event ID
        unsigned longint; // Value
    };
};
```

Here is an example of an 'aedt' resource:

```
resource 'aedt' (1) {
    {
    'PSM1', 'pref', cOpenPreferencesWindow;
    'PSM1', 'blow', cSetPartLocatorToBelow;
    'PSM1', 'next', cSetPartLocatorToNext;
    }
};
```

The event class value can be your application's signature. You must assign a unique four-character identifier to each event within the class. Finally, use the constant that you have defined for a command to associate that command with the event. (This command may be a command that you have already defined, such as the menu commands shown, or it may be a command that is only invoked from the Apple events interface. This section deals primarily with invoking menu commands from the Apple Events interface, but the principles are the same for all Apple events handled by MacApp.)

In the previous example, the command constants are used in the 'CMNU'resource in the same file in the following way:

```
resource 'CMNU' (mOptions,
#if qNames
"mOptions",
#endif
nonpurgeable) {
mOptions,
textMenuProc,
EnablingManagedByMacApp,
enabled,
"Options",
    {
    "Preferences_", noIcon, noKey, noMark, plain,
       cOpenPreferencesWindow;
    "Place New Parts Below", noIcon, noKey, noMark, plain,
       cSetPartLocatorToBelow;
    "Place New Parts Adjacent", noIcon, noKey, noMark, plain,
       cSetPartLocatorToNext;
    }
};
```

NOTE

You may remember that there is such a thing as the Apple Event Registry, which consolidates Apple Event suites and guarantees that every developer doesn't define similar events that use different identifiers and that behave in slightly different ways. Before adding Apple Events to your application, you should check the Apple Event Registry to see whether there are events defined that do what you want to do, in which case you can implement them yourself but reuse the standard identifiers.

When you are creating Apple Events that simply correspond to interface commands of your application, you can make the argument that these are unique, unsharable events that are specific to your application. If you define a suite that is identified with your application's signature, you should not step on anyone else's toes. Commands that are not unique to your application, such as new document, print, and so on, should use the standard event identifiers in the Registry.

Adding a DoAppleCommand Method to Your Application

MacApp takes the Apple Events that it receives and extracts the data they contain. It then calls DoAppleCommand with the event and its data. The syntax for DoAppleCommand is as follows:

```
void DoAppleCommand (
    CommandNumber aCommandNumber,
    const AppleEvent &message,
    const AppleEvent &reply);
```

DoAppleCommand is a method of both TEventHandler and TBehavior. It is called in the same way in which DoMenuCommand is called: for all of the event handler's behaviors, then for the event handler itself. If the event handler does not handle the event, its inherited method calls the next handler in the chain, up to the application object.

In the case of these light-weight interface-based events that you implement for Apple Guide's convenience, the event corresponds simply to a menu command and has no data associated with it. Although it is easy to extract the data from the *message* parameter, there is no need to in this case. In fact, all that your DoAppleCommand method need do is pass the command number on to the appropriate DoMenuCommand method that you have already implemented, as the following example shows:

```
pascal void TDanteApplication::DoAppleCommand(CommandNumber
aCommandNumber,  const AppleEvent& message,  const AppleEvent&
reply)
{
    switch (aCommandNumber)
    {
        case cKioskDocumentParms:
        {
            if (fKioskDocument)
```

```
                        fKioskDocument->DoMenuCommand
                                (cKioskDocumentParms);
                        break;
                };
                case cSetPartLocatorToBelow:
                case cSetPartLocatorToNext:
                {
                        this->DoMenuCommand (aCommandNumber);
                        break;
                };

                default:
                {
                        inherited::DoAppleCommand (aCommandNumber, message,
                                reply);
                        break;
                };
        }; //end switch
};
```

This is so easy to do that you may get carried away with adding more Apple Events to your application, including some that actually pass data in the message parameter.

Adding an 'aete' Resource to Your Application

The 'aete' resource in your application describes the events that you support. It is what the Script Editor application reads and displays when you choose the **Open Dictionary** command. Although the 'aete' resource structure is complex, the Aete Editor Stack on the Mac OS SDK and E.T.O. lets you enter the data easily into a HyperCard stack and store it either directly as a resource into your application (not recommended) or to DeRez it into a file, which you can then paste into your application's .r file (recommended). The Aete Editor Stack is self-explanatory and easy to use.

If you do not add the 'aete' resource to your application, no one will be able to see the Apple Events that you have so carefully added. Before casually dismissing this as a nonproblem (because you are adding these events only for your use in guide files), remember that others may want to add Apple Guide to your application, either itself or as part of a custom solution. Take the few minutes necessary to add the 'aete' resource to your application for their sake, and for your own, when the documentation is lost or eaten by space aliens.

BUILDING THE GUIDE MENU

Somewhat more challenging, but still well within the capabilities of any MacApp programmer is building your own Guide menu. You do this most often when you want to place guide files in nonstandard locations. The coresidency requirement of Apple Guide's default behavior is satisfactory in many cases. In some cases, however, you must build the menu yourself: cases where users may move the application around, forgetting to take guide files with it, or where guide files are to be put in the Guide menu only when certain documents are opened.

In this section, the most complicated case is presented: that of an application that has several different menu bars (an application menu bar, a separate menu bar that is displayed when the active document is text-based, another one for graphics documents, and so on). To further complicate things, the application picks up guide files from two locations: the Preferences folder and guide files that are coresident with the document opened. (This is based on Symposium Explorer's design. Because Apple Guide assistance can be added to the multimedia content of a Symposium, the assistance for the application itself is stored in guide files in the Preferences folder. The document-specific guide files are coresident with the documents.)

To implement this design, the following steps are required:

1. Check whether Apple Guide is installed in your IMyApplication method.

2. Find the appropriate guide files when documents are opened that may have guide files coresident with them.

3. Override TApplication::InstallHelpMenuItems to place the guide files in the Guide menu.

4. Add code to TMyApplication::DoMenuCommand to handle the commands you added to the Guide menu.

To facilitate the implementation, a light-weight object, TAGDB (Apple Guide database) is created for each guide file.

The TAGDB Object

The TAGDB object is a light-weight object that stores the FSSpec and name for each guide file. In this design, two TList objects are maintained with TAGDB objects in them: one list for the application's guide files, and one for the document's guide files. The interface and implementation of the object is as follows:

```
class TAGDB : public TObject{
    private:
          FSSpec          fFSSpec;
          CStr255         fDBName;
    public:
          TAGDB();
          virtual pascal void IAGDB (CStr255& theName, FSSpec&
             theFSSpec);
          virtual pascal void Initialize (void); //Override
          virtual pascal void GetFSSpec (FSSpec& theFSSpec);
          virtual pascal void GetMenuName (CStr255& theName);
};
TAGDB::TAGDB() {
}
#pragma segment AOpen
pascal void TAGDB::Initialize (void)//Override
{
    inherited::Initialize ();
    fDBName = gEmptyString;
}
#pragma segment ARes
pascal void TAGDB::GetMenuName (CStr255& theName)
{
    theName = fDBName;
}
#pragma segment AOpen
pascal void TAGDB::IAGDB (CStr255& theName, FSSpec& theFSSpec)
{
```

```
inherited::IObject ();
    fDBName = theName;
    fFSSpec = theFSSpec;
}
#pragma segment ARes
pascal void TAGDB::GetFSSpec (FSSpec& theFSSpec)
{
    theFSSpec = fFSSpec;
}
```

N O T E   The segments are standard MacApp segments and reflect the times when the various methods are usually called. Normally an object's methods reside in a number of different segments, not in a single segment. For some reason, several myths and mysteries have grown up around MacApp's segmentation strategy, such as that all of a class's methods should be in the same segment. This is a typical use of that strategy.

Checking for Apple Guide

The code in this section is the first code that uses Apple Guide API calls. In order to compile it, you must include AppleGuide.h in your source code as follows before you reference any of the Apple Guide API calls:

```
#ifndef __APPLEGUIDE__
#include <AppleGuide.h>
#endif
```

You must also move AppleGuide.h into your CInterfaces folder if it is not already there.

While you are at it, move the AGFileLib library so that it can be included in your application and move the AGFile.h header file into CInterfaces as well. (AGFileLib is needed in the next section.)

All of these files are on the CD-ROM.

N O T E

In your application's initialization method (IMyApplication, not the override of Initialize), you can test for Apple Guide's presence and do anything that is necessary, such as find guide files for a Guide menu:

```
long gestaltResult;
OSErr myOSErr = Gestalt(gestaltHelpMgrAttr, gestaltResult);
if ((myOSErr == noErr) && (gestaltResult &
(1 << gestaltAppleGuidePresent)))
    {
    //install coach marks and context checks
    this->LoadAppAGDBList ();
    };
```

In order to implement the design discussed here, the application object has a TList member, fAGDBList, containing a list of TAGDB objectsone for each application guide file. All that remains is to find them and build the list. That is what LoadAppAGDBList does. It is described in the next section.

Finding Guide Files

In this design, guide files are loaded from two locations, and at two different times. At application startup, the application's guide files are loaded.

Loading Application Guide Files

LoadAppAGDBList is a routine that uses the AGFileLib routines to look at guide files and determine whether they should be loaded into the Guide menu. First, of course, a bunch of local variables are defined:

```
long     myDirID;
short    myVolID;
FSSpec   fileSpec;
short    newFileCount = 0;
```

```
Boolean  wantMixin = FALSE;
Str63    menuName;
TAGDB*   theAGDB = NULL;
OSType   theType = '    ';
```

The fAGDBList is set to a new empty list:

```
fAGDBList = NewList ();
```

The Toolbox FindFolder routine is used to locate (and create if necessary) the Preferences folder, returning its volume and directory identifiers:

```
myOSErr = FindFolder(kOnSystemDisk,kPreferencesFolderType,
   kCreateFolder, myVolID, myDirID);
```

Using the AGFileGetDBCount from AGFile, the number of guide files in the Preferences folder is found:

```
wantMixin = FALSE;
newFileCount = AGFileGetDBCount (myVolID, myDirID,
   kAGFileDBTypeAny, wantMixin);
```

For each guide file found, the AGFileGetIndDB routine is used to get its FSSpec. If the guide file turns out to be usable, this will be stored in an AGDB object.

To determine whether this guide file should be used, the AGFileGetHelpMenuAppCreator routine is used to get the value set with <App Creator> command in Guide Maker. In a more general case, you might want to check the Gestalt selectors in the guide file to test whether it is still usable for the Guide menu. Further, you could check the guide file's type in order to enforce the standard that only one Help, Shortcuts, or Tutorial guide file appear in the Guide menu. In this case, only the test for the creator is used. If it passes the test, AGFileGetDBMenuName returns the name that should appear in the Guide menu, and a TAGDB object is created with that name and the FSSpec and inserted into the fAGDBList.

```
if (newFileCount >0)
    for (short i = 1; i <= newFileCount; i++)
```

```
if (AGFileGetIndDB (myVolID, myDirID, kAGFileDBTypeAny,
    wantMixin, i, &fileSpec) == noErr)
{
    myOSErr = AGFileGetHelpMenuAppCreator (&fileSpec,
        &theType);
    if (theType == kSignature)
        if (AGFileGetDBMenuName(&fileSpec,
            menuName)==noErr)
        {
            CStr255 itsName = menuName;
            theAGDB = new TAGDB;
            theAGDB->IAGDB (itsName, fileSpec);
            fAGDBList->InsertLast (theAGDB);
        };
};
```

Document Guide Files

Guide files that are coresident with documents are loaded when each document is opened. The document has an fAGDBList variable similar to the application's; the document's fAGDBList contains its guide files. The document's LoadAGDBList method is called at the end of its DoRead method. The DoRead method has the document's TFile object passed in as a parameter. It is also passed as a parameter to the document's LoadAGDBList method:

```
pascal void TMyDocument::LoadAGDBList (TFile* aFile)
```

This method is identical to the method shown previously except that the directory and volume identifiers are taken from the *aFile* parameter, rather than from the Preferences folder:

```
myDirID = aFile->GetDirID ();
myVolID = aFile->GetVolRefNum ();
```

Building the Guide Menu

Your application's InstallHelpMenuItems is used to add any items to the Guide menu. It is called at appropriate times by MacApp. Using the structures created, you can quickly add the relevant guide files to the menu with the following override of InstallHelpMenuItems:

```
pascal void TVirgil::InstallHelpMenuItems (void)
{
    TList*      theAGDBList = NULL;
    if ((fAGDBList) && (fAGDBList->GetSize () > 0))
    {
        CStr255     tempString (gEmptyString);
        short    j = 0;
        CObjectIterator iter(fAGDBList);

        for (TAGDB* aAGDB  = (TAGDB*)iter.FirstObject();
        iter.More(); aAGDB =(TAGDB*)iter.NextObject())
        {
            aAGDB->GetMenuName (tempString);
            gMenuBarManager->AddHelpMenuItem(tempString,
            cHelpCommandNumber + j);
            j ++;
            };
        };

    if (fKioskDocument)
        theAGDBList = ((TKioskDocument*)fKioskDocument)
        ->GetAGDBList ();

    if (theAGDBList)
        {
        CStr255     tempString (gEmptyString);
        short     j;
        if (fAGDBList)
            j = (short)fAGDBList->GetSize();
        if ((fAGDBList) && (fAGDBList->GetSize () > 0) &&
            (theAGDBList->GetSize() > 0))
            gMenuBarManager->AddHelpMenuItem( "-",
            cNoCommand);
```

```
CObjectIterator iter(theAGDBList);
for (TAGDB* aAGDB  = (TAGDB*)iter.FirstObject();
iter.More(); aAGDB =(TAGDB*)iter.NextObject())
        {
        aAGDB->GetMenuName (tempString);
        gMenuBarManager->AddHelpMenuItem(tempString,
        cHelpCommandNumber + j);
        j ++;
        };
    }
  }
};
```

Each TAGDB object in the application's fAGDBList is iterated through; the guide file's name is added to the menu using the gMenuBarManager routine AddHelpMenuItem. The only item of additional interest is the constant *cHelpCommandNumber*, which is declared only as a base from which the guide file commands can be found. Each guide file added to the menu has a command number one greater than the previous one. This command number is used when the command is handled.

Handling Guide Menu Commands

Processing commands from the Guide menu is done in your application's DoMenuCommand method. Just as whenever you have to access the menu rather than a command number (as in handling commands from variable menus like Font menus), you convert the command number to a menu and item identifier:

```
CommandToMenuItem(aCommandNumber, menu, item);
switch (menu)
{
    case kHMHelpMenuID:
    {
        this->OpenAGDatabase (item);
        break;
    };
```

All that remains is to open the guide file in the OpenAGDatabase method. This method relies on the Help Manager routine HMGetHelpMenuHandle to return a handle to the Help/Guide menu, so it has to check gConfiguration.hasHelpMgr to make certain that the Help Manager is installed. Having gotten the Guide menu, it is possible to convert the *item* parameter to an individual guide file. Because MacApp and Apple Guide have inserted menu items at the top of the Guide menu, these have to be skipped over. Although it is easy to see that there will be four menu items above the guide files that are added here, it is not necessarily safe to rely on that, so this routine calculates the number of items at the top of the Guide menu. The method is to count the total number of items in the Guide menu (using CountMItems), and then to subtract the number of items added from the AGDB lists.

After the appropriate guide file is found, a previous guide file (whose reference number is stored in the application variable fLastAGRefNum) is closed if necessary and the new file is opened.

```
pascal void TVirgil::OpenAGDatabase (short      item)
{
      AGErr          myErr = noErr;
      FSSpec         fileSpec;
      AGRefNum       resultRefNum;

      if( gConfiguration.hasHelpMgr) // should always be true
      {
            MenuHandle     helpMenu = NULL;
            OSErr          err = HMGetHelpMenuHandle( helpMenu );
            short          nHelpItems = CountMItems( helpMenu );
            TAGDB*         theAGDB = NULL;
            short          nOtherHelpItems = 0;

            if (fKioskDocument)
                {
                nOtherHelpItems = nHelpItems
                ((TKioskDocument*)fKioskDocument)
                    ->GetAGDBListSize();
                if (((TKioskDocument*)fKioskDocument)
                    ->GetAGDBListSize() > 0)
```

```
            nOtherHelpItems = nOtherHelpItems - 1;
            //dividing line
    if (fAGDBList)
            nOtherHelpItems = nOtherHelpItems -
            fAGDBList>GetSize ();
    item = item - nOtherHelpItems;

    if ((item > 0) && (item <= fAGDBList->GetSize()))
            theAGDB = (TAGDB*) fAGDBList->At (item);

    if (!theAGDB)
        {
        if (fAGDBList)
            {
            if (fAGDBList->GetSize () > 0)
                    item = item - 1; //dividing line
            item = item - fAGDBList->GetSize ();
            };

        if ((item > 0) && (item <=
            ((TKioskDocument*)fKioskDocument)
            ->GetAGDBListSize()))
            theAGDB =
            ((TKioskDocument*)fKioskDocument)
            ->GetAGDBAt (item);
        };
    }
else
    { // no kiosk document
    if (fAGDBList)
        nOtherHelpItems = nHelpItems - fAGDBList
        >GetSize ();
    item = item - nOtherHelpItems;
    if ((item > 0) && (item <= fAGDBList->GetSize()))
        theAGDB = (TAGDB*) fAGDBList->At (item);
    };
```

```
        if (theAGDB)
            {
            if (fLastAGRefNum)
                {
                myErr = AGClose (&fLastAGRefNum);
                if (myErr == noErr)
                    fLastAGRefNum = 0;
                };
            theAGDB->GetFSSpec (fileSpec);
            myErr = AGOpen (&fileSpec, (UInt32)0, NULL,
            &resultRefNum);
            if (myErr)
                {
                theAGDB->GetMenuName (gErrorParm3);
                Failure (kMissingAGFile, 0);
                }
            else
                fLastAGRefNum = resultRefNum;
            };
        };
    }
```

Once again it should be pointed out that you may never need to do this. Apple Guide can build the Guide menu successfully in many cases. Even if you do need to manipulate the Guide menu, you are most likely to pick up guide files from one specific location, not two, as is shown in this example. Nevertheless, by walking through an almost worst-case scenario, you can see that you should not be frightened about undertaking such an operation.

OBJECT COACH MARKS

Adding coach marks to an application was described in Chapter 17, "The Apple Guide API," using MacApp examples from Symposium Explorer. Here is a large section of a coach mark handler that is used in that application so that you can see how it all fits together. The sections of the code that have been removed are additional case statements that repeat the logic of those shown here. They are essential for functioning of the routine, but do not use different logic than that shown here.

Without having a familiarity with the entire application, nevertheless you should be able to follow these points in the routine:

- The A5 world is saved off for restoration at the end.

- The *refCon* parameter was set to the application object when the coach mark handler was installed. From the application object, accessor routines allow the coach mark handler to find the main document (kiosk document), as well as several application-defined interface objects (a Controller window, a tear-off Colors palette, and so forth).

- The *pNameIn* pointer is parsed into two parts, separated by a dash. The first letter of the first word is used to control an outer switch statement. The second word (if it exists) is used to further control the switch statement.

- The appropriate object is asked to return the rectangle for the coach mark. Note the encapsulation here: the coach mark routine knows nothing about where the rectangle might be, except in one case (as follows).

- For the Colors palette, this routine does in fact calculate the rectangle that bounds the torn-off palette. Because Apple Guide wants the rect returned in global coordinates, code is included here to do that conversion. As you can guess, the methods called elsewhere in this method perform that conversion themselves.

- The A5 world is restored.

```
pascal OSErr CoachMarkCallBack (Rect* pItemRect, Ptr pNameIn, long
refCon)
{
  OSErr   result=kAGErrItemNotFound;
  long    restoreGlobals = SetA5(*(long*)CurrentA5);
  TVirgil*ourApp = (TVirgil*)refCon;
  char    pNameLocal[64];
  Ptr     pName1=pNameLocal;
  Ptr     pName2;
  char    chooser = ' ';
```

```
// This parsing of the pNameIn Ptr into two pieces
// separated by a - is taken from the MoGuide example
// on the Mac OS SDK.  Thanks, John.
// Split pNameIn into pName1 and pName2.
// Copy first name to pNameLoc (pName1).
while(*pNameIn && *pNameIn!='-')
  *pName1++ = *pNameIn++;
// Set terminator for first name at delimiter.
*pName1 = 0;
// Reset first name to the beginning.
pName1 = pNameLocal;
// If delimiter, then set pName2 to second name.
// Otherwise, set pName2 to point to null.
if(*pNameIn)
  pName2 = pNameIn+1;
else
  pName2 = pNameIn;

if(ourApp)
  {
  TDocument*    aDocument = ourApp->GetKioskDocument();
  if (aDocument)
    aKioskDocument = (TKioskDocument*) aDocument;
  };

switch (pNameLocal [0]) //only the first character is needed
  {
  case 'N': //notes
    {
    if (aKioskDocument)
      // Get the Note window bounds
      result = aKioskDocument->GetNoteWindowRect(pItemRect);
    break;
    };
```

```
case 'P': //part
  {
  if (aKioskDocument)
    //ask the Controller for the rect of pName2 part
    result = (aKioskDocument->GetController())
    ->GetRectForPartButton (pName2, pItemRect);
  break;
  };

case 'M': //menu
  {
  chooser = *pName2;
  switch (chooser)
    {
    case 'C': //the Colors palette can be torn off
      {
      VRect  theVRect (gZeroVRect);
      VPoint  theVPoint (gZeroVPt);
      if (((TVirgil*)gApplication)->GetColorsWindow())
        {
        ((TVirgil*)gApplication)->GetColorsWindow()
        ->GetExtent (theVRect);
        ((TVirgil*)gApplication)->GetColorsWindow()
        ->ViewToQDRect (theVRect, (CRect&)*pItemRect);
        GrafPtr  savePort;
        // Return the rectangle in global coordinates
        GetPort(savePort);
        // Get the GrafPort.
        SetPort(((TVirgil*)gApplication)->GetColorsWindow()
        ->GetGrafPort ());
        // Top-left
        LocalToGlobal(((CPoint&)(pItemRect->top));
        // Bottom-right
        LocalToGlobal(((CPoint&)(pItemRect->bottom));
        SetPort(savePort);
        result = noErr;
```

```
              break;
                };
            }; //case color menu

            default:
              break;
          };
        break;
        };
      };
    SetA5(restoreGlobals);
    return (result);
  }
```

Remember to install your coach mark handler in the IMyApplication method using the AGInstallCoachHandler routine.

CUSTOM CONTEXT CHECKS

Custom context checks were also discussed extensively in Chapter 17. A large section of one of Symposium Explorer's context check handlers is presented here so that you can see how it all works together. You should be able to follow the logic as the routine does the following steps:

- Save the A5 world.
- Convert the *hAppInfo.refCon* to the application object and set *hasKioskDocument* to the proper value. (This is to make the code more readable. *hasKioskDocument* is used in a number of the context checks, including those that are not shown in this excerpt.)
- Use the *hAppInfo.eventID* to determine which context check is to be done. Note that these constants were used in the installation process to associate the particular context check with this call-back routine.
- *kAreNotesOpen* is a context check with no parameters.
- The *kTornOffMenu* context check expects an OSType in the *pInput* parameter to specify which of two tear-off menus should be questioned to

determine whether it is torn off.

- The *kControllerTool* context check asks the Controller whether the OSType in the *pInput* parameter is the currently selected tool. This OSType corresponds to a subview identifierthe same one that is used in the coach mark handler shown above. Once again, the context check handler knows nothing about these subviews.

- The *ppOutput* pointer is created, pointing to a Boolean that contains the value to be returned from the context check. The A5 world is restored and the result of the context check (noErr in all cases here) is returned.

```
pascal OSErr ReplyToWindowsContext(Ptr pInput,
                Size inputDataSize,
                Ptr *ppOutput,
                Size *pOutputDataSize,
                AGAppInfoHdl hAppInfo)
{
  //based on the MoGuide ReplyToContext method. Thanks, John.
  OSErr       err=noErr;
  OSErr       myOSErr = noErr;
  Boolean     result = FALSE;
  OSType      inputType='    ';
  Boolean     hasKioskDocument = FALSE;
  TComponent* currentComponent = NULL;
  TKioskDocument* aKioskDocument = NULL;
  long        gestaltResult = 0;
  TController* theController = NULL;

  long restoreGlobals = SetA5(*(long*)CurrentA5);

  TVirgil*  ourApp = (TVirgil*)(**hAppInfo).refCon;
  if(ourApp)
    {
    TDocument*  aDocument = ourApp->GetKioskDocument();
    if (aDocument)
```

```
      {
    hasKioskDocument = TRUE;
    aKioskDocument = (TKioskDocument*) aDocument;
    theController = aKioskDocument->GetController();
    currentComponent = theController->GetCurrentComponent ();
      };
    };
// Which event id?
switch ((**hAppInfo).eventId)
{
  case kAreNotesOpen:
    {
    if (aKioskDocument)
      result = aKioskDocument->HasNoteDocument();
    break;
    };

  case kTornOffMenu:
    {
    VPoint  theVPoint (0, 0);
    if(pInput && inputDataSize>0)
      inputType = *((OSType*)pInput);
    switch (inputType)
      {
      case 'colr':
        {
        if (ourApp)
          if (ourApp->GetColorsWindow())
            result = ourApp->GetColorsWindow()->IsShown();
        break;
        };

      case 'tool':
        {
        if (ourApp)
```

```
              if (ourApp->GetToolsWindow())
                result = ourApp->GetToolsWindow()->IsShown();
            break;
            };

         default:
            break;
         }; // switch inputType
       break;
       };

    case kControllerTool:
      {
      if (theController)
        {
        if(pInput && inputDataSize>0)
          inputType = *((OSType*)pInput);

        result = theController->IsToolSelected (inputType);
        };
      break;
      };

    default:  // An unknown event will be ignored.
      break;
    }

// Create storage for our result.
*ppOutput = NewPtr(sizeof(Boolean));
if(*ppOutput)
{
  // Set the result and its size.
  **ppOutput = result;
  *pOutputDataSize = sizeof(Boolean);
}
```

```
    SetA5(restoreGlobals);
    return err;
}
```

Remember to install the context check handler using AGInstallContextHandler during your IMyApplication method. If you are implementing several context checks, you may want to create several different handlers, each of which deals with different types of checks.

SUMMARY

Using Apple Guide with MacApp, even doing extensive integration as shown in the examples here, is not at all difficult. The somewhat long code excerpts included here give you an idea of precisely what you have to do in the various cases discussed. Remember that rarely will you need all of the code samples shown here.

After providing extensive Apple Guide support in your applications, there's nothing left but to add Apple Guide support to other people's applications, both to add to existing assistance from the developer as well as to create custom solutions. The next part of this book deals with those issues.

CHAPTER 20

Adding Apple Guide to Custom Solutions

Custom solutions range from an insurance company's customer support center, which integrates communications, word processing, database, and in-house applications, to the receptionist's interoffice routing slip, which was created in one afternoon using a word processing program. Because Apple Guide can be added to any and all of these applications, it can be used to tie together the multiple-application solution as well as to document the single-application solution.

All of the arguments for adding Apple Guide to applications apply equally well to solutions. Some arguments are even more persuasive. Documentation is often a weak spot with custom solutions. The development and implementation phases of a project can be so intensive and involve so many people in an organization that "everyone knows" how the system works. Over time, "everyone" may forget or be transferred, and modifications to the system may not be reflected in updated documentation. Solutions that are inherently complex, such as those used in heavily regulated industries or used by a work force with a high rate of turnover, lend themselves easily to the addition of Apple Guide. Apple Guide, by providing a uniform, electronic system of support, can be a key to keeping solutions documented and supported.

Because Apple Guide can work with the Finder as well as multiple applications, Apple Guide can even *become a* solution: create a guide file of type Other that appears in the Guide menu and walks the user through various applications. Applications that provide support for Apple events allow you to automate the process with **Do It for Me** buttons. If the applications involved integrate Apple

Guide closely with application-based context checks and coach marks, you can provide even more impressive and useful guide files.

The examples in this section demonstrate different ways of adding Apple Guide support to applications that are often used singly or in combination to provide custom solutions: HyperCard, 4th Dimension, WordPerfect, Microsoft Word, and Microsoft Excel. Each chapter can be read in two ways: as a template for adding Apple Guide support to that specific application, or as a model for how to handle generic problems and challenges that many applications share. Thus, the chapter on HyperCard shows not only how to add Apple Guide support to HyperCard, but how to deal with any application that supports Apple Script and the Object Support Library (OSL). The chapter on 4th Dimension addresses not only the issues posed by that application, but also the issues of any application in which window titles are not known in advance (but where you still want to do context checks) and where the menu bar is not actually a menu bar, and where Apple events are not used as they are in HyperCard. The other chapters similarly have dual purposes, which are described at the beginning of each chapter.

Although Apple Events and AppleScript are in no way necessary to the guide files that you write, they can be so useful, and enough applications now support at least a few Apple Events that the next chapter discusses the Apple Guide Core Suite of Events, which you can access through AppleScript.

Finally, the last chapter in this section addresses the issues involved in adding Apple Guide to multimedia content. Some of those issues are unique to that problem, but others are relevant to many Apple Guide situations in which the interplay of the task and the tool must be clarified.

By the end of this part of the book, you will have seen how to create Apple Guide assistance, how to integrate it closely with applications, and how to use it to support and link third-party applications.

Apple Guide features and services, available through guide files and Guide Maker commands, through the API calls described in the previous part of the book, and through the AppleScript commands discussed in this part, are an impressive array of user support features. The ease with which you can invoke them from so many different environments and the ease with which you can coordinate them with any application, makes it easier than ever to provide users with the tools they need to do their work.

CHAPTER 21

The Apple Guide Core Suite of Events

What, more syntax? More commands? More Apple Guide?

The answer is "no." A somewhat nuanced "no" to be sure. This chapter contains descriptions of 32 Apple events that you can use with AppleScript, but there really is no new syntax described in this chapter. Apple Guide's functionality is accessible to you through Guide Maker commands and through the Apple Guide API, as well as through AppleScript and Apple events. Because the functionality is made available through so many different means, you should never find yourself struggling with an unfamiliar tool. Use whichever method is most convenient. The design of Apple Guide, with its services open to everyone, is an excellent example of how the pieces of the Mac OS can be tied together. If all applications were as open, the world would be a much better place.

You use the Apple Guide events the same way you use the API and for many of the same reasons. If you want to open an Apple Guide database from your AppleScript script (rather than from the Guide menu), you need to use these events. If you want to manipulate a guide file from the script (going to certain panels, showing the Access window at specific points, and so forth), you need to use these events. Finally, if you are testing and debugging either guide files or applications that manipulate them with the API, you may find it faster and easier to send events directly from a script to Apple Guide and watch the results.

USING SCRIPT EDITOR TO BROWSE THE SUITE

If you are not used to working with AppleScript, you may not be familiar with Script Editor's ability to show you the events and syntax for any application's events. From the File menu of Script Editor, choose Open Dictionary (see Figure 21.1).

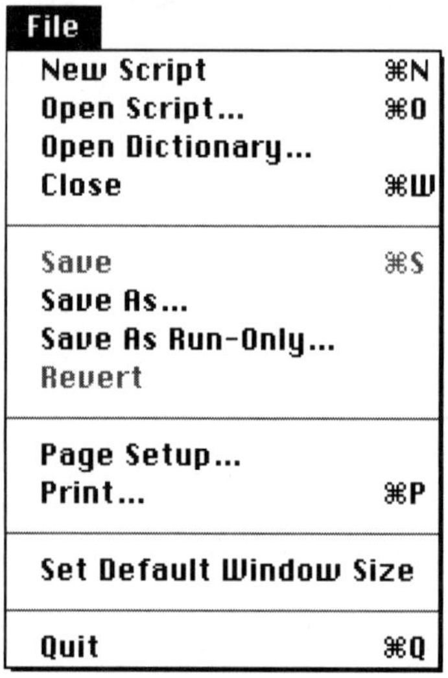

File	
New Script	⌘N
Open Script...	⌘O
Open Dictionary...	
Close	⌘W
Save	⌘S
Save As...	
Save As Run-Only...	
Revert	
Page Setup...	
Print...	⌘P
Set Default Window Size	
Quit	⌘Q

Figure 21.1 Script Editor's File menu.

Script Editor will ask you which application's dictionary you want to browse. In this case, open Apple Guide itself. It is located in the Extensions folder of your System folder. You will see the window shown in Figure 21.2.

Clicking on any event in the left pane of the window will show you its syntax to the right. Figure 21.3 demonstrates the display if you click DoCoach.

If you click the first item in the panel at the left, Apple Guide Core Suite, the entire list will be highlighted. The panel at the right will show the entire syntax for the suite in a scrolling view, suitable for printing and keeping close at hand (see Figure 21.4).

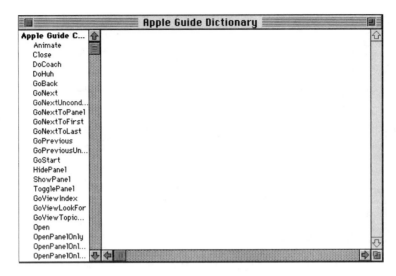

Figure 21.2 Apple Guide core suite of events.

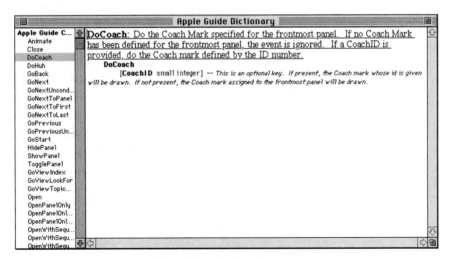

Figure 21.3 DoCoach syntax.

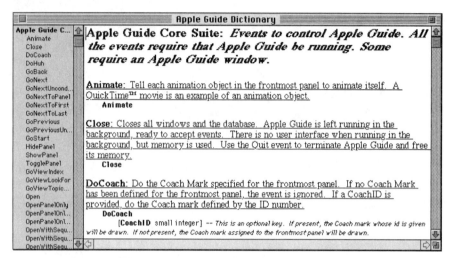

Figure 21.4 Complete Apple Guide core suite syntax.

Whenever you are developing an AppleScript script, get in the habit of using Script Editor to look at the application's events. More and more applications are supporting AppleScript now, and their suites can be quite extensive.

If you have added Apple event support to an application, you have probably included an 'aete' resource, which contains the sort of information shown here. In fact, Script Editor simply reads an application's 'aete' resource to produce the dictionary listing.

The syntax for AppleScript commands differs somewhat from the syntax described previously. Parameters for Guide Script commands and the Apple Guide API functions are specified in a given order; their order determines which is which. AppleScript uses the convention in which each parameter is identified by a keyword. These keywords are part of the syntax and, as such, are presented in boldface type: :

```
OpenWithSequence Database database, SequenceID sequence,
    [PanelID panel]
```

The command can be implemented as

```
OpenWithSequence Database "myDatabaseName" SequenceID 14
```

or

```
OpenWithSequence Database "myDatabaseName" SequenceID 14 PanelID 2
```

N O T E

Many of the events described in this chapter may return various error codes. In addition to standard Mac OS error codes, they can return specific Apple Guide error codes. Many of these were discussed in Chapter 17, "The Apple Guide API." A complete listing is provided in the interface file AppleGuide.h on the RealWorld Apple Guide CD-ROM. Error codes are mentioned in this section only if they are likely to occur.

Each event described in this chapter corresponds to an event in Apple Guide's core suite (the 'help' suite). Each event within a suite has its own four-character event ID. These event IDs are provided here. You never use them from Apple Script, but if you want to send one of these events from another application or with the AGGeneral routine in the Apple Guide API, they are useful to know.

As with the terminology in the API, "guide file" and "database" are used interchangeably, except where "database" appears in a event's syntax. The preference here is to use "guide file."

STARTING APPLE GUIDE

Even though the Apple Guide extension is installed when you start up your machine, Apple Guide needs to be running in order to be used. Normally, you start up Apple Guide automatically when you choose an item from the Guide menu. If you are writing a script, however, you need to start Apple Guide so that you will have an application to send messages to (with the tell command). During the computer's startup process, the AGStart scripting addition is added to the Scripting Additions folder inside the Extensions folder. It adds the AGStart event to the system.

AGStart Event

It may take a few moments for Apple Guide to start up after you issue the AGStart event. Because there is no way to test whether Apple Guide is running (except indirectly), you may need to take some precautions to make certain that Apple Guide has indeed started up before issuing additional events to it. Some of the strategies are as follows:

- Call AGStart before you need it—at the beginning of a script, for example, rather than immediately before the first Apple Guide event.
- Call AGStart several times. Once Apple Guide is running, repeated calls to AGStart have no effect and produce no errors.
- Insert a pause after the call to AGStart.

Timing problems are always pesky on computers. Because different processors run at different speeds and because random events (printing, network requests, and so forth) can influence results in a way that cannot be measured, these problems can be hard to diagnose and track down. One or more of these strategies should prevent the problem.

Syntax:	**AGStart**
EventID:	agst
Result Codes:	If Apple Guide is not installed, you will get the following result:
	errAEEventNotHandled -1708
When to Use:	Before using any Apple Guide events in AppleScript. Thereafter, all events should be sent directly to Apple Guide using the syntax tell application "Apple Guide"

OPENING A GUIDE FILE

You use the Open event to open a guide file from AppleScript, rather than having the user open it from the Guide menu. Any other Apple Guide windows are closed.

Open Event

The *databaseFile* parameter is either a string containing the full path name of the guide file or an FSSpec. If it is omitted, a currently open database is closed and reopened. If it is omitted and there is not currently open database, an error is returned.

The *lookForString* parameter is a string that is placed in the Look For phrase in the Look For view of a Full Access window.

The *startupView* parameter, a short integer, specifies the startup view. Its values are as follows:

Full Howdy	1
Topic Areas	2
Index	3
LookFor	4
Single Howdy	5
Single Topics	6

Syntax:	**Open** [*Database* databaseFile][, *String* lookForString] [,*ViewNumber* startupView]
EventID:	open
Result Codes:	If the *databaseFile* parameter is missing and no database is currently open, you will get the following result code: -2914
Example:	Open database "HF:MyApp:MyGuideFile"
When to Use:	As needed to open an Apple Guide database other than from the Guide menu.

The **GoStart** event is a synonym for the Open event in the case where a database is already open.

Although the **Open** event opens a guide file to its startup view, the **OpenWithSequence** event opens the guide file and immediately displays a sequence within it. Like the **Open** event, it closes other Apple Guide windows.

OpenWithSequence Event

The databaseFile parameter is either a string containing the full path name to the guide file or an FSSpec. The parameter sequence is the id number of the sequence that you want to display. If you specify a panel parameter, that panel of the sequence will be shown. Panels are numbered sequentially from 1 in each sequence. To find the sequence, you need to use Guide Maker's reporting facility.

Syntax:	**OpenWithSequence database** *databaseFile* , **sequenceID** *sequence* [,***panelNumber*** *panel*]
EventID:	stpr
Example:	OpenWithSequence database "HF:MyApp:MyGuideFile" sequenceID 12
When to Use:	As needed.

NAVIGATING IN OPENED GUIDE FILES

The events in this section all require a guide file to be open. They allow you to navigate:

- to Access windows
- to a specific sequence
- from panel to panel

Displaying Access Windows

Three events are used to toggle among the different views of the Full Access window. They have the same effect as that of the user clicking the Topics, Index, or Look For buttons. In each case, the Access window in one of its views must be displayed. In other words, an error is returned if a presentation panel rather than the Access window is open.

GoViewTopicAreas Event

This event displays the Topics view of the Access window.

Syntax:	**GoViewTopicAreas**
EventID:	gotp
Result Code:	no Access window open -2902
When to Use:	As needed.

GoViewIndex Event

This event displays the Index view of the Access window.

Syntax:	**GoViewIndex**
EventID:	goin
Result Code:	no Access window open-2902
When to Use:	As needed.

GoViewLookFor Event

This event displays the Look For view of the Access window. If the optional *lookForString* parameter is present, it is put into the entry field.

Syntax:	**GoViewLookFor *string*** lookforstring
EventID:	golf
Result Code:	no Access window open -2902
Example:	GoViewLookFor string "disk"
When to Use:	As needed.

Displaying Sequences in a Guide File

Normally when you open a sequence in a guide file, you want to close the current sequence, leaving the new sequence's presentation panel as the only Apple Guide window open. You use the OpenWithSequenceReplacement event for this purpose.

OpenWithSequenceReplacement Event

The *sequence* parameter is the number of the sequence to open (which you obtain from Guide Maker's reports). The optional *panel* parameter identifies which panel of the sequence (starting from 1) is to be shown.

Syntax:	**OpenWithSequenceReplacement sequenceID** sequence [, **panelNumber** panel]
EventID:	stpc
Example:	OpenWithSequenceReplacement sequenceID 12 panelNumber 1
When to Use:	As needed, but not for Oops sequences (see next event).

OpenWithSequenceAnother Event

To open a sequence from the current guide file while leaving the existing sequence open, use the **OpenWithSequenceAnother** event.

The parameters are the same as for the **OpenWithSequenceReplacement** event previously described.

Syntax:	**OpenWithSequenceAnother sequenceID** sequence [, **panelNumber** panel]
EventID	:stps
Example:	OpenWithSequenceAnother sequenceID 12
When to Use:	As needed, but not for Oops sequences (see next event).

OpenWithSequenceOops Event

Most commonly when you want to open a second sequence, it is because you want to launch an Oops sequence. That is done with the **OpenWithSequenceOops** event.

The window of the currently open sequence is hidden (not closed) when an Oops sequence is opened. To return from the Oops sequence to the first sequence, you use the GoBack event.

Syntax:	**OpenWithSequenceOops sequenceID** sequence
EventID:	stop
Example:	OpenWithSequenceOops sequenceID 14
When to Use:	As needed.

GoBack Event

Normally sequences in a guide file are either closed by the user or are closed automatically as part of the opening of a new sequence or guide file. The one exception to this rule is when an Oops sequence is closed. Its windows are closed and the sequence whose windows were hidden when it was opened is shown again.

The GoBack command is used to return from an Oops sequence.

Syntax:	**GoBack**
EventID:	gobk
When to Use:	As needed.

Displaying Panels in a Guide File

The events used to display panels in a guide file fall into two broad categories:

- relative events (next/previous)
- absolute events (display a specific panel)

Relative Panel Navigation

When users interact directly with Apple Guide, they normally use the left and right arrows to move to adjacent panels. You can use events to have the same effects.

GoNext Event

The GoNext event is the event triggered when the user clicks the right arrow. All of the conditions and constraints that come into play at that time (Show If, Skip If, and Make Sure) are performed.

Syntax:	**GoNext**
EventID:	gonp
When to Use:	As needed.

GoNextUnconditionally Event

Sometimes you want to go to the next panel in a sequence bypassing the conditions and constraints that are performed with the GoNext event.

Syntax:	**GoNextUnconditionally**
EventID:	gons
Example:	GoNextUnconditionally
When to Use:	For testing.

Another pair of events is available to perform the functions associated with the left arrow.

GoPrevious Event

This is the event triggered by the left arrow. Although the left arrow is dimmed and unavailable for the first panel in a sequence, this event is available at that time; using it will close the window. Any context checks that would be evaluated with the left arrow are performed with this event.

Syntax:	**GoPrevious**
EventID:	gopp
When to Use:	As needed.

You can also go to the previous panel without performing any context checks.

GoPreviousUnconditionally Event

Syntax:	**GoPreviousUnconditionally**
EventID:	gops
When to Use:	As needed.

Displaying Specific Panels

The events in this section let you open specific panels in a sequence.

GoNexttopanel Event

This event goes to the panel specified by panel, where the first panel in a sequence is 1. The Show If, Skip If, and Make Sure tests are performed. If they fail, the next panel in the sequence that satisfies its conditions is shown.

Syntax:	**GoNextToPanel *panelNumber* panel**
EventID:	goup
Example:	GoNextToPanel panelNumber 4
When to Use:	As needed.

GoNextToFirst Event

To go to the first panel in a sequence, use the GoNextToFirst event.

This is equivalent to GoNextToPanel panelNumber 1. The context checks of the GoNextToPanel are performed.

Syntax:	**GoNextToFirst**
EventID:	gofp
When to Use:	As needed.

To go to the last panel in a sequence, performing the appropriate context checks, use GoNextToLast.

GoNextToLast Event

If the context checks fail for the last panel in a sequence, no panel will be shown.

Syntax:	**GoNextToLast**
EventID:	golp
When to Use:	As needed.

Opening Panels For Diagnostics and Alerts

Finally, it is possible to open a guide file directly to an individual panel. This is often done when you are testing a guide file. It also may be necessary if you are opening a guide file directly to information that the user will need to solve a problem you have detected. In such case you may use Apple Guide to put up a presentation panel that serves as an alert box would serve in the standard Mac OS interface.

OpenPanelOnly panelID panel, database databaseFile

The *panel* is the actual resource ID of the panel as stored in the guide file (type 'ppUA'). It is not the panel sequence number used in the previous events. The *databaseFile* is either a string containing the full path name of the guide file or an FSSpec.

Syntax:	**OpenPanelOnly *panelID* panel, *database* databaseFile**
EventID:	stpo
Example:	`OpenPanelOnly panelID 15, database "HD:MyApp:MyGuideFile"`
When to Use:	Testing.

OpenPanelOnlyAnother Event

When you have a guide file open, you can use OpenPanelOnlyAnother to display a panel without its title bar or navigation bar while leaving other Apple Guide windows open.

The *panel* is the resource ID of the panel.

Syntax:	**OpenPanelOnlyAnother panelID** *panel*
EventID:	stpq
Example:	OpenPanelOnlyAnother panelID 4
When to Use:	Testing.

OpenPanelOnlyReplacement Event

The last event in this section is the same as the previous event, but it does close other Apple Guide windows.

Syntax:	**OpenPanelOnlyReplacement panelID** *panel*
EventID:	stpp
Example:	OpenPanelOnlyReplacement panelID 4
When to Use:	Testing.

Working with Open Panels

After you have a panel open, a set of events lets you manipulate it.

DoCoach coachID coachMark Event

If no value is specified for *coachMark*, this event draws the coach mark for the panel that is open. If no coach mark has been defined, the event is ignored (no error is returned). If the *coachMark* is included, the coach mark specified by that identifier is drawn, whether it is the coach mark for the open panel or not.

Syntax:	**DoCoach coachID** *coachMark*
EventID:	doco
Example:	DoCoach coachID 42
When to Use:	As needed.

DoHuh Event

You can simulate the user clicking the Huh? button on the open panel with the DoHuh event.

If no Huh? button is provided for the open panel, the event is ignored (no error is returned).

Syntax:	**DoHuh**
EventID:	dhuh
When to Use:	As needed.

Animate Event

If a QuickTime movie is present in a presentation panel shown, you can start it with an event.

All animation objects in the currently open panel are started with this event. (Currently, only QuickTime movies are animation objects.)

Syntax:	**Animate**
EventID:	paan
When to Use:	As needed.

Three events are used to support the actions taken when the user clicks the zoom box of a presentation window.

TogglePanel Event

This is the event that occurs when the user clicks the zoom box.

Syntax:	**TogglePanel**
EventID:	patg
When to Use:	As needed.

HidePanel Event

If a panel is maximized (full size), this event minimizes it. If the panel is already minimized, the event is ignored (no result is returned).

Syntax:	**HidePanel**
EventID:	pahi
When to Use:	As needed.

ShowPanel Event

This is the reverse of the HidePanel event.

Syntax:	**ShowPanel**
EventID:	pash
When to Use:	As needed.

PlaySound Event

Given the resource ID of a 'snd' resource in the guide file, you can play that sound with the PlaySound event.

Syntax:	**PlaySound soundID** *resourceID*
EventID:	psnd
Example:	`PlaySound soundID 432`
When to Use:	As needed.

Closing and Quitting Apple Guide

The final events in the Apple Guide core suite are used to close and quit Apple Guide.

Close Event

This event closes the guide file and all of its windows. Apple Guide is still running in the background in sleep mode and uses memory. After closing guide files with this event, you do not need to send a new AGStart event before communicating with Apple Guide again.

Syntax:	**Close**
EventID:	slep
When to Use:	As needed.

Quit Event

This event terminates Apple Guide. After sending this event, you will need to send a new AGStart event before sending additional events to Apple Guide.

Syntax:	**Quit**
EventID:	quit
When to Use:	As needed.

QuitFront Event

This event closes the front-most Apple Guide window, if one exists. If no Apple Guide windows are open, this event functions identically to the Quit event.

Syntax:	**QuitFront**
EventID:	ktop
When to Use:	As needed.

Summary

With Apple Guide's features and functionality available equally through Guide Maker commands, the API, and Apple events, you may come to the conclusion that it is inexcusable not to use these features wherever appropriate in your applications and custom solutions. Right.

Now that you have seen what you can do with Apple Guide, it is time to move on and see how this functionality can be used with several real-world applications.

CHAPTER 22

Adding Apple Guide to HyperCard Stacks

By now, just about everyone has heard about HyperCard. In case you've been living in a modemless cave, this blurb from the back of the HyperCard box should fill you in:

> HyperCard version 2.2 lets you develop powerful standalone applications for customizing business solutions, education courseware, interactive multimedia presentations, and more. HyperCard, the leading tool for creating custom software, has been integrated with AppleScript, so you can easily control scriptable off-the-shelf applications (and automate repetitive tasks) with the click of a button.

One word should jump out at you from that paragraph: AppleScript. Apple Guide relies heavily on Apple events for its functioning and the Apple Guide core suite of events, which is described in Chapter 21, lets you access each and every one of them from AppleScript. Does that make Apple Guide itself a "scriptable off-the-shelf application" that you can "easily control" from HyperCard? You've got it. (In fact, as you will see later in this chapter, you can send Apple events from Apple Guide to HyperCard as well as in the other direction. Control passes easily between the two applications.)

In this chapter, you will see how to integrate Apple Guide with HyperCard stacks. You may want to develop a HyperCard stack and attach one or more guide files (Help, Tutorial, and so on) to it to provide one of those customized solutions just referred to. Alternatively, you may want to integrate one or more HyperCard stacks into a more complex solution, one that may also involve other applications. The tips and techniques in this chapter apply to both cases.

You can provide unintegrated assistance for a stack without taking any special steps. Simply create a guide file that provides whatever assistance is necessary and place it in the folder with HyperCard itself. Apple Guide will automatically add it to the Guide menu when HyperCard is launched. You can do quite a lot with such a guide file:

- You can coach windows and menus with the <Define Window Coach> and <Define Menu Coach> commands.
- You can use the external code modules in Standard Resources to check that specific windows are open or active.
- You can execute HyperCard scripts with **Do It for Me** buttons in Apple Guide.

The limits of unintegrated assistance are quickly apparent, as you discover:

- When you put a guide file in the folder with HyperCard, it shows up in the Guide menu whenever HyperCard is opened whether the stack you care about is opened or not.
- If a user moves a field or button on a stack, your <Define Window Coach> command will coach the previous location.
- You cannot check to see whether a button on a card is clicked. Only the standard context checks are available.

In this chapter you will see how to create an integrated guide file that addresses those issues.

NOTE

Although this chapter is specifically directed at HyperCard, you can reuse many of these techniques with other applications that support AppleScript.

THE APPLE GUIDE COMMAND STACK

The commands from Guide Maker have been assembled into a self-running HyperCard stack that is included on the CD-ROM that comes with this book. That stack comes with an Apple Guide Help file, which is tightly integrated with the stack. Both the stack and that guide file are used as examples in this chapter. The stack is shown in Figure 22.1.

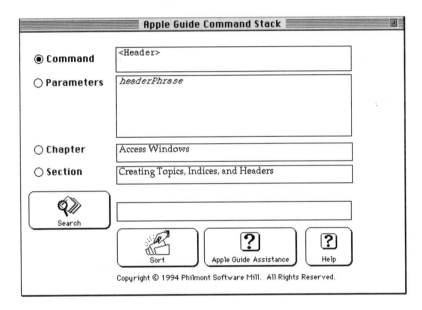

Figure 22.1 The Apple Guide command stack.

The four radio buttons at the left are used to control the **Search** and **Sort** buttons. When you click the **Sort** button, the stack is sorted on whichever field is clicked. For example, to sort the stack by commands within sections of chapters, you click **Command** and then **Sort**, **Section** and then **Sort**, and finally **Chapter** and then **Sort**. To search for a word or phrase, you enter it in the field next to the

Search button. You click the radio button that corresponds to the field in which you want to search for the word or phrase. All of this is very common in HyperCard stacks.

Also common is a **Help** button, such as the one at the lower right of the stack. If you click on the button, a hidden field with locked text is shown, as demonstrated in Figure 22.2.

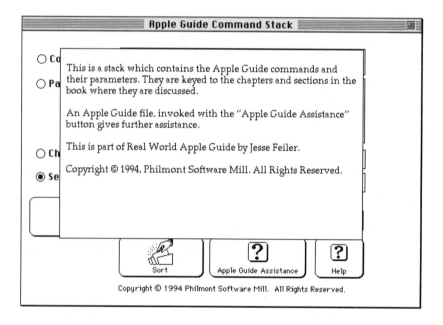

Figure 22.2 Apple Guide command stack help button.

Less common, at least for now, is the **Apple Guide Assistance** button in this stack. Clicking it opens a guide file, one of whose panels is shown in Figure 22.3.

In fact, Figure 22.3 does not adequately demonstrate what is happening. If you were to modify this stack, moving the entry field for the search string to another location, you would find that the coach mark that underlines the field moves as well.

The guide file and stack demonstrate how the limitations of unintegrated guide files can be overcome. The rest of this chapter details the methods used.

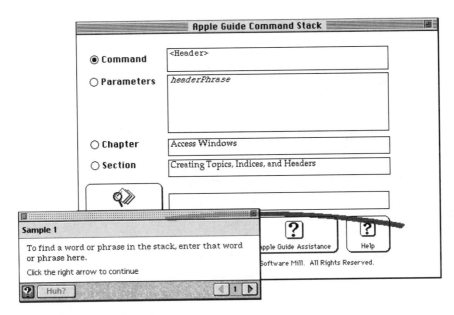

Figure 22.3 Apple Guide assistance for Apple Guide command stack.

OPENING GUIDE FILES FROM HYPERCARD BUTTONS

Any button or field in HyperCard can have a script attached to it. Scripts can now be written either in HyperTalk or in AppleScript. A pop-up at the top of each script window lets you choose which one you use. This stack uses both HyperTalk and AppleScript scripts, because each is more useful in some cases. Because Apple Guide supports AppleScript, it is very easy to add the Apple Guide core events to AppleScript scripts that are attached to HyperCard objects.

Starting Apple Guide

In Chapter 21, "The Apple Guide Core Suite of Events," the AGStart command is described. It must be sent to make certain that Apple Guide is running and is identifiable as an application to which AppleScript events can be sent. As noted, sometimes there is a lag between the time that you issue the AGStart event and the time that Apple Guide gets itself up and running. Because it is likely that Apple Guide will be needed when this stack is opened, the AGStart command is placed in an on OpenBackground handler, as shown in Figure 22.4. That generally provides enough time for Apple Guide to start running before other commands are sent to it from the stack.

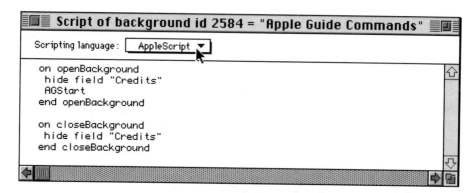

Figure 22.4 The on OpenBackground handler.

In a case where a stack will probably not use Apple Guide, this is a wasteful design. Apple Guide uses memory when it runs, and it takes a small but definite amount of processor power to start it up. If you copy this design, make certain that you apply it in a case like this where Apple Guide is likely to be needed by a stack. In other cases, you can place AGStart in other locations in your stack where it is called only when needed but sufficiently in advance of its being needed. If all else fails, you can call AGStart exactly at the moment when you need Apple Guide to be running; experiment with inserting a pause that is sufficiently long to let Apple Guide start up but not long enough to waste the user's time.

Remember that if you are writing guide files that will be opened from the Guide menu, you do not have to include the AGStart event in your stack.

Finding a Guide File's Name

It is basic HyperCard script-writing to attach a handler to a button. In fact, when you open a script window for a newly created button, you have the shell of an on mouseUp handler waiting for you. In Figure 22.5 you can see the code for the on mouseUp handler of the button that opens a guide file.

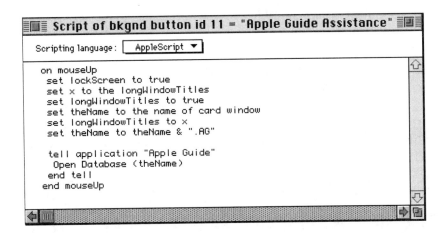

Figure 22.5 Script to open a guide file from a button.

If you do not have guide files coresident with HyperCard (and thus automatically added to the Guide menu by Apple Guide whenever HyperCard is running), you must decide where to place them. This stack's design makes the guide file coresident with the stack itself. Furthermore, the guide file in question is assumed to have the same name as the stack, but with the suffix ".AG" appended to it. This allows this section of code to work in any case where this design is used, regardless of the name of the stack.

Having made that assumption, it is now necessary to implement it. All that is necessary is to find the name of the stack and to add the ".AG" to it. Because the Open Database AppleScript event that will eventually be used to open the guide files requires a fully qualified file name, it is necessary to get the fully qualified name of the stack (that is, the name of the stack with its parent folder, that folder's parent, and the name of the hard disk on which they all reside.) HyperCard has a global attribute, *longWindowTitles* that allows you to have the fully qualified stack name shown in the window title. This little script first locks the screen (so that no changes will be visible to the user). Then the current value of *longWindowTitles* is stored temporarily, and the parameter is set to TRUE. Having done that, you can then copy the name of the window title to a local variable (*theName* in this script) and append the ".AG" to it. You restore *longWindowTitles* to the value it had before and unlock the screen.

At this point, you have available the name of the guide file that you want to open. You then tell Apple Guide to open that file using the **Open Database** command, as shown in the script.

You don't have to worry about whether Apple Guide is running, because AGStart was called when this background was opened. If the guide file is not found, an error will be returned to the user: Apple Guide got an error: a result of -2914 was returned. Depending on the circumstances (the likelihood of files being moved, the sophistication of your users), you could check for such a result in your script.

That's all you have to do to open guide files from HyperCard buttons.

COACHING HYPERCARD BUTTONS AND FIELDS

You can use the <Define Window Coach> command to create coach marks based on known locations in a window. That is fine for coaching buttons and fields that don't move. However, often they are moved around on HyperCard stacks. If the users don't move them, you yourself may move and resize them frequently in the course of stack development and maintenance. Coaching buttons and fields by name rather than location keeps your coach marks consistent.

The <Define AppleScript Coach> command lets you associate a script with a coach mark. As long as the script returns a rectangle, Apple Guide is happy. Because HyperCard is scriptable and because the attributes of buttons and fields are available through AppleScript, you can write a coach mark script such as the one shown in a Script Editor window (see Figure 22.6).

You start by telling HyperCard to get the bounds of the field requested and the location of the window. The remaining code is used to add the horizontal and vertical coordinates of the window's location to the appropriate coordinates of the button's rectangle. This is because Apple Guide expects the coach mark in global coordinates and HyperCard has returned the values in window coordinates.

Compile this script and save it with a meaningful name. Many people have a Scripts folder in the folder with their Guide Maker files. Within the Scripts folder you can have meaningfully named scripts. To use this coach mark, you use the Guide Maker command <Define AppleScript Coach> as follows.

```
<Define AppleScript Coach> "CoachMarkForSearchField", REDCIRCLE,
   ":Scripts:Search Field Coach"
```

As long as Guide Maker can find the compiled script when you compile your guide file, everything will be set.

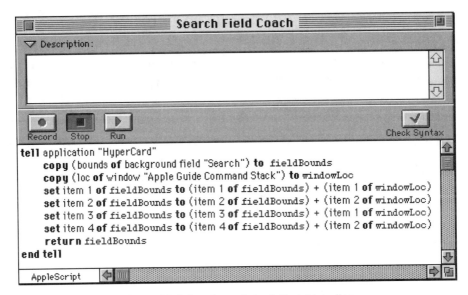

```
tell application "HyperCard"
    copy (bounds of background field "Search") to fieldBounds
    copy (loc of window "Apple Guide Command Stack") to windowLoc
    set item 1 of fieldBounds to (item 1 of fieldBounds) + (item 1 of windowLoc)
    set item 2 of fieldBounds to (item 2 of fieldBounds) + (item 2 of windowLoc)
    set item 3 of fieldBounds to (item 3 of fieldBounds) + (item 1 of windowLoc)
    set item 4 of fieldBounds to (item 4 of fieldBounds) + (item 2 of windowLoc)
    return fieldBounds
end tell
```

Figure 22.6 Coach mark AppleScript handler.

NOTE It takes a noticeable amount of time to load and run an AppleScript script. On some machines with slower processors, you may decide that the time it takes to evaluate an AppleScript coach mark is excessive. In such a case, you can always revert to the <Define Window Coach> with its limitations.

Since users cannot move fields and buttons in self-running stacks, you may want to replace your AppleScript coach marks with <Define Window Coach> commands in self-running stacks. The Real World Apple Guide CD-ROM contains several HyperCard stacks that use both techniques for comparison.

PROVIDING CONTEXT CHECKS FOR HYPERCARD BUTTONS AND FIELDS

If you want to provide context checks for objects in your HyperCard stacks, the context checks provided in the external code modules in Standard Resources will be of no help; they don't know about HyperCard and its objects. HyperCard, because it is scriptable, is just dying to tell the world everything it knows about its stack objects, and you can use that fact to implement context checks.

Using an External Code Module to Implement Context Checks Using Apple Events

In this scenario, you must first find a programmer. If you do not have a programmer who can write an external code module, you should skip to the next section.

Although the code involved in this process is not particularly complicated, its full explication is beyond the scope of this book, so this section is particularly cursory.

You write an external code resource that performs the context check by sending an Apple event to HyperCard inquiring about the state of the object(s) in question, and then returns the appropriate result. Because you can pass a number of parameters to a context check, you can design a single external code module that is general enough to handle the various context checks that your stack requires.

To do this, you need to be familiar with *Inside Macintosh: Interapplication Communications*, particularly the sections on sending and responding to Apple events and placing and extracting objects from the events. This is not complicated after you are used to it, but may be more effort than you want to exert.

Using an External Code Module To Implement Context Checks Using Apple Events

If only you could use a <Define AppleScript Context Check> command to associate an AppleScript with a context check. The AppleScript would return a Boolean value that indicated whether the context check passed or failed, and all would be well. Unfortunately, there is no such command, and you need to simulate its function, if you want to use it.

You can create an external code module that runs an AppleScript script. The AppleScript script returns a Boolean value to the external code module, which, in turn, passes it back to Apple Guide. Use the OSAExecute function described in *Inside Macintosh:Interapplication Communications* to execute the script. For many people, this requires less study than the previous method.

This process takes longer to execute than the previous method, but requires a much less complicated external code module.

Context Checks Using Apple Events

It is easy enough to use AppleScript to query the attributes of objects in HyperCard. You saw how to get field and window locations in the script shown in Figure 22.6. The problem is managing the mechanics of evaluating the context check and possibly launching an Oops sequence. The solution is simple: perform the context check in the AppleScript script as you would naturally think of doing. Then, rather than returning a Boolean result to Apple Guide, which would use it in evaluating a <Make Sure>, <Skip If>, or other condition, you evaluate it yourself in the AppleScript code and if it fails, you send the OpenWithSequenceOops event to Apple Guide. The script shown in Figure 22.7 demonstrates this.

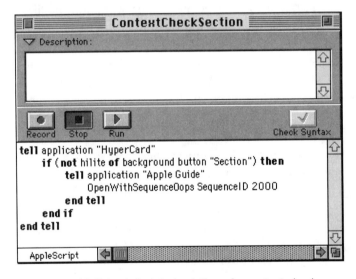

Figure 22.7 AppleScript simulation of a context check.

Apple Guide doesn't care how the Oops sequence is launched. An **OK** or **Continue** button will return the user to the appropriate place.

N O T E   Remember that Guide Maker normally does not compile sequences that are not referenced in a guide file. Thus, if your Oops sequence is referenced only from an AppleScript script, Guide Maker will not find any references to its use in your source file. Use the <Build Sequence> with the name of the sequence to force the sequence to be compiled.

You cause the pseudo context check to be evaluated by attaching it to an <On Panel Show> command or other event-handling procedure. (Use <Define Event> with the DoAppleScript event function to do this.) Then, when the event function is called, the script will be executed, and the Oops sequence will be launched if necessary.

In using this simulation of context checking, you may have to test several times to find the right event-handler to use to launch the AppleScript. <On Panel Show> often produces an appropriate result, but since it is called when a panel is expanded with the zoom box, it may evaluate the context check too often. More seriously, you may find unacceptable the fact that the panel is shown before the Oops sequence (which is different from the standard behavior in which the panel is not shown before the Oops sequence is launched). Depending on the context check in question, the users that you are dealing with, and the likelihood of the context check actually failing, you may make other decisions.

An even more serious problem may present itself on some machines. Because it takes time for an AppleScript to be loaded and executed, the swift user may be able to open a panel with a failed AppleScript context check and then click on to the next panel before the AppleScript has finished executing. The AppleScript context check, if it fails, will then launch the Oops sequence on the wrong panel. And then won't your user be confused?

On top of this, remember that context checks are called repeatedly. You may seriously degrade system performance on some machines with this strategy.

For all these reasons, you should be careful about using AppleScript scripts alone to handle context checks. With proper planning, they can be very effective; without that planning (and extensive testing) they can be misleading and annoying, which is worse than no context check at all.

The main reason to consider their use is that, if you have a context check that you simply must perform, you can, in fact, carry it out without having to find a programmer to write code.

EXECUTING HYPERCARD SCRIPTS

The final integration of Apple Guide and HyperCard is the ability to attach AppleScript scripts to buttons and panels in Apple Guide. Using the DoAppleScript event function, you can define an event either with the <Define Event> command alone or with <Define Event> and <Define Event List>. This event can then be attached to a panel object or invoked with a handler, such as <On Panel Create>. As shown previously, the script can carry out a context check, but it can also be used for more traditional purposes:

- going to a specific card
- entering data in a given field
- clicking a button

and so forth.

SUMMARY

HyperCard, Apple Guide, and AppleScript can give a solution provider an unparalleled combination of tools. You can limit your stacks to what is necessary for everyone, placing optional features, "hand-holding", and other forms of assistance in Apple Guide files. Where once you might have considered having "expert" and "beginner" modes in stacks, with different conditions determining how the interface looks, now you can write just one stack, and let the user choose an appropriate guide file that will provide the level of assistance required.

Integrating Apple Guide with HyperCard is fairly easy and interesting. The techniques outlined in this chapter apply to any application that is scriptable and whose objects are open to view with Apple events. Many, many applications fall into this category, and more are being written and enhanced to take advantage of these technologies.

But not every application falls into this category. Some very powerful, very popular, and very useful applications are not scriptable and do not expose their innards to view by Apple events and AppleScript. Should you give up on tightly integrating them with Apple Guide? Foolish question.

In the next chapter, you'll see how to integrate 4th Dimension with Apple Guide.

CHAPTER 23

Adding Apple Guide to 4th Dimension

4th Dimension, the integrated database environment by Laurent Ribardière, is published by ACI/ACI US. It is one of the most widely used products for providing custom solutions on the Macintosh. As of version 3.1.1, 4th Dimension itself did not provide support for AppleScript. (Third-party add-on products do offer AppleScript support.)

In this chapter, you will see how to integrate Apple Guide with 4th Dimension without using Apple events. The integration cannot be so tight as the integration with HyperCard described in the last chapter, but it still can provide you with coach marks and context checks that you can use in developing guide files. As with HyperCard, this allows you to add assistance (often with guide files of varying levels of support) to your custom solution.

Use the chapter as a guide for integrating Apple Guide with other applications that do not provide support for Apple events, or for cases where you do not want to use AppleScript as in the previous chapter.

With 4th Dimension you can provide coach marks for windows and menus as well as certain context checks. There are problems and solutions for each.

Complete code for the example discussed in this chapter in provided on the *Real World Apple Guide* CD-ROM.

NOTE

COACH MARKS

Coach marks are the most visible and appealing part of Apple Guide. Certainly you should want to add them to your guide files for a 4th Dimension application.

Menu Coaches

If you define a menu coach for the 4th Dimension menu bar, you will discover (if you did not know before) an interesting fact: the menu bar isn't a menu bar. Although it looks and functions like a menu bar, it is not a menu bar, and the <Define Menu Coach> command does not work.

Fortunately, there's another way of defining a coach mark for the menu bar. The <Define Window Coach> lets you specify DESKTOP for the *targetWindow* parameter. If you can identify the location of the menu that you want to coach, you can specify that rectangle in the *windowRect* parameter, and Apple Guide will coach the menu appropriately.

This method is not perfect, and it is not foolproof. If the application's menu bar changes as a result of a revision, your coach mark will coach the wrong location. More troublesome is that, using this technique, you can coach only the name of the menu; the menu command that is normally underlined or shown in red when the menu is pulled down cannot be coached. But you *can* provide menu coaches.

Window Coaches

Window coach marks are handled exactly as they are in other applications, except for the fact that you often will have to rely on the FRONT parameter rather than the window title. Just as when coaching unsaved windows called Untitled-1 in a word processing program, you often do not know the name of the windows in 4th Dimension. For example, the Structure window for the Video Store example is titled Structure for Video Store. If you can be certain that the front-most window is the Structure window, then there is no problem in using the FRONT parameter for the <Define Window Coach> command.

The context checks in the next section allow you to know what the front-most window is.

CONTEXT CHECKS

The external code modules supplied in Standard Resources on the *Real World Apple Guide* CD-ROM include the 'WIND' context check module, which is able to check the title of open and active windows (among other things). One of the parameters that is passed to these and other context checks controls the way in which the comparison of the window title to the string in the context check is performed. A value of 10 means that the context check should return TRUE if the title matches the string. A value of 11 means that the context check should return TRUE if the title *contains* the string.

The first two following context checks are used to check whether the title of the active or open window contains a string. The last two are used to check whether the title exactly matches the string.

You may want to use these four context checks in your Apple Guide assistance for 4th Dimension (as well as many other applications). ('4D05' is 4th Dimension's application signature. As always, you are best served if you direct your context checks to a specific application rather than whichever one is front-most.)

```
<Define Context Check> "ActiveWindowContains", 'WIND', '4D05',
    LONG:0, LONG:0, LONG:11, LPSTRING
<Define Context Check> "OpenWindowContains", 'WIND', '4D05',
    LONG:1, LONG:0, LONG:11, LPSTRING
<Define Context Check> "ActiveWindowExact", 'WIND', '4D05',
    LONG:0, LONG:0, LONG:10, LPSTRING
<Define Context Check> "OpenWindowExact", 'WIND', '4D05', LONG:1,
    LONG:0, LONG:10, LPSTRING
```

When you invoke each context check, you pass it a single parameter, which is the string you want tested, as in:

```
ActiveWindowContains("Structure")
```

Returning to the 4th Dimension case, remember that the name of the Structure window will be "Structure for *databaseName*". For that reason, you can check whether the Structure window is open or active by using:

```
OpenWindowContains("Structure")

    or

ActiveWindowContains("Structure")
```

You can even use the Structure window to test which environment has been selected in the Use menu, as in the following Apple Guide example.:

```
Define Sequence> "4D Demo"
<Panel> "Intro"
<Skip If> OpenWindowContains("Structure")
<Panel> "4D Panel 1"
<Make Sure> OpenWindowContains("Structure"), "Oops: Structure"
<Panel> "4D Panel 2"
<End Sequence>

<Define Sequence> "Oops: Structure"
<Define Panel> "Oops: Structure"
<Format> "Tag"
Oops
<Format> "Body"
You must choose Design from the Use menu.
<Coach Mark> "Use menu"
<Standard Button> "OK", CENTER, ReturnBack()
<End Panel>
<End Sequence>

<Define Panel> "Intro"
This is the beginning of a 4D demonstration of Apple Guide.
<End Panel>

<Define Panel> "4D Panel 1"
<Format> "Tag"
```

```
Do This
<Format> "Body"
Choose Design from the Use menu.
<Coach Mark> "Use menu"
<End Panel>


<Define Panel> "4D Panel 2"
<Coach Mark> "Structure Window"
This is a coach mark for the title bar of the Structure window.
<End Panel>
```

As with all indirect context checks, the farther you get from testing the thing that you are asking about, the more risks there are of reporting an erroneous result. For example, if an architect or engineer has created a database of projects, it is quite possible that a database file could be called "Structures." In such a case, the above code would erroneously suggest that the Structure window was open, when in fact one of the database files named "Structures" was the open or active window.

Depending on the circumstances and use to which you are putting your guide file, you may be able to predict such problems. If, for example, you are providing Apple Guide assistance for a 4th Dimension application you have designed (the most likely case), you will probably know whether it is possible for a window other than the Structure window to contain the word "structure."

OPENING GUIDE FILES

Finally, there is the question of opening the Apple Guide files for your 4th Dimension application. Without writing special code, the easiest way to install guide files in the Guide menu is to make them coresident with the 4th Dimension application. This poses the problem of your guide files being opened when any 4th Dimension database is opened.

Again, this problem may not matter in the case of a custom solution. If it is a problem, you may be able to use the context checks described previously to check whether a certain database is open. If it is, you can launch a new sequence to provide specific assistance.

SUMMARY

In this chapter you have seen how to integrate Apple Guide, particularly context checks and coach marks, to 4th Dimension and by extension to any application that does not support Apple events and that may even not use some of the standard interface objects (such as menus that Apple Guide can recognize).

In the next chapter, you will see another approach to integration. WordPerfect already contains Apple Guide assistance and is aware of Apple events and AppleScript. Unlike HyperCard, however, the interface itself is not exposed to Apple events. It, too, poses challenges and provides rewards to the Apple Guide author.

Adding Apple Guide to WordPerfect or Microsoft Word

In this chapter, you will see a middle road between the integration of Apple Guide with HyperCard, a scriptable application with standard Mac OS controls, and 4th Dimension, a nonscriptable application (in its basic form), which uses some nonstandard controls.

For WordPerfect 3.1, you will see how to write a tutorial to guide a user through spell-checking a document, but the principles are applicable to many other cases in these and other applications, from word processors to spreadsheets and others. For Microsoft Word version 6.0, you will see how to write a tutorial to assist a user in using the **Font Format** command. You will also see how to incorporate Apple Scripts to run macros defined in each application.

The tutorials shown here are designed to illustrate the interaction between the applications and Apple Guide. In reality, more panels and more detailed instructions would most likely be given to users.

NOTE

WordPerfect 3.1 is scriptable, and includes Apple Guide assistance. Microsoft Word version 6.0 is also scriptable, but does not include Apple Guide assistance. In this chapter, you will see how you can add assistance to each of the products.

As in most scriptable applications, AppleScript scripts are able to access and control document and data elements of WordPerfect. The interface objects, however, which are exposed to view in HyperCard (fields, buttons, and so on) are not available to the AppleScript writer who is dealing with WordPerfect. This is a very common situation. Except with applications such as HyperCard, in which the interface elements can actually represent data (a button's being on can represent a Boolean value of TRUE), these are rarely relevant to script writers.

Complete code for the examples discussed in this chapter in provided on the *Real World Apple Guide* CD-ROM.

N O T E

OVERVIEW OF THE WORDPERFECT SPELLING TUTORIAL

This tutorial coaches the user through the process of spell-checking a document. As is common with most word processing applications, the user first opens a document, and then chooses a menu command that opens a window that controls the process. The window is shown in Figure 24.1.

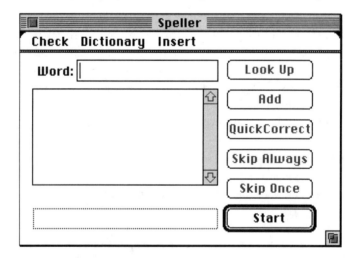

Figure 24.1 WordPerfect Speller window.

Coach Marks

Two coach marks are needed for this tutorial. The first is an ordinary menu coach to coach the **Speller** command in the Tools menu, which opens the Speller window.

```
<Define Menu Coach> "Spell Command", 'WPC2', REDCIRCLE, "Tools",
  "Speller"
```

The second coach mark is for the **Start** button in the Speller window. Because the window is defined as a dialog in WordPerfect's file, you can use the DialogID function to identify the **Start** button, as follows:

```
<Define Item Coach> "OK to Spell", 'WPC2', REDCIRCLE , "Speller",
  DialogID(1)
```

These coach marks are used in the panels shown here:

```
<Define Panel> "WP Panel 1"
<Coach Mark> "Spell Command"
<Format> "Tag"
Do This
<Format> "Body"
Choose Speller from the Tools menu.
<End Panel>

<Define Panel> "WP Panel 2"
<Coach Mark> "OK to Spell"
Click Start to start spelling.
<End Panel>
```

N O T E   You can use ResEdit to examine an application's resources and to identify the ID numbers of items in a dialog list (DITL). As always, if you do this, you must make a copy of the application and perform your investigations on the copy. This prevents any accidental corruption of the application itself.

If you do not want to use ResEdit, you can use a <Define Window Coach> command for the Start button's coach mark, identifying the rectangle by the pixel coordinates of the button. You can do this by making a screen shot of the Speller window and copying the screen shot to a drawing program. Set the rulers to pixels and draw a rectangle around the image of the Start button, noting the pixel coordinates of each corner.

Context Checks

The ActiveWindowExact context check defined in the previous chapter is used again here to make certain that the Speller window is open. As is common with this sort of sequence, the user is prompted to open the Speller window (in WP Panel 1), but if the window is already open and active, that instruction is skipped.

After displaying WP Panel 1, which asks the user to open the Speller, the <Make Sure> command guarantees that the window is open before displaying WP Panel 2, which contains the instruction to click the **Start** button. Following is the code, including the Oops: Speller sequence that is invoked if necessary from the <Make Sure> command.

```
<Skip If> ActiveWindowExact("Speller")
<Panel> "WP Panel 1"
<Make Sure> ActiveWindowExact("Speller"), "Oops: Speller"
<Panel> "WP Panel 2"
<End Sequence>


<Define Sequence> "Oops: Speller"
<Seq Nav Button Set>        NONE
<Define Panel> "Oops: Speller"
<Coach Mark> "Spell Command"
<Panel Prompt> NONE
<Format> "Tag"
Oops
<Format> "Body"
Choose Speller from the Tools menu.
<Standard Button> "OK", CENTER, ReturnBack()
<End Panel>
<End Sequence>
```

These commands require no special knowledge of WordPerfect and use no unusual Apple Guide commands. Adding the Spelling Tutorial to WordPerfect is almost child's play.

Adding the Spelling Tutorial to the Guide menu

WordPerfect's Guide menu is shown in Figure 24.2 with the spelling tutorial inserted.

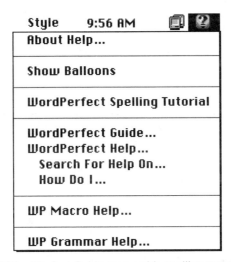

Figure 24.2 WordPerfect Guide menu with spelling tutorial inserted.

Adhering to the standards, you should make the spelling tutorial a guide file of type OTHER, letting Apple Guide insert it appropriately in the menu.

As you can see from the WordPerfect Guide menu, the menu is a hybrid of traditional help and Apple Guide files, and must be built by the application. If you make the guide file of type OTHER, it will not be added to the menu by WordPerfect. You must make it type HELP, and WordPerfect will add it to the Guide menu, albeit in a location that is not standard. Nevertheless, it is there and clearly labeled.

OVERVIEW OF THE MICROSOFT WORD 6.0 FONT FORMATTING TUTORIAL

In version 6.0 of Microsoft Word, spelling is integrated with other grammar checks, so no special Speller window is shown before spell-checking starts. As a result, a spelling tutorial would be significantly shorter. The **Font Format** command has a similar structure to the WordPerfect **Speller** command, and is demonstrated here.

Coach Marks

The coach mark for the **Font Format** command for Microsoft Word is as follows:

```
<Define Menu Coach> "Font Format Command", 'MSWD', REDCIRCLE,
   "Format", "Font"
```

The **OK** button on the Font Format window needs to be coached using coordinates as previously described (a screen shot of the window was taken and pasted into a graphics program where pixel positions could be found).

```
<Define Window Coach> "OK Button", 'MSWD', REDCIRCLE , "Font",
   Rect(72, 400, 100, 520)
```

These two coach marks are used in the following panels for the font formatting tutorial:

```
<Define Panel> "WP Panel 1"
<Format> "Tag"
Do This
<Format> "Body"
Choose Font from the Format menu.
<Coach Mark> "Font Format Command"
<End Panel>

<Define Panel> "WP Panel 2"
<Coach Mark> "OK button"
Click OK to close the window.
<End Panel>
```

Context Checks

Just as in the WordPerfect spelling tutorial shown above, you can provide a context check to make certain that the user has, in fact, opened the Font Format window. The logic of the context check is identical; following is its definition and its use:

```
<Define Sequence> "WP Demo"
<Panel> "Intro"
<Skip If> ActiveWindowExact("Font")
<Panel> "WP Panel 1"
<Make Sure> ActiveWindowExact("Font"), "Oops: Font"
<Panel> "WP Panel 2"
<End Sequence>


<Define Sequence> "Oops: Font"
<Seq Nav Button Set>       NONE
<Define Panel> "Oops: Font"
<Coach Mark> "Font Format Command"
<Panel Prompt> NONE
<Format> "Tag"
Oops
<Format> "Body"
Choose Font from the Format menu.
<Standard Button> "OK", CENTER, ReturnBack()
<End Panel>
<End Sequence>
```

Invoking the Guide File

Once again, the only fly in the ointment is making the guide file available to users. Microsoft Word does not support Apple Guide and builds its own Guide menu without regard to any guide files that may exist. Accordingly, you must open the guide file in some other way.

A rather heavy-handed approach would be to place it in the Extensions folder of the System folder so that it is opened with the Finder's Apple Guide files. This is a poor place for a tutorial on such an arcane subject as font formatting for Microsoft Word, but if the tutorial is embedded in a substantially larger guide file that contains all of a company's tips and techniques for all of its applications and projects, that might just be the right place for it.

Another possible way of opening the guide file is from an AppleScript script or another application's guide file. The different techniques for opening guide files described in this book can each be used in various ways. Because the coach marks and context checks in the guide file explicitly reference the application's signature (rather than the front-most window or application), you need have no qualms about coaching one application from a guide file opened by another.

There will be some context-switching going on because the opened guide file is associated with another application rather than Microsoft Word, but except for the fact that it prevents the menu command (**Font**) from being coached as well as the menu title (Format), there is little noticeable effect.

USING APPLESCRIPT AND MACROS

Like many applications, WordPerfect 3.1 and Microsoft Word 6.0 have their own scripting language in which you can create automated tasks for the application to perform (macros). These macros are available to AppleScript using the Do Script AppleScript event. This enables you to do something like the following.

This macro is very simple; it turns the bold attribute on, and then types **Name:** as you might do for a data entry form. It then turns bold off so that the text you enter, after the execution of the macro, will be in plain type.

WordPerfect and Microsoft Word use different syntax for their macros. Fortunately, both support a Record function, so you can do what you want and let the applications record the actions in their own syntax. For reference, however, here are the two macros. First, from WordPerfect:

```
Attribute (On;Bold)
Type (Name:)
Attribute (Off;Bold)
```

Here is the macro from Microsoft Word:

```
Sub MAIN
Bold
Insert "Name:"
Bold
End Sub
```

If the macro is stored under the name "Enter Bold Name," the following AppleScript script invokes that macro:

```
tell application "WordPerfect"
    Do Script "Enter Bold Name"
end tell
```

or

```
tell application "Microsoft Word"
    Do Script "Enter Bold Name"
end tell
```

If you store that AppleScript in a file called "WP Script" inside a folder called "Scripts" that is coresident with your Guide Maker source code, you can write either of the following lines of code:

```
<On Panel Create> DoAppleScript("Scripts:WP Script")
```

or

```
<Standard Button> "Enter Name", CENTER, DoAppleScript("Scripts:WP
    Script")
```

In the first case, the macro will be executed via the AppleScript code whenever the panel is created. This is a common construction for a Continue panel. In the second case, if the user clicks the **Enter Name** button, the code will be executed.

You can use this method of executing a macro via an AppleScript script wherever an event can be used in Guide Maker, on buttons, in Oops and Continue sequences, for radio buttons and check boxes, and so on.

This method is available for many applications in which their native macro language is accessible from an AppleScript event.

SUMMARY

The integration of Apple Guide with WordPerfect and Microsoft Word shown here is common to many applications. The coach marks and context checks are straightforward, and the use of their own macro languages, through AppleScript and its Do Script event, is a common example.

After you have mastered the basic Apple Guide functionality as described in Part 2, you can add this type of assistance to most applications running on the Mac OS, often in a very brief period of time.

CHAPTER 25

Adding Apple Guide to Content

In this chapter, you will see how to add Apple Guide to interactive multimedia content. Some of the design issues will also be explored, because they are somewhat different from those involved with adding Apple Guide to applications.

N O T E You can make a very clear distinction between applications (the programs that you run) and their content (the documents that they deal with). With many programs, you buy the application and provide the content (for example, you type your own letters). In the world of interactive multimedia, you generally buy the two together—the content together with the software that presents it. In this chapter, the jaw-breaking phrase, "interactive multimedia content," which is frequently used to refer to all content provided by publishers (often on CD-ROM), is replaced by the word "content."

OVERVIEW OF CONTENT AND ASSISTANCE

Adding Apple Guide to content lets you provide a rich environment for the user in which the content is supported by a broad bandwidth of assistance. You can divide this broad bandwidth of support into several layers, of generally increasing complexity and abstraction:

- Interface Identification (a fancy word for Balloon Help and similar technologies). This lets users answer the question, "*What is* this thing and what will it do?"

- Application Assistance. This layer comprises all application support, whether provided by printed materials, traditional on-line help, or Apple Guide. This layer lets users answer the question, *"How do I* navigate?" and similar ones.

- Content Assistance. This layer (which can very appropriately be provided by content-specific Apple Guide) answers such questions as, *"What's a good way* to approach this content?" or *"What should I learn first?"*.

- Content Commentary. This layer is often present when the content is published in traditional forms. It consists of material that is presented in books in footnotes or appendices. Typical questions that this layer answers are "What reference works provide *further information* on this issue?" or *"Why* is this?"

- Interactive Annotation. Many applications that support content presentation have annotation tools that let users do the equivalent of writing notes in the margins of a book. This layer provides the facility to *write* notes, questions, comments, and ideas. As teachers have found, this intense interaction with the material being presented greatly contributes to people's learning.

If you consider these layers of support for content, you should be able to see how they can be delivered most effectively. The first, Interface Identification is the service provided by Balloon Help and is generally delivered by the application itself.

Application Assistance is also provided as part of the application itself, often in the form of Apple Guide. Adding this sort of assistance to interactive multimedia applications is no different than adding it to any other sort of application. Whether provided as part of a shrink-wrapped product or as an add-on from a third party, it is focused on the application and not on a specific set of content.

Content Assistance is the subject of this chapter.

Content Commentary is generally provided by the author of the content. The facility for their display and coordination with the content currently being displayed is provided by the application.

Interactive Annotation is a facility provided by the application. The substance of the annotations is provided by the user who uses the annotation feature.

CONTENT ASSISTANCE

There are two cases of providing Content Assistance. In the first, an application is used that presents content but provides no special facilities for content-based assistance. In the second, an application is used that explicitly provides Apple Guide assistance "hooks."

The first case is exemplified by HyperCard, and is demonstrated and discussed at length in Chapter 22, "Adding Apple Guide to HyperCard."

The second case is exemplified by Symposium Explorer, and is demonstrated in Josef Albers's *Interaction of Color* interactive CD-ROM edition, which is used as an example in this chapter.

N O T E

A demo version is provided on the *Real World Apple Guide* CD-ROM.

ADDING CONTENT-SPECIFIC GUIDE FILES TO THE GUIDE MENU

The only difficulty in adding assistance to content is making the Guide menu reflect the appropriate guide files (those for the application as well as those for the content). As discussed in Chapter 19, "MacApp and Apple Guide," Symposium Explorer places its own guide files in the Preferences folder, and opens content-specific guide files that are coresident with its documents. Figure 25.1 shows Symposium Explorer's Guide menu before any documents are opened.

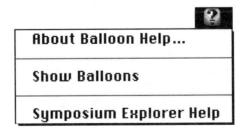

Figure 25.1 Symposium Explorer's Guide menu with no open documents.

As soon as you open a document (in this case *Interaction of Color*), any guide files coresident with the document are added programmatically to the Guide menu, as shown in Figure 25.2.

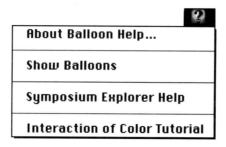

Figure 25.2 Interaction of Color's tutorial in the Symposium Explorer Guide menu.

Believe it or not, that is the only technical issue of any significance in adding Apple Guide to content! If you are adding Apple Guide to content in an application where this explicit support is not provided, you still have two alternatives:

- Launch Apple Guide assistance from an application event, such as a button or menu command, as described in Chapter 22, "Adding Apple Guide to HyperCard."
- Launch Apple Guide assistance as you would for any application that doesn't add the appropriate guide files to its Guide menu. This was discussed in Chapter 24, "Adding Apple Guide to WordPerfect or Microsoft Word."

WHAT GOES WHERE

When you add Apple Guide assistance to content, it is important to make certain that the right information is provided in the right way. As a demonstration of how assistance can be provided, consider Figure 25.3, which shows Study VII-7 from *Interaction of Color*, which is quite clearly the content layer.

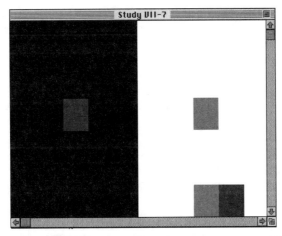

Figure 25.3 Study VII-7 from Josef Albers's *Interaction of Color*.

In the notes shown in Figure 25.4, Josef Albers's commentary on the study is shown. This is an example of Content Commentary and demonstrates one of the points made: the facility is provided by the application, but the content is provided by the author of the content. In this case, Josef Albers died a number of years before the Symposium Explorer software was written.

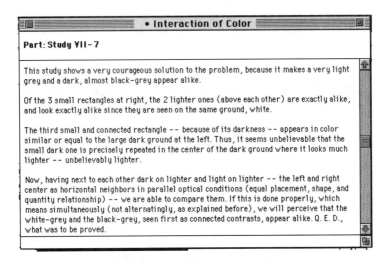

Figure 25.4 Notes for Study VII-7.

The Apple Guide panel shown in Figure 25.5 is part of the Symposium Explorer Application Assistance and is provided by the application regardless of the content. It assists the user with the use of the program, not with the content being presented.

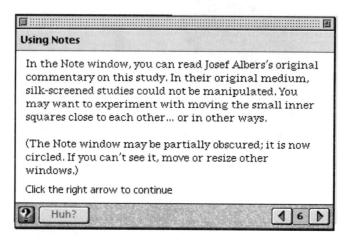

Figure 25.5 Using Notes Apple Guide Assistance from Symposium Explorer.

If you are developing your own multimedia presentations using a product such as HyperCard, keeping these distinctions in mind will help you to provide the most useful service to your users while also allowing your guide files to be reused as appropriate.

APPLICATION SUPPORT FOR APPLE GUIDE

When you start to develop Apple Guide assistance that will work with an application (either with its content or the application itself), two sets of "hooks" can make your life easier:

- Apple events (which have been discussed previously)
- application-specific Apple Guide APIs

As you saw in Part 3, it is very easy to modify applications to support Apple Guide with custom coach marks and context checks. In a situation that is parallel to an application's providing access to its functionality through Apple events, applications that have custom coach marks and context checks can publish them so that guide file authors can take advantage of them.

When users can resize and scroll windows, coaching objects in these windows can be very difficult because they are in different places at different times. When you can use object coach definitions that refer to coach mark rectangles computed by an application you can avoid these problems. The coach mark definitions in Symposium Explorer's Apple Guide API let Apple Guide authors coach buttons on the Controller, including items that may have been scrolled out of view. Only by used object or AppleScript coach marks can you handle such variably located coach marks.

Similarly, custom context checks can be very useful. Consider the following context check definition for Symposium Explorer:

```
<Define Context Check> "ColorPaletteTorn", 'torn', 'PSM3',
   OSTYPE:'colr'
```

This context check returns TRUE if the color palette is torn off the menu bar. (Much of its code is provided in Part 3.) It is obviously of use to authors of tutorials for content who want to walk users through the manipulation of specific content with the color palette (rather than with the general techniques of manipulating generic drawing objects).

SUMMARY

As with Apple events shortly after the introduction of System 7, application support of Apple Guide is spotty and very much a chicken-or-egg issue. Application developers are unlikely to provide custom callbacks for Apple Guide authors until they clamor for them. And until they realize how powerful they can be, the authors won't know to raise a fuss. Meanwhile, users who see this service that provides a helping hand, an assist, or a reassuring guide continue to smile and be even less fearful of their computers. Apple Guide is a powerful technology, truly a substantially different technology than "on-line help." To make it available to more people, there are tools and techniques that let Apple Guide authors reach out to the world. They are discussed in the next part of this book.

CHAPTER 26

Apple Guide and Windows Help

Guide Maker provides a conversion utility to convert Windows Help source files to Guide Maker source files. In many cases the conversion can be automatic, but in a large number of cases a certain amount of tweaking is necessary. In this chapter you will see a very brief comparison of Guide Script and Windows Help syntax, as well as some tips and strategies for making conversions and synchronization of files easier.

SIMILARITIES AND DIFFERENCES BETWEEN APPLE GUIDE AND WINDOWS HELP

Without in any way detracting from the remarks in the Introduction (Apple Guide isn't help, it is a service to the user), the fact of the matter is that Apple Guide and Windows help do often provide help, and they provide a number of similar features and functionalities.

Both provide the concept of topics that organize information, and both provide key-word searching. Both can incorporate graphics. Despite these similarities, the approach to the user interface is quite different in the two systems, as is the approach to the creation of the assistance files.

Although automated systems exist for building Windows help, many people develop help systems directly from within Microsoft Word. Where Apple Guide has a language—Guide Script—that you use to create your Apple Guide source files for Guide Maker, with Windows Help some standard word processing symbols and codes are used by the help compiler.

A Comparison of Some Common Commands

The purpose of this section is to very quickly present some of the Windows Help terminology and contrast it with Apple Guide terminology. It is designed to help if you are an Apple Guide author coordinating your work with a Windows Help author, or if you are a Windows Help author trying to work with an Apple Guide author or trying to learn Apple Guide's terminology yourself.

Windows Help Topics Are Apple Guide Sequences

In source files, each Windows Help topic is a single page of text, with the page terminated by a hard page break. The title appears at the top of the page, and footnotes with specified symbols are inserted before the title. These specified symbols have meaning. Thus, a topic from a Windows Help file might consist of the following:

```
#$K+Maintenance
The printer requires minimum maintenance, but the ink cartridge
needs to be changed periodically. In addition, the rollers
occasionally need replacement. You should clean the outside of the
printer on a regular basis.
```

```
# PrintMaintenance
$ Maintenance
K printer
+ 004
```

The characters #$K+ are Microsoft Word footnote identifiers; their text appears below the end-of-page symbol in the example above. The # creates a context string that uniquely identifies the topic. The $ creates a title for the topic, the K creates the key-words for this topic, and the + determines the topic's position in a browse sequence.

Guide Maker would convert the above to the following:

```
<Define Sequence> "PrintMaintenance", "Maintenance"
<Define Panel> "Panel 1"
The printer requires minimum maintenance, but the ink cartridge
needs to be changed periodically. In addition, the rollers
```

```
occasionally need replacement. You should clean the outside of the
printer on a regular basis.
<End Panel>
```

Elsewhere in the guide file, you would find:

```
<Index> "printer"
    <Topic> "Maintenance", "PrintMaintenance"
```

This conversion, which creates single-panel sequences when it gets to Apple Guide, occasionally causes problems because the panels that are created are too tall. If your Windows Help topics are incomplete after conversion, take the converted source file and split the panels into two (or more) panels. Apple Guide panels are typically smaller than Windows Help topics.

Jumps and Cross-References are Hot Text and Launch New Sequence

A jump or cross-reference in Windows Help implements hot text. The Windows Help author implements this functionality by double-underlining the hot text and then entering the context string of the desired topic in hidden text. The user sees simply the double-underlined text and knows that it is hot.

For example, the Windows Help author might rewrite the text above as follows:

```
Choose one of the following topics to learn more about printer
maintenance.
    Changing ink cartridges
    Replacing rollers
    Cleaning the outside of the printer
```

Invisible text following "ink cartridges" might be INKCARTRIDGE:desc. Similar invisible text items would follow the other choices. If that were the case, Guide Maker would convert the code to the following:

```
Choose one of the following topics to learn more about printer
maintenance.
<Hot Text> "changing ink cartridges", ALL,
    LaunchNewSequence("INKCARTRIDGE:desc)
```

```
        Changing ink cartridges
   <Hot Text> "replacing rollers", ALL,
     LaunchNewSequence("ROLLERS:desc)
        Replacing rollers
   <Hot Text> "cleaning the outside of the printer", ALL,
     LaunchNewSequence("CASE:desc)
        Cleaning the outside of the printer
```

Presumably the topics referenced in invisible text in the Windows Help file will appear somewhere in the source code and will have been converted by Guide Maker. If you want to preserve the similarity between your assistance on two platforms, you can leave this converted code alone. However, this conversion demonstrates a difference in the interface between Windows Help and Apple Guide.

With Windows Help, the topic window generally both presents the information and provides navigation. In Apple Guide, navigation and organization of the information is provided by the navigation bar and by the access window. In-panel navigation with buttons and hot text is common, but is by no means so prevalent as it is in Windows Help. The information and navigational tools are separated. If your mandate does not require you to keep assistance for two platforms looking similar, you may decide to take advantage of Apple Guide's navigation bar and access windows to move some of the navigational features shown in the example out of the Apple Guide panels.

Pop-Ups are LaunchNewSequenceNewWindow

Pop-Ups, which in Windows Help source files are defined with single underscore characters followed by invisible text, cause a small window to open in front of the primary help window. For this Windows Help excerpt:

```
   Open the door of the printer.
```

(where PrintDoor:Def is in invisible text after "door"), Guide Maker's conversion utility would produce:

```
   <Hot Text> "door", ALL,
     LaunchNewSequenceNewWindow("PrintDoor:Def")
   Open the door of the printer.
```

In this example, the underscoring of the text that the Windows Help user sees is brought forward during the conversion. In Apple Guide, however, the functionality is provided not by the underscore itself, but by the preceding <Hot Text> command.

Learning More

To learn more about how Apple Guide converts Windows Help to Guide Maker source, you can take a simple Windows Help file—perhaps a demo version that comes with a Windows Help tutorial—and convert it using Guide Maker's conversion utility. Compare both versions to find comparable structures. You can create a "translation table" for your own reference.

Different Functionalities

Although there are commonalties as shown above, there are a number of differences between Windows Help and Apple Guide, and you need to be aware of them and to plan how to deal with them. The major problems that arise occur because of the different approaches to assistance taken by the two systems. If you have to develop or maintain assistance for both Windows and the Mac OS, you must choose between implementing only the basic functionality common to both or using each platform's tools to the utmost.

Color and Text Appearance

One of the biggest differences is that from the user's perspective, colors and underlining symbols have different meanings in the Windows Help panels. Guide Maker has no trouble replacing these formats with the appropriate Apple Guide commands. The problem may occur in the other direction: as an Apple Guide author, you may use underlining or color for emphasis on a word and find that you have inspired users to click frantically on text that is not hot.

Access Windows

The Apple Guide system of Access windows does not exist in a comparable form in Windows Help. As a result, you must manually create them, including topic areas and headers, during the conversion process. You may choose not to use the Full Access window to minimize the amount of additional work that you have to do at this stage. This also minimizes the functionality that you provide. Given the relative ease with which you can create topic areas, you should consider providing a full access interface.

Keyword Searching

Windows Help provides a list of keywords that the user can select for information. Apple Guide lets you enter a keyword, and provides the stemming and parsing features described in Chapter 7, "Access Windows." As a result, in order to produce a usable keyword searching capability for a Full Access window, you should devote time to developing your keywords. Again, by not using the Full Access window you can minimize the additional work required, at the cost of providing less Apple Guide assistance than you could.

Guide Maker's Conversion Process

Guide Maker converts RTF files that are of type 'TEXT'. Make sure that your Windows Help files are in that format and are assigned that type. If you have text that is both underlined and hidden, remove one of those attributes (usually the underline) before starting the conversion process.

Assumptions Apple Guide Makes

Because Apple Guide and Windows Help take such different approaches, some assumptions must be made during the conversion process. These include:

K control codes are used to create Apple Guide index terms

and $ control codes are required for every Windows Help topic

Apple Guide assumes that a Windows Help topic starts with a # control code and ends just before the next one (or at the end of file)

What Is Ignored

Some Windows Help features are not converted. These include:

! control codes (which create Macro references)

+ control codes (which determine the order of topics in a browse sequence)

tables

List commands

SUMMARY

Your choices are constrained by circumstances. You may be implementing assistance for a new application that will run under the Mac OS and Windows, or you may be adding Windows Help to an application that has Apple Guide in its Windows version—or vice versa. Each circumstance requires different choices. Remember that help or assistance should not be an add-on, and can make a critical difference in a use"'s experience with an application.

You may want to take a leaf from the book of developers who develop applications for multiple platforms. You could create a core set of help and assistance that will run under Windows and the Mac OS. Use Guide Maker to convert the files from one format to another. Then, plan to add additional functionality on each platform's assistance, so that the full-blown help in the Windows world and the complete assistance in the Apple Guide world both take advantage of the features available to them. (The core help code is only for internal use, but remains the basis for additions.)

Whatever you do, on any platform, do not approach the issue of providing cross-platform help as a religious or political platform from which to prove the unworthiness of your unfavored environment. With help and assistance—more perhaps than with any other aspect of your application or solution—you owe it to your users to focus as much on them, their problems, and their tasks as you can, using the tools that are available to you to their best advantage.

Localizing Apple Guide

Apple Guide can be viewed as an interface layer that is closer to the user than an application's interface itself. The panels float in front of all other interface elements, physically closer than the application interface; in elaborating on the features of the interface and providing explanations, tutorials, and tips, Apple Guide can also seem psychologically closer to the user than the more distant, more general, and terse elements of the menus and commands of an application's interface.

In developing a level of assistance that is closer to the user, you focus on the needs of the user, the particular tasks that are undertaken, and the terminology that is appropriate for the user. "Document" may be an appropriate terminology for a mass-market word processing application, but "memo" or "quote sheet" is a more appropriate ("closer") terminology for the user in the office of a lumberyard.

Part of providing the appropriate terminology for a user is using the language and cultural references that are most appropriate. From its inception, the Mac OS has provided localization tools and techniques so that applications can be modified for different countries and regions of the world with little effort. Apple Guide is no exception, and Guide Maker provides simple tools for localization. ResEdit and AppleGlot can be used to ease the conversion process.

LOCALIZATION ISSUES

Several general principles apply when you are writing assistance that will be localized:

- Translated text is often longer than the original.
- Avoid placing text in graphics if at all possible.
- When choosing icons and images be careful to avoid cultural and political biases that are unwanted.

Translated Text May Require More Space than the Original

Text translated from English to another language often takes up more space and requires more words to express the same idea. To a certain extent, any translation from any language may be more verbose than the original—it is the nature of translations to be less simple than the originals. Additionally, different languages have different strengths in terms of the concepts that they represent simply and succinctly. (These strengths have often arisen from fairly obvious influences. The famous notion that Inuit have 50 words for snow is an example—albeit discredited—of such an influence. There are two Eskimo words for snow: one describes snow on the ground, the other describes snow in the air—snowflakes.)

Since translated text may take up more space than the original, dialog boxes in application programs sometimes need to be modified as part of a localization process. Fortunately, Apple Guide sizes panels to fit the text that is displayed, so you don't have to worry about this. Your only concern should arise if you have a panel that is lengthy in the original; the translated text may push the panel's size beyond the value specified in <Max Height> (or its default), and Apple Guide may be forced to split the text into two panels.

Avoid Placing Text in Graphics

Editing text is much easier than editing graphics—whether they be icons, PICT graphics, or QuickTime movies. For this reason, you should attempt to eliminate text from the images in your guide file if you plan to reuse these images in a localized version. Since you indicate elements of the interface with coach marks, you should be able to avoid duplicating screen shots of your interface in various languages in your guide file—rarely do you need a screen shot of the interface at all.

Where text is appropriately seen in a graphic, you should not go through contortions to eliminate it. Your goal should be to provide the best and fullest assistance in each localized version of your guide files. Some images may well have to be redone as part of the conversion process: compromising on the contents of these images may make your guide file less useful in every language. As with so many aspects of Apple Guide, you must use your own judgment in deciding where to draw the line.

Be Sensitive to Political and Cultural Ramifications of Icons, Images, and Metaphors

This point is obvious, and yet endless anecdotes illustrate how easily you can fall into traps. For the author of guide files, the issue is a broader one: the tone and style of the guide file contents should never detract from the contents themselves. "Cute" graphics and humorous text can wear out their welcome very quickly. Whimsy quickly palls, and last year's fads and phrases are as inscrutable as the Sphinx to this year's people.

This does not mean that your guide files should be dull and dry. By using terms that the user is comfortable with you can inspire trust and confidence. Humor can be appropriatem—ore so in the relaxed environment of a Tutorial guide file than a Help guide file. It is not merely a matter of judgment to decide on the tone and style of your guide files—it is once again the matter of understanding your user, the tasks being undertaken, and the application or process itself.

HOW TO LOCALIZE A GUIDE FILE

The basic process of localizing any Macintosh application is to remove the resources that contain text (dialog items, strings, etc.) and to translate them in one way or another to the target language. These resources are then replaced in the resource fork of the application, and it can run in the new language. (This is the ideal: dialog boxes often need to be slightly resized, and error messages constructed from phrases may need to be constructed differently.)

This process is similar for Apple Guide, but an additional step is provided. Instead of modifying the resources from the guide file (the equivalent of the compiled application), Guide Maker extracts the text from the source code of your guide files. You then translate the text as you would with an application, and Guide Maker restores the text to a new copy of the source code of your guide files. You must then recompile the source code into new Apple Guide files. This allows you to do the final tweaking and adjusting that is often needed in translation projects.

What is Extracted for Translation

The Guide Maker localization utility extracts text that needs to be translated or reviewed for localization. This text consists of:

- all quoted strings (in "double quotes"—four-character strings enclosed in single quotes such as 'TEXT' are not extracted),
- all panel text, and
- all parameters to context checks that are of type LPSTRING (as opposed to PSTRING).

Thus, the names of your panels will remain in the original language, and in a command such as:

```
<Topic> "Trouble-shooting the printer", "Seq: printer trouble
    shoot"
```

the phrase "Trouble-shooting the printer," which will appear in the topics list, will be extracted for translation; the phrase "Seq:printer trouble shoot," which identifies the sequence to be associated with this topic, will not be extracted.

N O T E

Since Guide Maker normally extracts all of the text that will be visible to the user, you can use the first step of the localization procedure—the extractionto produce files of text strings for review by editors who check spelling, consistency, and style. This can make life much easier for them, since they don't have to work around the Guide Script commands to do their copyediting.

Handling Extracted Files

Guide Maker's localization utility creates a file of TEXT resources that corresponds to each file of your source code for the guide file. Each text resource is named to let you know what it is: <Index>, <Panel: Intro to Printer>, and so forth. Using either ResEdit or AppleGlot, you translate each of the text strings as appropriate.

During the localization process, Guide Maker creates a localization library file, which it uses to keep track of which text resource belongs where in the source guide file. Once you have completed the translation, Guide Maker reconstructs the source guide files with the translated strings inserted in the appropriate places in the now-localized guide files.

If resources such as PICT graphics need to be modified for the localized assistance, these resources should be included in the new guide files either using the <Resource> command or by referring to the appropriate files in the source code folder.

While this process handles the bulk of the conversion issues, remember that stray pieces of untranslated text may appear from time to time. Does an AppleScript script display a dialog with text?—this process does not examine the contents of scripts associated with events. Have you used the syntax that allows you to position objects in a panel at specific locations rather than in Apple Guide's natural flow?—you may be surprised at the results.

You should recompile the guide files and test the new assistance just as thoroughly as you would test an original version.

SUMMARY

There are two basic steps to successfully localizing Apple Guide assistance. The first step takes place during the initial design process, when you are sensitive to the possibility of translation and are careful to choose tone, images, and text that can be easily translated and that are not likely to distract from the content of the assistance (while being careful to avoid a dull, boring, and distancing tone).

The second step occurs when you actually localize your guide file. The basic steps of using Guide Maker for localization are discussed here.

Afterword

Apple Guide plays a significant role in the evolution of the computer from an "electronic brain"—an object of interest and wonder—to an object as ordinary, unexceptional, and useful as a pencil or pair of scissors.

In some ways, the author of Apple Guide assistance needs a broader range of skills than anyone else on a development project. Ideally, the author should understand the application and its structure, the terminology and design of the implementation (so that context checks can be used to best advantage), the needs and wishes of the users, as well as the frames of reference that they have for their work. This wide-ranging purview, covering people, computers, and the work that they do together, can become fascinating: it is often the author of assistance who has a better sense of the big picture than anyone else on the project team.

At the same time, it is the task of the Apple Guide author to make Apple Guide and its assistance as well as the application or process itself invisible to the user. Despite the fears of some, this is not a self-defeating process for a commercial developer: people do indeed notice and appreciate excellent service that is personal, unobtrusive but always available. The apparent paradox of providing a service that is designed to be unnoticed is resolved whenever your spot a lapse. The English grande dame who looked down at her dessert ice cream in a fancy restaurant and loudly proclaimed, "What, no wafers!" was simply demonstrating the risks run by those who do not provide good service.

How your Apple Guide assistance presents itself—in its graphics, the tone of its text, and in the organization of its access windows—is a subject for much discussion and analysis. Far-fetched metaphors, decoration, and cuteness may serve you well—but more often they do not. Remember that the computer itself is a new invention—and the graphical user interface, active assistance and even your own application or solution are new inventions to many users. New technologies often begin by defining themselves in familiar terms—the vocabulary of a previous technology ("horseless carriages", "wireless", "frost-free refrigerators"). In their infancies, many technologies not only describe themselves as what they are not, but they hide their faces—look at illustrations of TV sets from the 1950's, hidden in elaborate cabinets, or consider early automobiles which look for all the world like the horseless carriages they were called). One of the signs of maturity of a technology is the use of its own terminology and its presentation of itself as itself. As we enter an era of maturity in the computer age, Apple Guide assistance has a large role to play in making these things happen.

Apple Guide assistance isn't an add-on or after-thought. Apple Guide is an intrinsic part of an intense user experience—one of assistance and cooperation between user and computer. Apple Guide opens the door to a new, more powerful, and ultimately much simpler way for people to use computers to do the things that they want to do.

And there's one more thing—

It's not help.

Jesse Feiler

Index

Using the CD-ROM

The CD-ROM that comes with this book has three sections:

* Resources
* Demos
* The Cookbook

RESOURCES

Inside the Resources folder you will find everything you need to put Apple Guide to use. The latest version of Apple Guide itself, the Apple Guide fonts, interfaces for programmers, and Apple's Guide Maker compiler and debugging utility are all there. You will also find a self-running References & Resources stack with more goodies. (Make sure to read the Read Me files before installing any of the tools in the Resources folder.)

DEMOS

The Demos folder contains a number of sample Apple Guide files - including several discussed in detail in this book. The guideWorker utility from guideWorks is included here. You can use it to directly open any Apple Guide file by simply dragging it on to the guideWorker icon. (Try dragging the Custom Solutions Examples guide file on to guideWorker to see a number of interesting examples from guideWorks.) Other demos demonstrate adding Apple Guide to interactive content and to HyperCard stacks, as well as a dealer's guide file providing post-sale assistance to customers.

THE COOKBOOK

The Cookbook contains recipes demonstrating various features of Apple Guide, as well as shells to help you create guide files. Most of the examples given in this book are presented in their entirety in the Cookbook.

ON-LINE RESOURCES

Philmont Software Mill has an area on eWorld. Information from the Resources folder on the CD-ROM is posted there and updated periodically. To reach the eWorld area, use the path Computer Center : Straight to the Source : Philmont Software Mill or the shortcut "Philmont." A discussion board about this book is also located in the eWorld area. If you have resources which you would like to see included in this folder, send details to ePhilmont@eWorld.com.

<Define Sequence> "Oops: some quotes are wrong"

<Define Panel> "Clarification"

Guide Script parameters that are enclosed in quotes (such as "Clarification" after the command <Define Panel> above) are always enclosed in straight quotes.

Some of the examples (particularly in Chapter 6 and 10) incorrectly show curly quotes ("like these").

As this sample demonstrates, you may use curly quotes within the text of your panels, but parameters for Guide Script commands (such as <Define Panel>, above) require straight quotes.

This sequence uses both kinds of quotes correctly.

<End Panel>